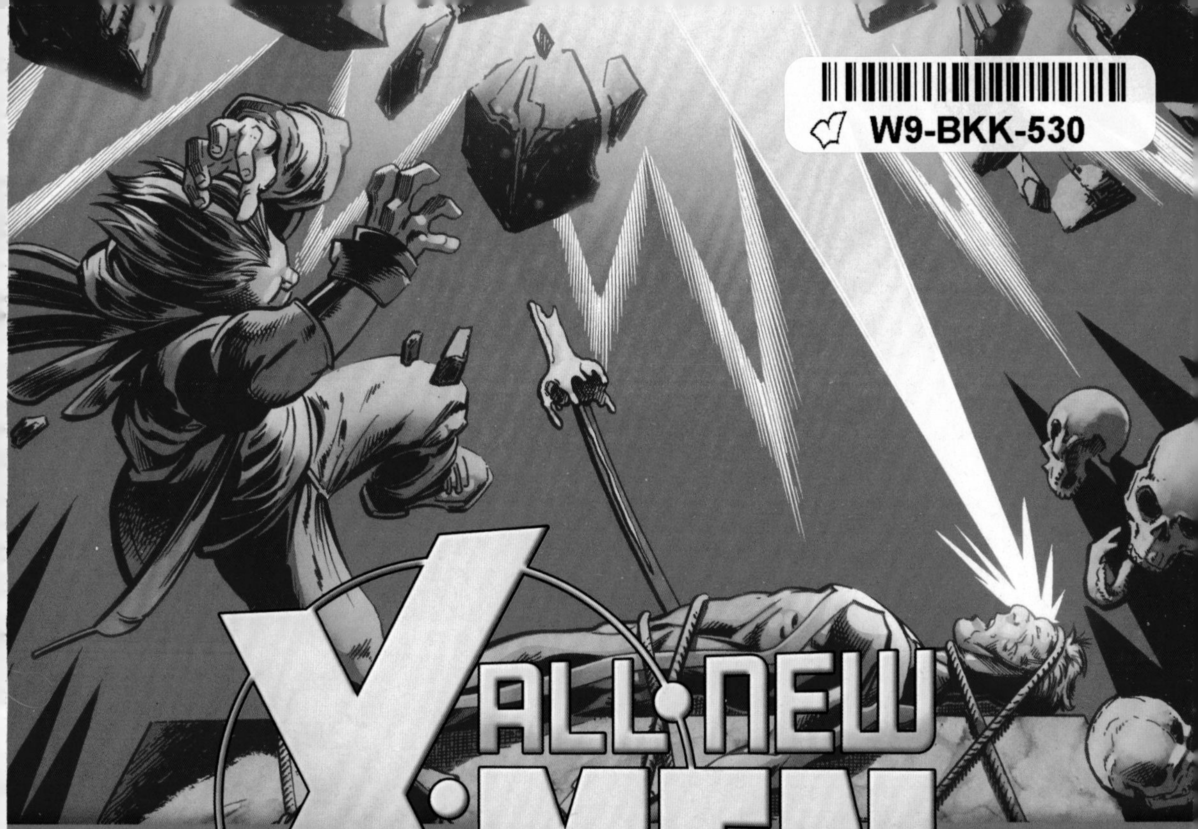

ALL-NEW X-MEN

APOCALYPSE WARS

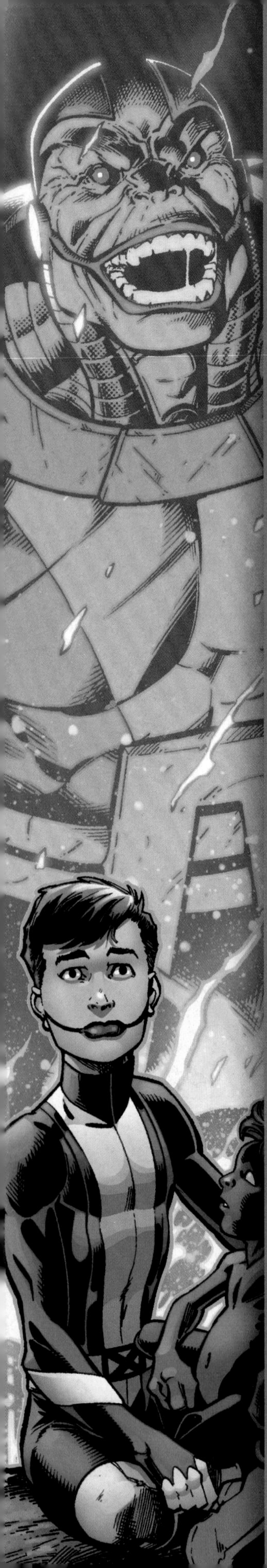

PLUCKED FROM THE PAST, THE ORIGINAL X-MEN—CYCLOPS, BEAST, ICEMAN AND ANGEL—ARE NOW TRAPPED IN THE PRESENT, IN A TIME WHEN MUTANTS ARE HATED AND FEARED MORE THAN EVER. DETERMINED NOT TO LET THE WORLD GET THE BETTER OF THEM, THEY'VE SET OUT TO WRITE THEIR OWN FUTURES AND BUILD A LEGACY THEY CAN BE PROUD OF.

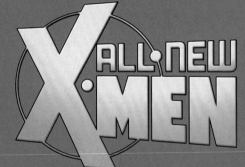

ALL-NEW X-MEN

WHILE STRUGGLING TO PUT AN END TO THE ENRAGED BLOB'S RAMPAGE THROUGH PARIS, THE X-MEN FAILED TO NOTICE THEIR TEAMMATE, CYCLOPS, WAS STRUCK BY A CAR AND ABDUCTED BY THEIR LONGTIME ADVERSARY, TOAD. WHEN THE UNCONSCIOUS SCOTT CAME TO, HE FOUND HIMSELF HELD PRISONER IN THE CATACOMBS BENEATH THE CITY...WITH HIS LIFE HANGING IN THE BALANCE!

APOCALYPSE WARS

DENNIS HOPELESS
WRITER

ISSUES #7, #9-11

MARK BAGLEY
PENCILER

ANDREW HENNESSY
INKER

NOLAN WOODARD
COLORIST

ISSUE #8

PACO DIAZ
ARTIST

RACHELLE ROSENBERG
COLORIST

VC's CORY PETIT
LETTERER

MARK BAGLEY, ANDREW HENNESSY & NOLAN WOODARD
COVER ART

CHRISTINA HARRINGTON
ASSISTANT EDITOR

DANIEL KETCHUM
EDITOR

MARK PANICCIA
X-MEN GROUP EDITOR

X-MEN CREATED BY **STAN LEE** & **JACK KIRBY**

COLLECTION EDITOR: **JENNIFER GRÜNWALD**
ASSOCIATE EDITOR: **SARAH BRUNSTAD**
ASSOCIATE MANAGING EDITOR: **KATERI WOODY**
EDITOR, SPECIAL PROJECTS: **MARK D. BEAZLEY**
VP PRODUCTION & SPECIAL PROJECTS: **JEFF YOUNGQUIST**
SVP PRINT, SALES & MARKETING: **DAVID GABRIEL**
BOOK DESIGNER: **ADAM DEL RE**

EDITOR IN CHIEF: **AXEL ALONSO**
CHIEF CREATIVE OFFICER: **JOE QUESADA**
PUBLISHER: **DAN BUCKLEY**
EXECUTIVE PRODUCER: **ALAN FINE**

ALL-NEW X-MEN: INEVITABLE VOL. 2 — APOCALYPSE WARS. Contains material originally published in magazine form as ALL-NEW X-MEN #7-11. First printing 2016. ISBN# 978-0-7851-9631-0. Published by MARVEL WORLDWIDE, INC., a subsidiary of MARVEL ENTERTAINMENT, LLC. OFFICE OF PUBLICATION: 135 West 50th Street, New York, NY 10020.

Printed in Canada. ALAN FINE, President, Marvel Entertainment; DAN BUCKLEY, President, TV, Publishing & Brand Management; JOE QUESADA, Chief Creative Officer; TOM BREVOORT, SVP of Publishing; DAVID BOGART, SVP of Business Affairs & Operations, Publishing & Partnership; C.B. CEBULSKI, VP of Brand Management & Development, Asia; DAVID GABRIEL, SVP of Sales & Marketing, Publishing; JEFF YOUNGQUIST, VP of Production & Special Projects; DAN CARR, Executive Director of Publishing Technology; ALEX MORALES, Director of Publishing Operations; SUSAN CRESPI, Production Manager; STAN LEE, Chairman Emeritus. For information regarding advertising in Marvel Comics or on Marvel.com, please contact Vit DeBellis, Integrated Sales Manager, at vdebellis@marvel.com. For Marvel subscription inquiries, please call 888-511-5480. **Manufactured between 8/19/2016 and 9/26/2016 by SOLISCO PRINTERS, SCOTT, QC, CANADA.**

10 9 8 7 6 5 4 3 2 1

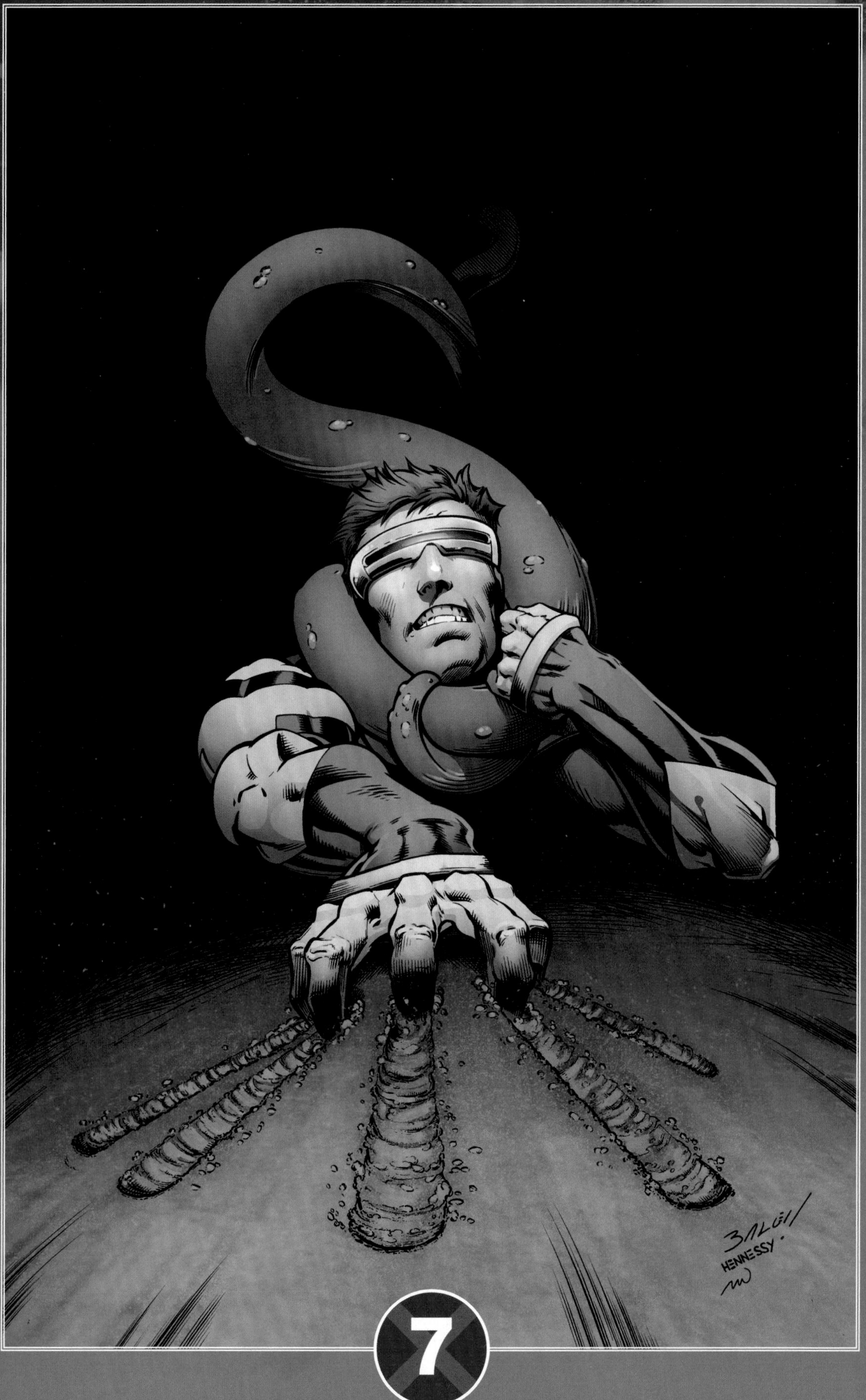
HENNESSY
7

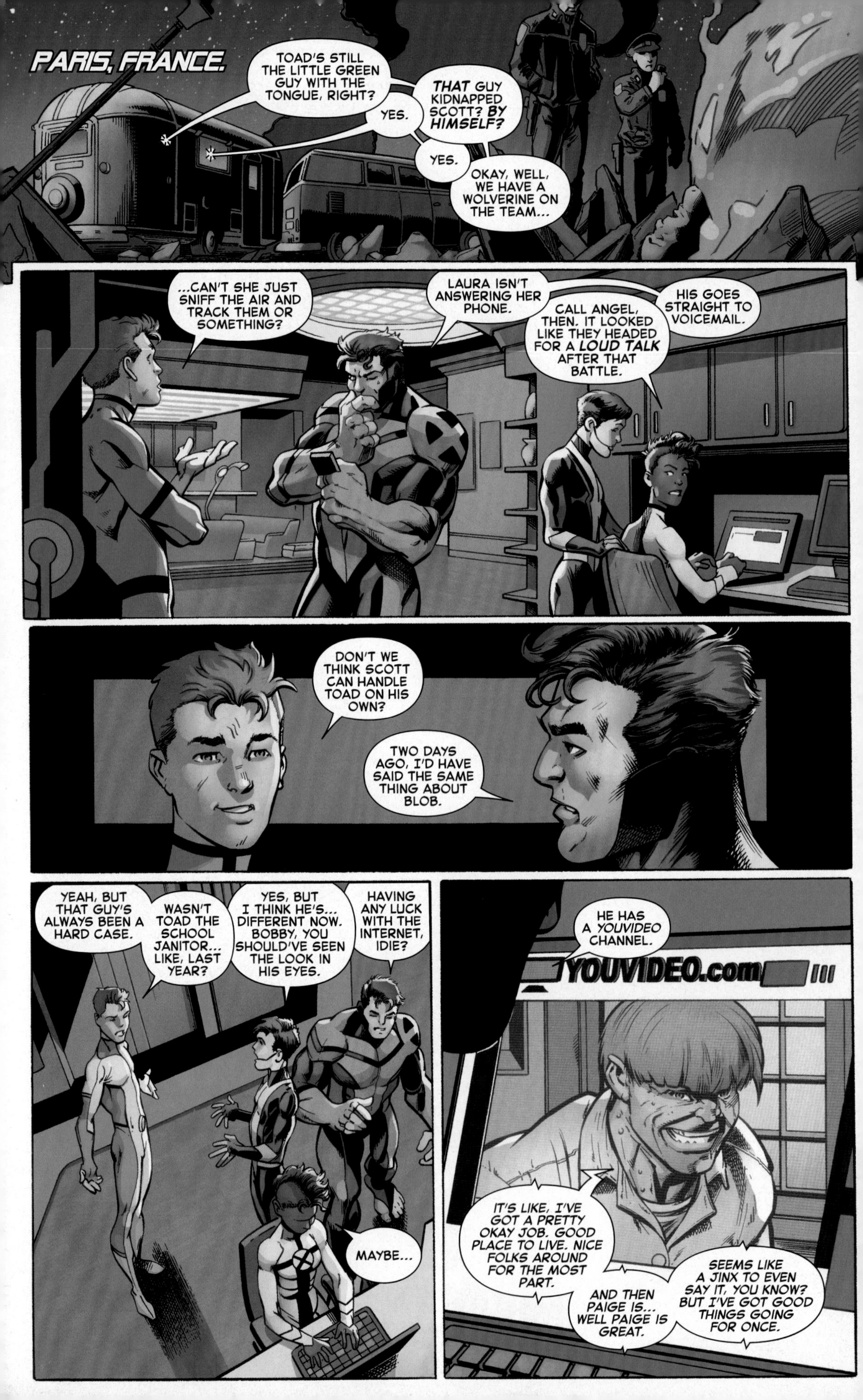
PARIS, FRANCE.
TOAD'S STILL THE LITTLE GREEN GUY WITH THE TONGUE, RIGHT?
YES.
THAT GUY KIDNAPPED SCOTT? BY HIMSELF?
YES.
OKAY, WELL, WE HAVE A WOLVERINE ON THE TEAM...
...CAN'T SHE JUST SNIFF THE AIR AND TRACK THEM OR SOMETHING?
LAURA ISN'T ANSWERING HER PHONE.
CALL ANGEL, THEN. IT LOOKED LIKE THEY HEADED FOR A LOUD TALK AFTER THAT BATTLE.
HIS GOES STRAIGHT TO VOICEMAIL.
DON'T WE THINK SCOTT CAN HANDLE TOAD ON HIS OWN?
TWO DAYS AGO, I'D HAVE SAID THE SAME THING ABOUT BLOB.
YEAH, BUT THAT GUY'S ALWAYS BEEN A HARD CASE.
WASN'T TOAD THE SCHOOL JANITOR... LIKE, LAST YEAR?
YES, BUT I THINK HE'S... DIFFERENT NOW. BOBBY, YOU SHOULD'VE SEEN THE LOOK IN HIS EYES.
HAVING ANY LUCK WITH THE INTERNET, IDIE?
MAYBE...
HE HAS A YOUVIDEO CHANNEL.
YOUVIDEO.com
IT'S LIKE, I'VE GOT A PRETTY OKAY JOB. GOOD PLACE TO LIVE. NICE FOLKS AROUND FOR THE MOST PART.
AND THEN PAIGE IS... WELL PAIGE IS GREAT.
SEEMS LIKE A JINX TO EVEN SAY IT, YOU KNOW? BUT I'VE GOT GOOD THINGS GOING FOR ONCE.

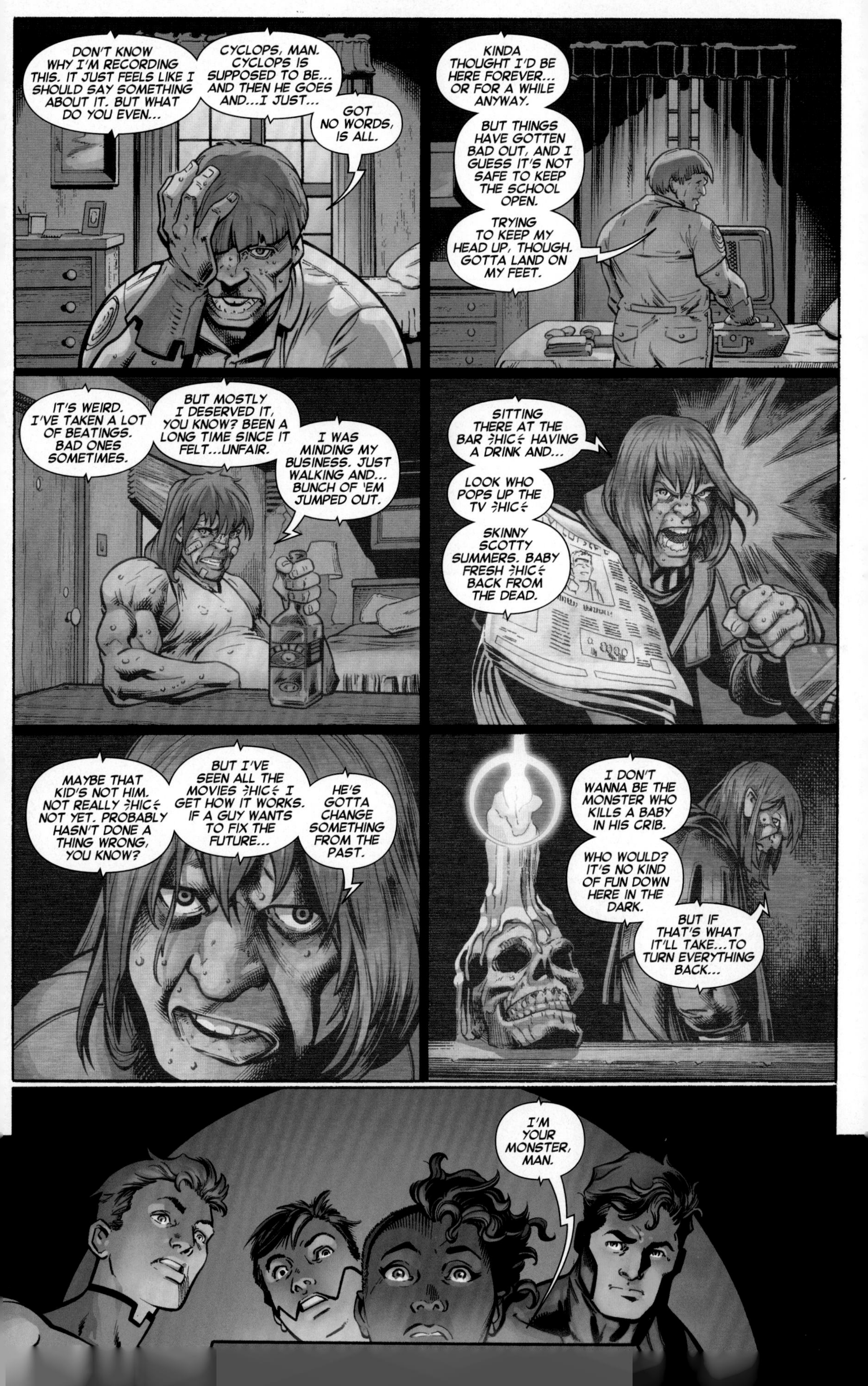

DON'T KNOW WHY I'M RECORDING THIS. IT JUST FEELS LIKE I SHOULD SAY SOMETHING ABOUT IT. BUT WHAT DO YOU EVEN...
CYCLOPS, MAN. CYCLOPS IS SUPPOSED TO BE... AND THEN HE GOES AND...I JUST...
GOT NO WORDS, IS ALL.
KINDA THOUGHT I'D BE HERE FOREVER... OR FOR A WHILE ANYWAY.
BUT THINGS HAVE GOTTEN BAD OUT, AND I GUESS IT'S NOT SAFE TO KEEP THE SCHOOL OPEN.
TRYING TO KEEP MY HEAD UP, THOUGH. GOTTA LAND ON MY FEET.
IT'S WEIRD. I'VE TAKEN A LOT OF BEATINGS. BAD ONES SOMETIMES.
BUT MOSTLY I DESERVED IT, YOU KNOW? BEEN A LONG TIME SINCE IT FELT...UNFAIR.
I WAS MINDING MY BUSINESS. JUST WALKING AND... BUNCH OF 'EM JUMPED OUT.
SITTING THERE AT THE BAR *HIC* HAVING A DRINK AND...
LOOK WHO POPS UP THE TV *HIC*
SKINNY SCOTTY SUMMERS. BABY FRESH *HIC* BACK FROM THE DEAD.
MAYBE THAT KID'S NOT HIM. NOT REALLY *HIC* NOT YET. PROBABLY HASN'T DONE A THING WRONG, YOU KNOW?
BUT I'VE SEEN ALL THE MOVIES *HIC* I GET HOW IT WORKS. IF A GUY WANTS TO FIX THE FUTURE...
HE'S GOTTA CHANGE SOMETHING FROM THE PAST.
I DON'T WANNA BE THE MONSTER WHO KILLS A BABY IN HIS CRIB.
WHO WOULD? IT'S NO KIND OF FUN DOWN HERE IN THE DARK.
BUT IF THAT'S WHAT IT'LL TAKE...TO TURN EVERYTHING BACK...
I'M YOUR MONSTER, MAN.

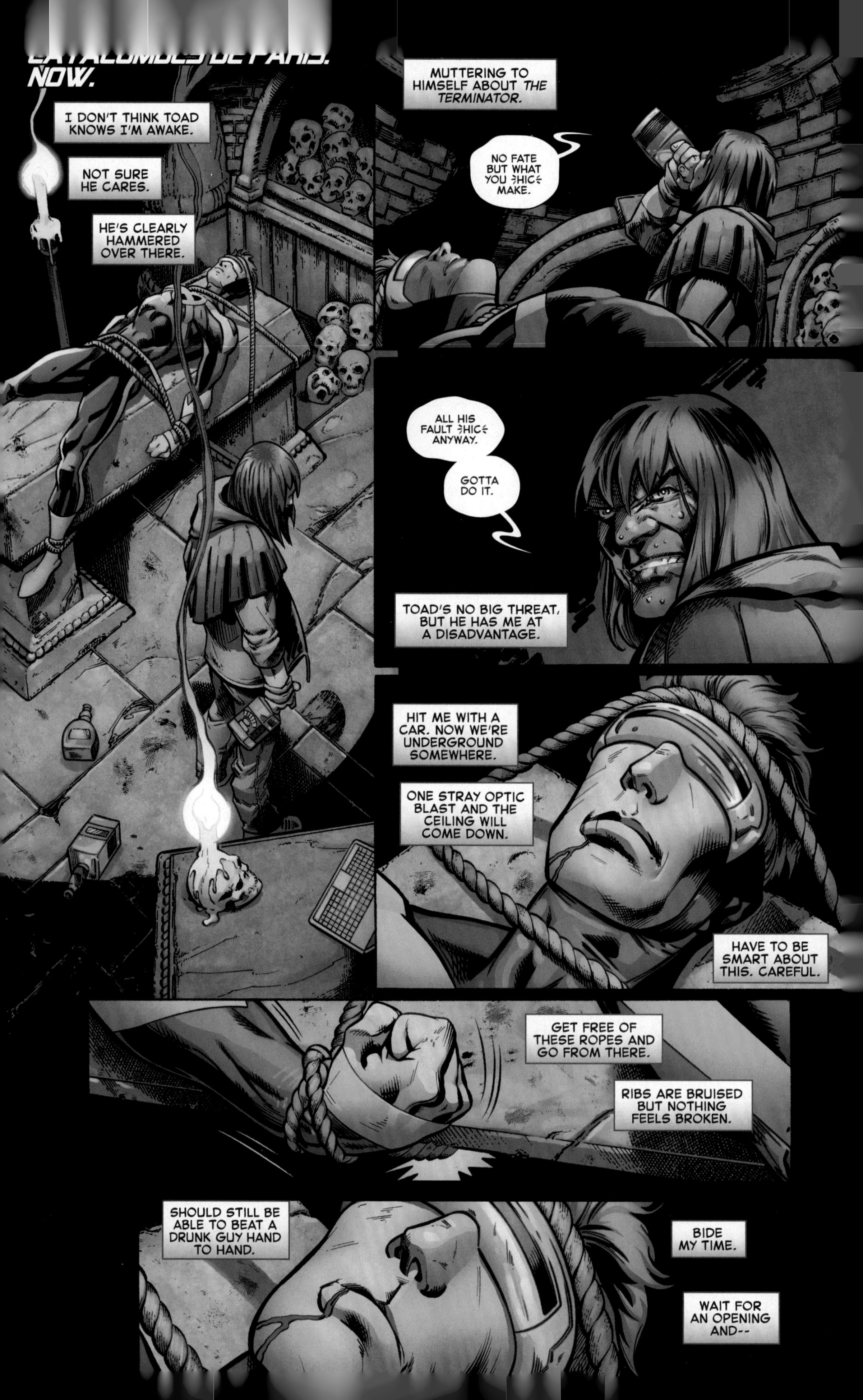
NOW.
I DON'T THINK TOAD KNOWS I'M AWAKE.
NOT SURE HE CARES.
HE'S CLEARLY HAMMERED OVER THERE.
MUTTERING TO HIMSELF ABOUT *THE TERMINATOR*.
NO FATE BUT WHAT YOU ≯HIC≮ MAKE.
ALL HIS FAULT ≯HIC≮ ANYWAY.
GOTTA DO IT.
TOAD'S NO BIG THREAT, BUT HE HAS ME AT A DISADVANTAGE.
HIT ME WITH A CAR. NOW WE'RE UNDERGROUND SOMEWHERE.
ONE STRAY OPTIC BLAST AND THE CEILING WILL COME DOWN.
HAVE TO BE SMART ABOUT THIS. CAREFUL.
GET FREE OF THESE ROPES AND GO FROM THERE.
RIBS ARE BRUISED BUT NOTHING FEELS BROKEN.
SHOULD STILL BE ABLE TO BEAT A DRUNK GUY HAND TO HAND.
BIDE MY TIME.
WAIT FOR AN OPENING AND--

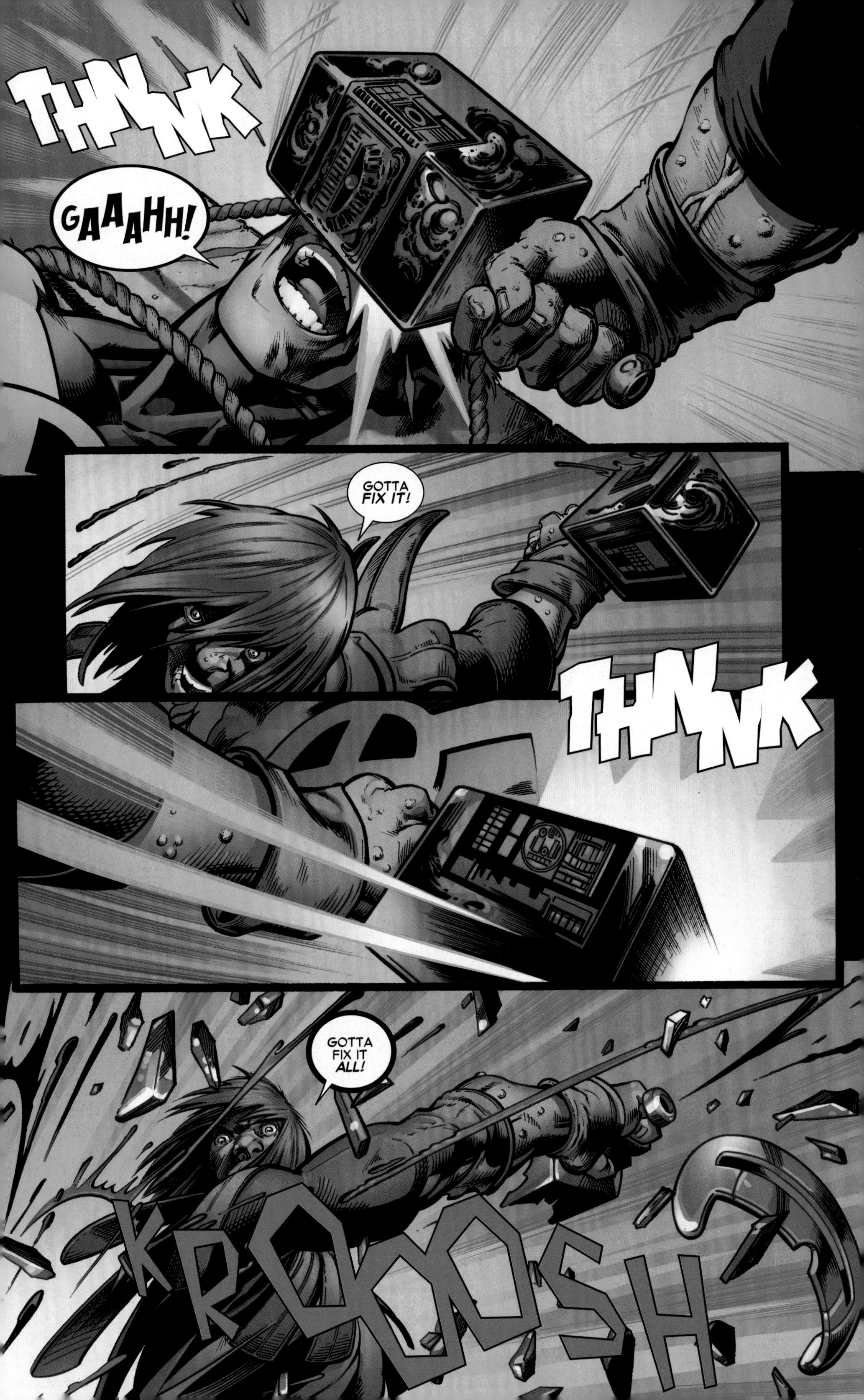
THNNK
GAAAHH!
GOTTA FIX IT!
THNNK
GOTTA FIX IT ALL!
KROOOSH

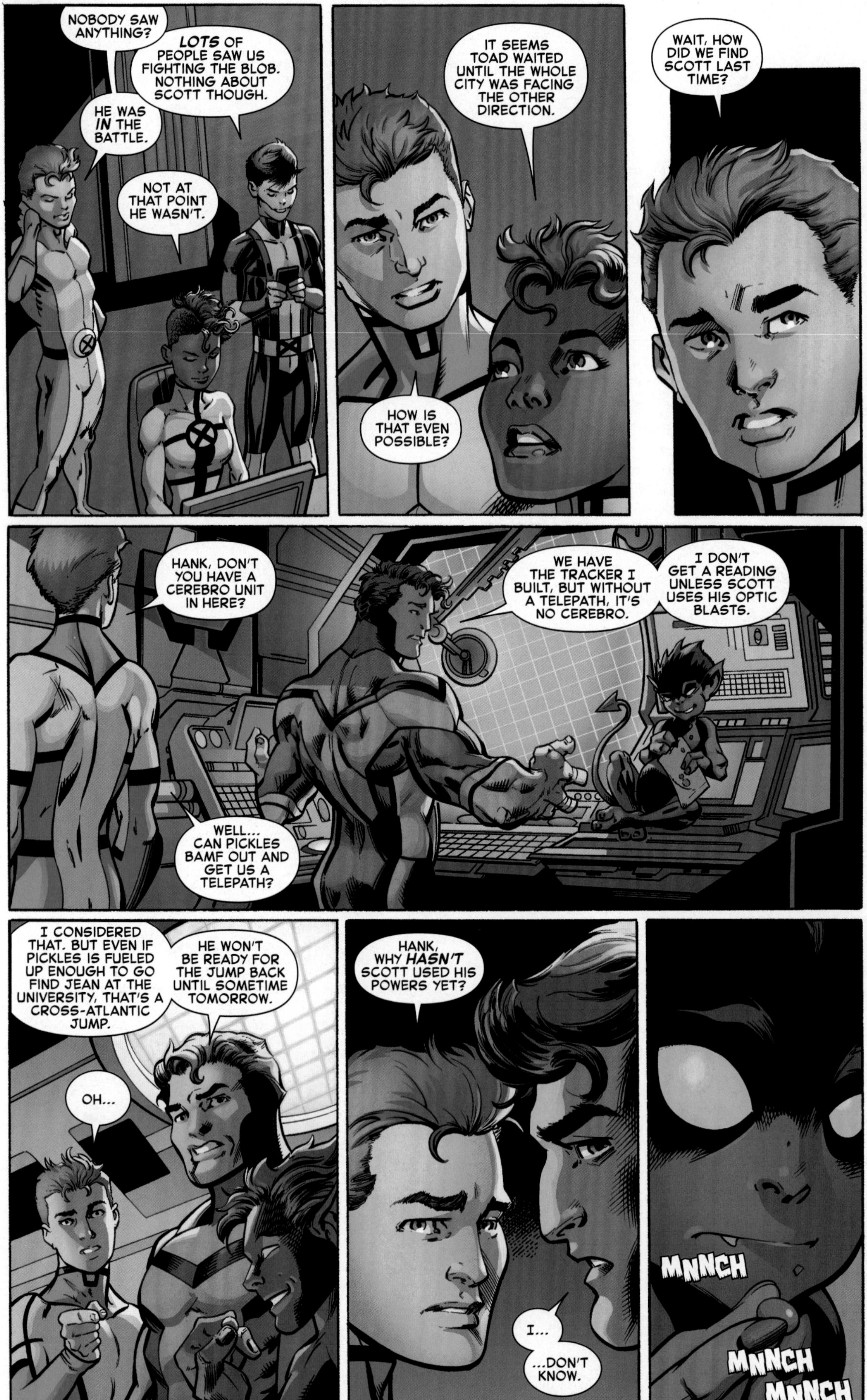
NOBODY SAW ANYTHING?
HE WAS *IN* THE BATTLE.
LOTS OF PEOPLE SAW US FIGHTING THE BLOB. NOTHING ABOUT SCOTT THOUGH.
NOT AT THAT POINT HE WASN'T.
IT SEEMS TOAD WAITED UNTIL THE WHOLE CITY WAS FACING THE OTHER DIRECTION.
HOW IS THAT EVEN POSSIBLE?
WAIT, HOW DID WE FIND SCOTT LAST TIME?
HANK, DON'T YOU HAVE A CEREBRO UNIT IN HERE?
WE HAVE THE TRACKER I BUILT, BUT WITHOUT A TELEPATH, IT'S NO CEREBRO.
I DON'T GET A READING UNLESS SCOTT USES HIS OPTIC BLASTS.
WELL... CAN PICKLES BAMF OUT AND GET US A TELEPATH?
I CONSIDERED THAT. BUT EVEN IF PICKLES IS FUELED UP ENOUGH TO GO FIND JEAN AT THE UNIVERSITY, THAT'S A CROSS-ATLANTIC JUMP.
HE WON'T BE READY FOR THE JUMP BACK UNTIL SOMETIME TOMORROW.
OH...
HANK, WHY *HASN'T* SCOTT USED HIS POWERS YET?
I...
...DON'T KNOW.
MNNCH
MNNCH
MNNCH

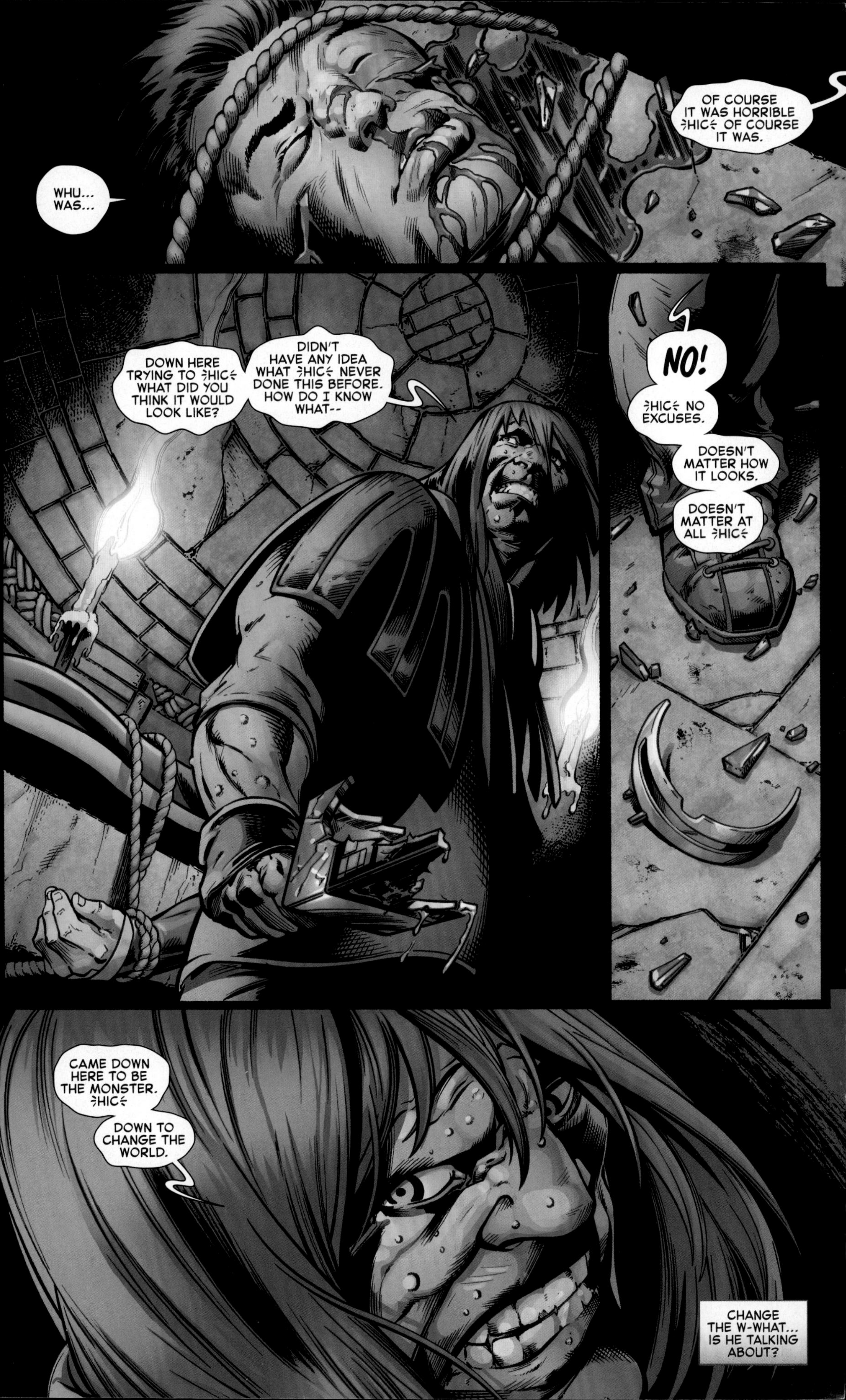
OF COURSE IT WAS HORRIBLE ⋡HIC⋠ OF COURSE IT WAS.
WHU... WAS...
DOWN HERE TRYING TO ⋡HIC⋠ WHAT DID YOU THINK IT WOULD LOOK LIKE?
DIDN'T HAVE ANY IDEA WHAT ⋡HIC⋠ NEVER DONE THIS BEFORE. HOW DO I KNOW WHAT--
NO!
⋡HIC⋠ NO EXCUSES.
DOESN'T MATTER HOW IT LOOKS.
DOESN'T MATTER AT ALL ⋡HIC⋠
CAME DOWN HERE TO BE THE MONSTER. ⋡HIC⋠
DOWN TO CHANGE THE WORLD.
CHANGE THE W-WHAT... IS HE TALKING ABOUT?

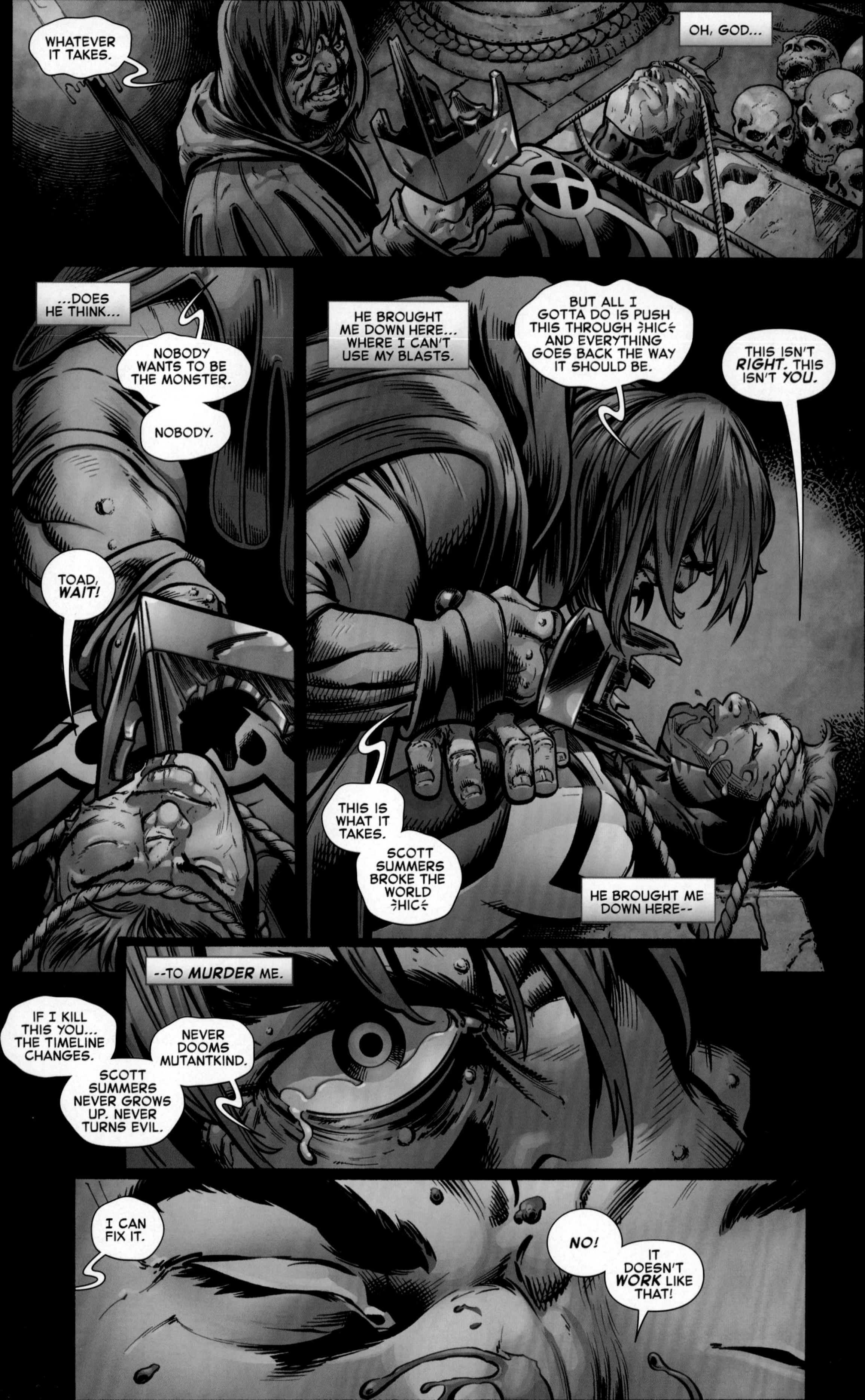
WHATEVER IT TAKES.
OH, GOD...
...DOES HE THINK...
NOBODY WANTS TO BE THE MONSTER.
NOBODY.
TOAD, WAIT!
HE BROUGHT ME DOWN HERE... WHERE I CAN'T USE MY BLASTS.
BUT ALL I GOTTA DO IS PUSH THIS THROUGH *HIC* AND EVERYTHING GOES BACK THE WAY IT SHOULD BE.
THIS ISN'T RIGHT. THIS ISN'T YOU.
THIS IS WHAT IT TAKES.
SCOTT SUMMERS BROKE THE WORLD *HIC*
HE BROUGHT ME DOWN HERE--
--TO MURDER ME.
IF I KILL THIS YOU... THE TIMELINE CHANGES.
NEVER DOOMS MUTANTKIND.
SCOTT SUMMERS NEVER GROWS UP. NEVER TURNS EVIL.
I CAN FIX IT.
NO!
IT DOESN'T WORK LIKE THAT!

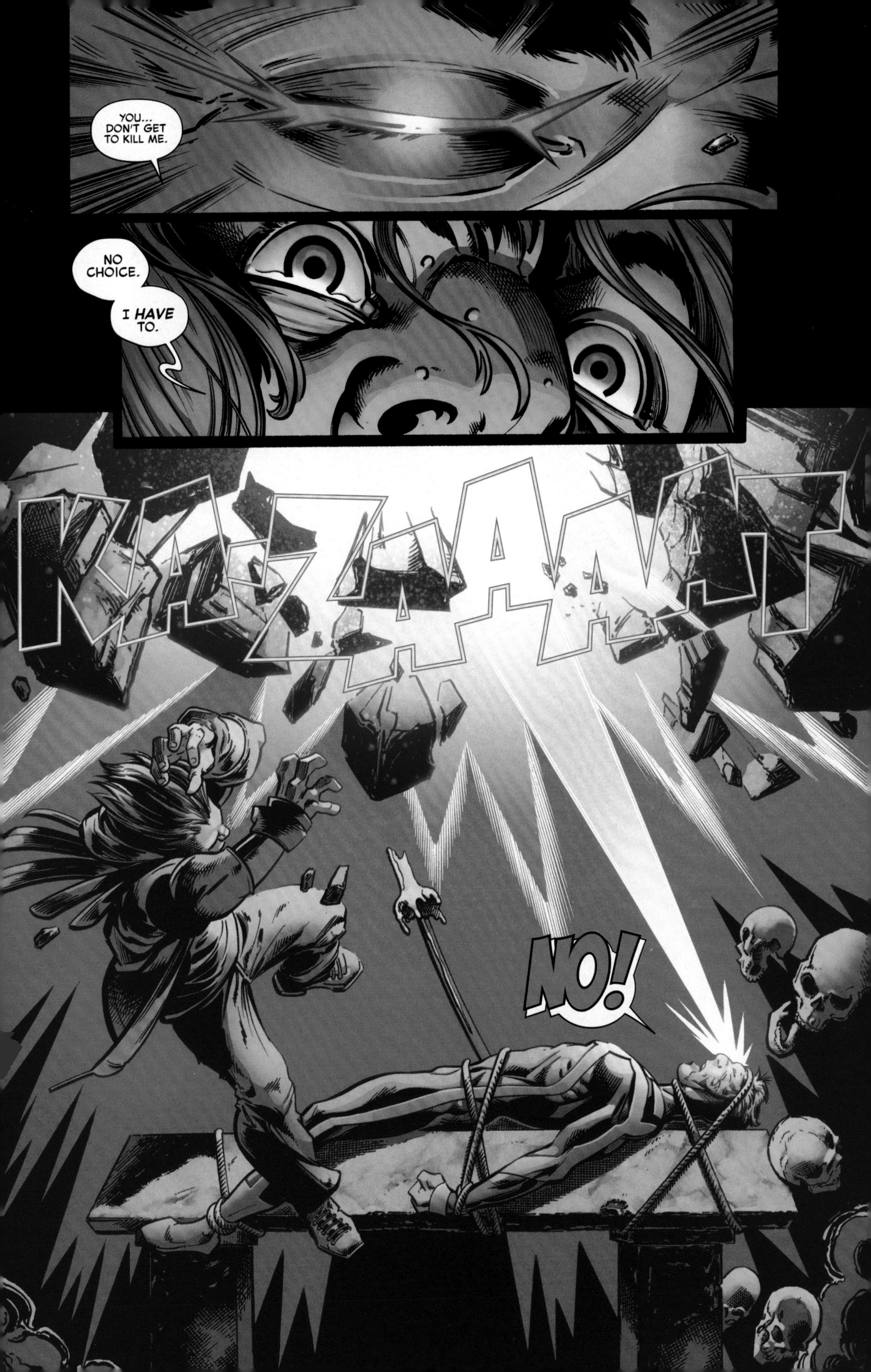
YOU... DON'T GET TO KILL ME.
NO CHOICE.
I HAVE TO.
KAZZAAAT
NO!

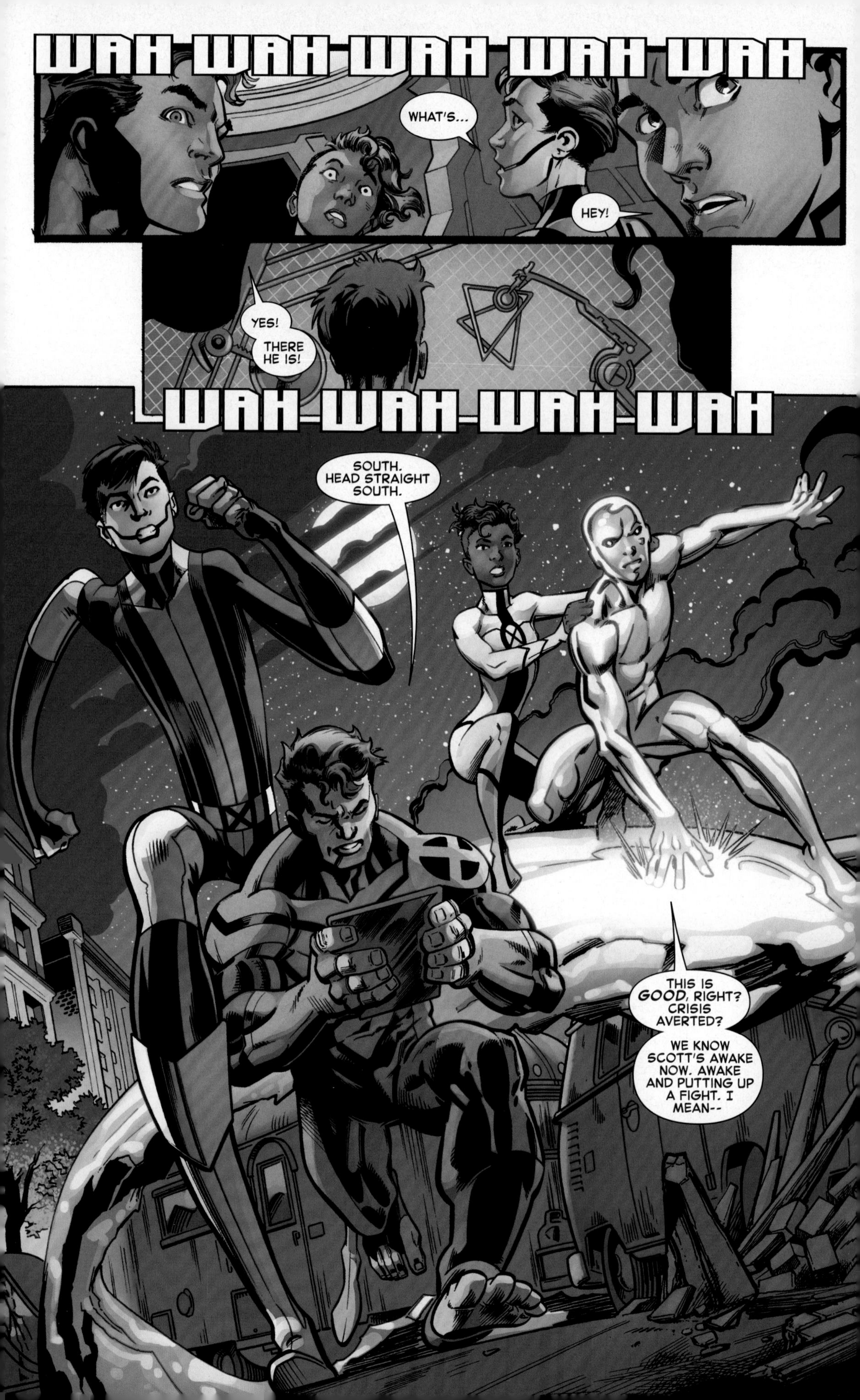
WAH WAH WAH WAH WAH
WHAT'S...
HEY!
YES!
THERE HE IS!
WAH WAH WAH WAH
SOUTH. HEAD STRAIGHT SOUTH.
THIS IS *GOOD*, RIGHT? CRISIS AVERTED?
WE KNOW SCOTT'S AWAKE NOW. AWAKE AND PUTTING UP A FIGHT. I MEAN--

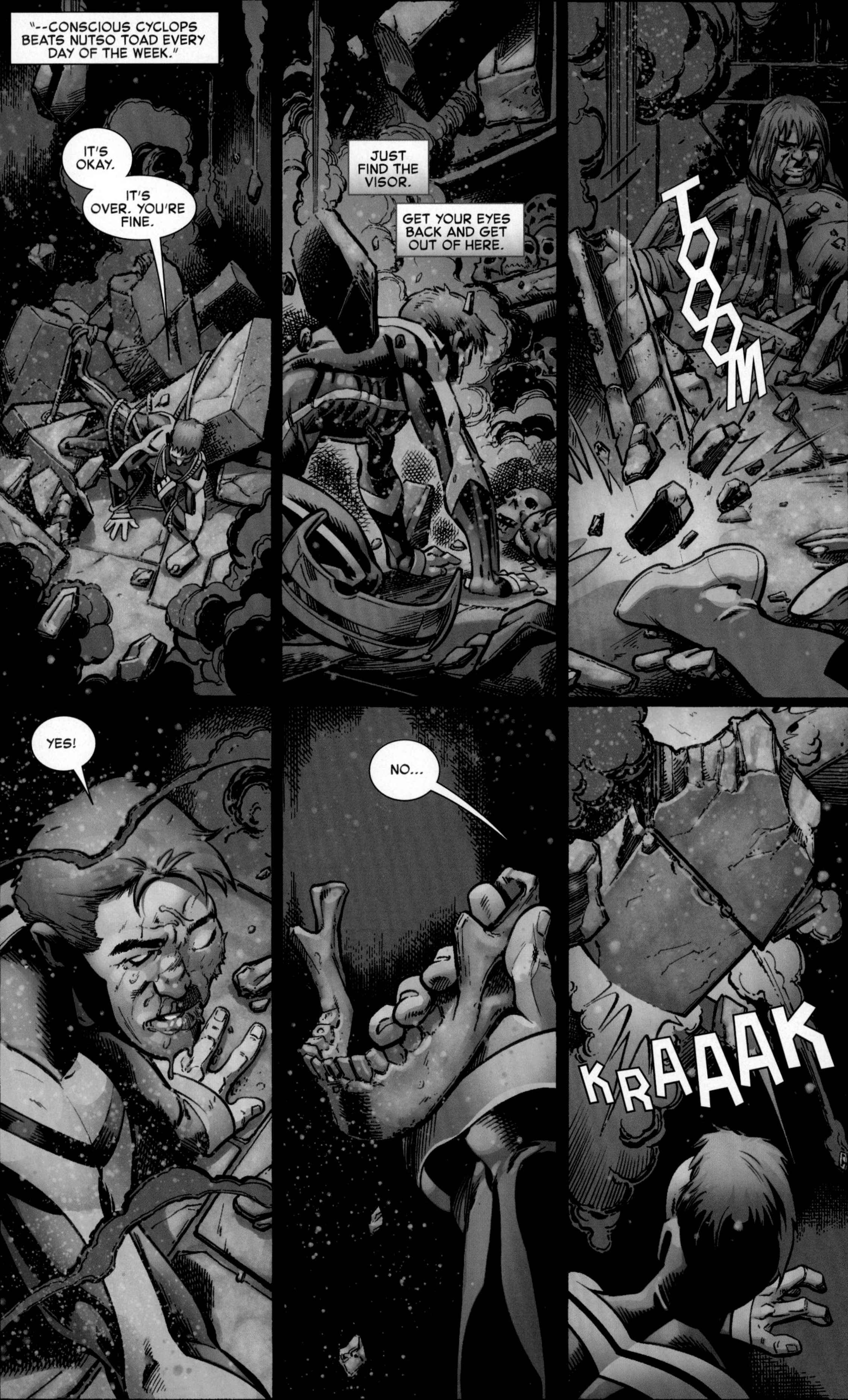
"--CONSCIOUS CYCLOPS BEATS NUTSO TOAD EVERY DAY OF THE WEEK."
IT'S OKAY.
IT'S OVER. YOU'RE FINE.
JUST FIND THE VISOR.
GET YOUR EYES BACK AND GET OUT OF HERE.
TOOOM
YES!
NO...
KRAAAK

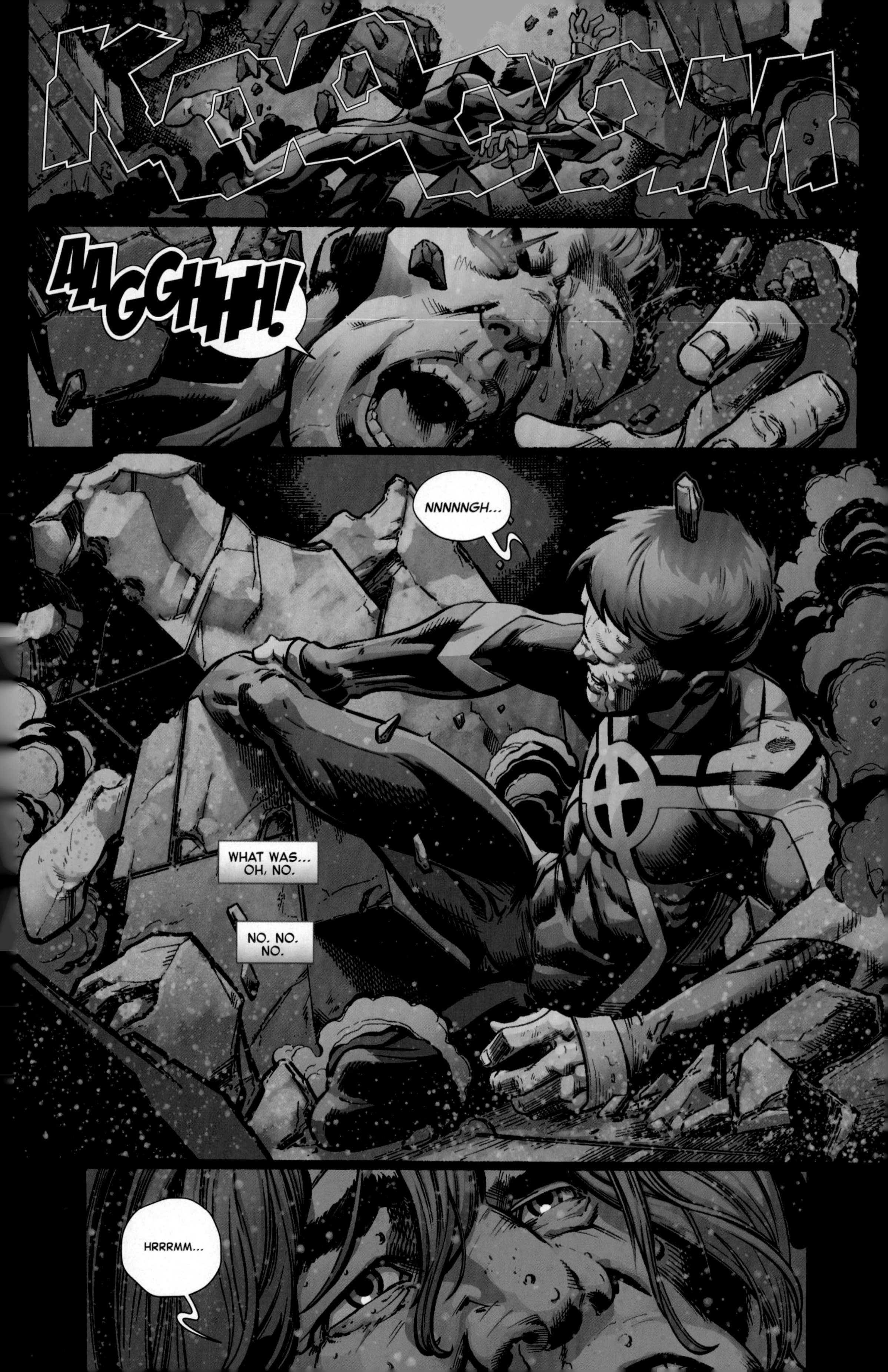
KA-BOOM
AAGGHHH!
NNNNNGH...
WHAT WAS... OH, NO.
NO. NO. NO.
HRRRMM...

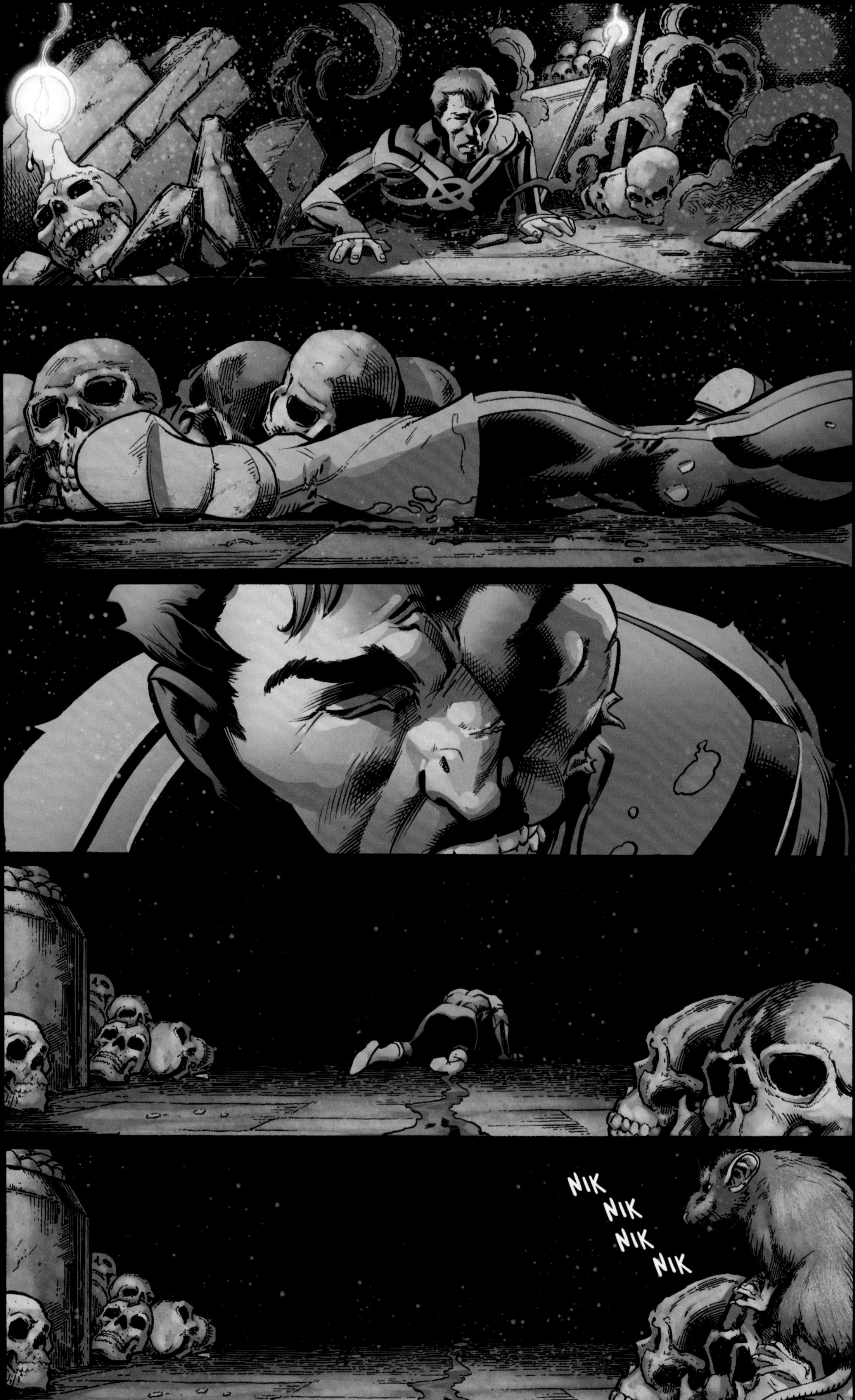
NIK
NIK
NIK
NIK

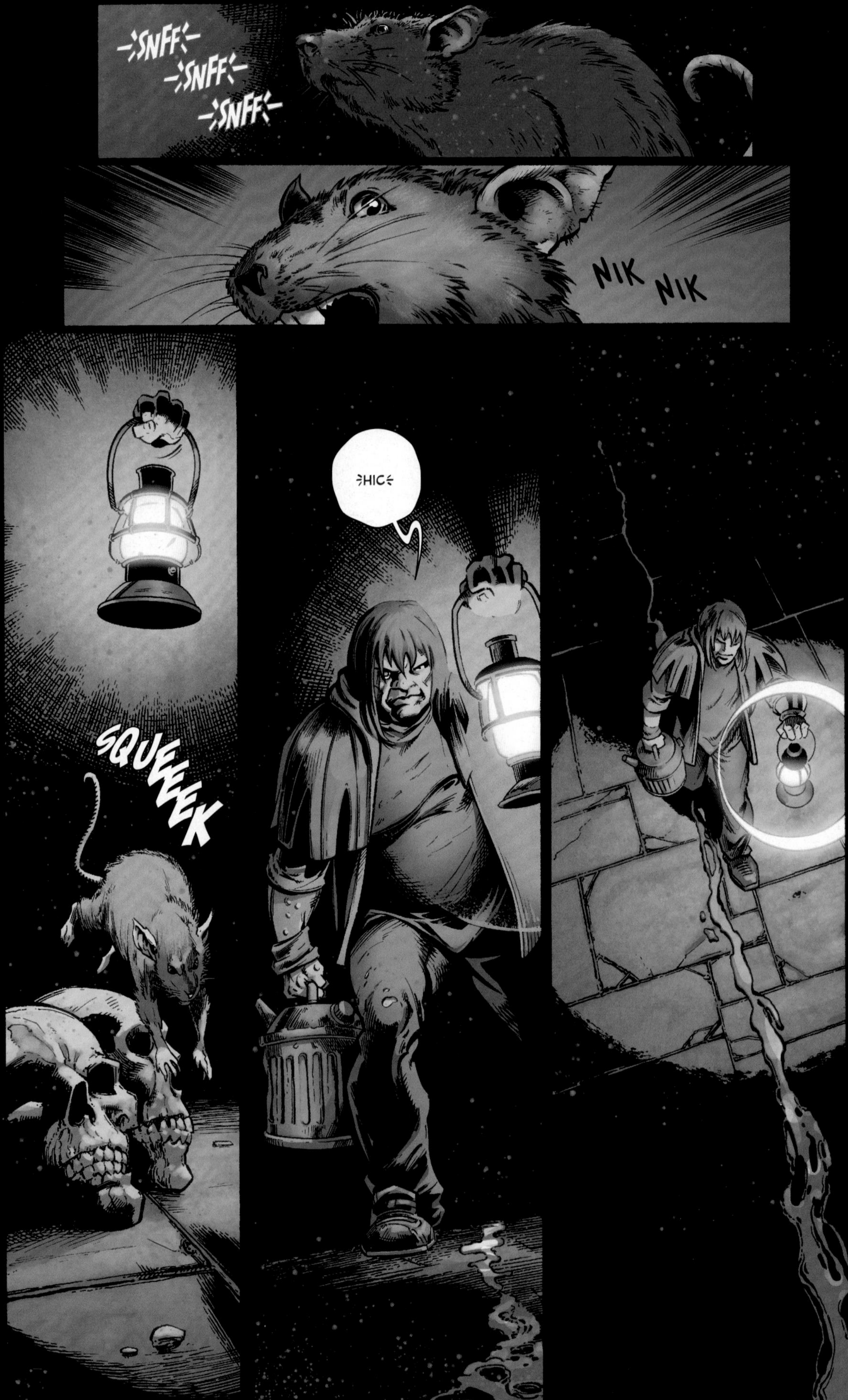
SNFF
SNFF
SNFF
NIK NIK
SQUEEEK
HIC

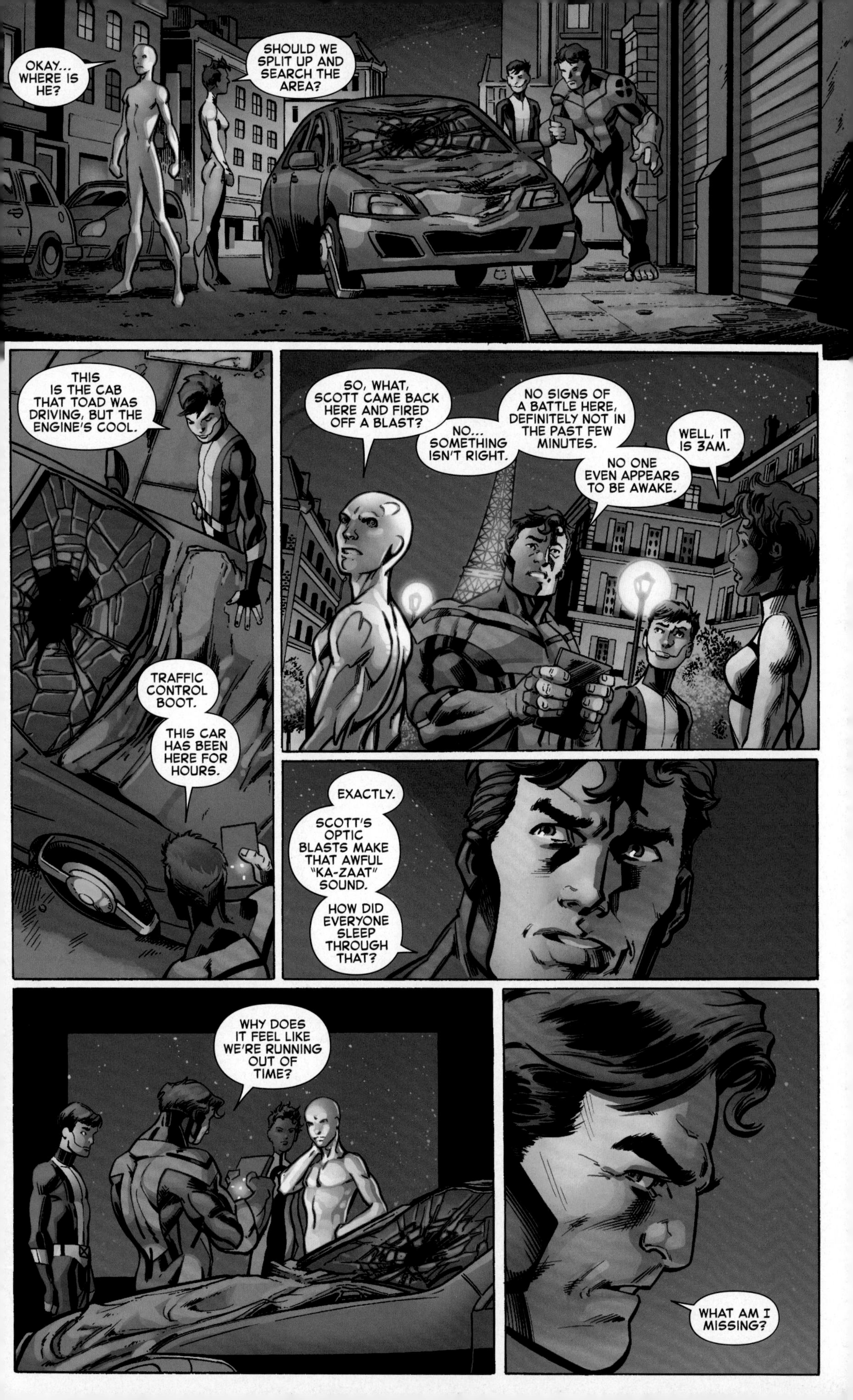
OKAY... WHERE IS HE?
SHOULD WE SPLIT UP AND SEARCH THE AREA?
THIS IS THE CAB THAT TOAD WAS DRIVING, BUT THE ENGINE'S COOL.
TRAFFIC CONTROL BOOT.
THIS CAR HAS BEEN HERE FOR HOURS.
SO, WHAT, SCOTT CAME BACK HERE AND FIRED OFF A BLAST?
NO... SOMETHING ISN'T RIGHT.
NO SIGNS OF A BATTLE HERE, DEFINITELY NOT IN THE PAST FEW MINUTES.
NO ONE EVEN APPEARS TO BE AWAKE.
WELL, IT IS 3AM.
EXACTLY.
SCOTT'S OPTIC BLASTS MAKE THAT AWFUL "KA-ZAAT" SOUND.
HOW DID EVERYONE SLEEP THROUGH THAT?
WHY DOES IT FEEL LIKE WE'RE RUNNING OUT OF TIME?
WHAT AM I MISSING?

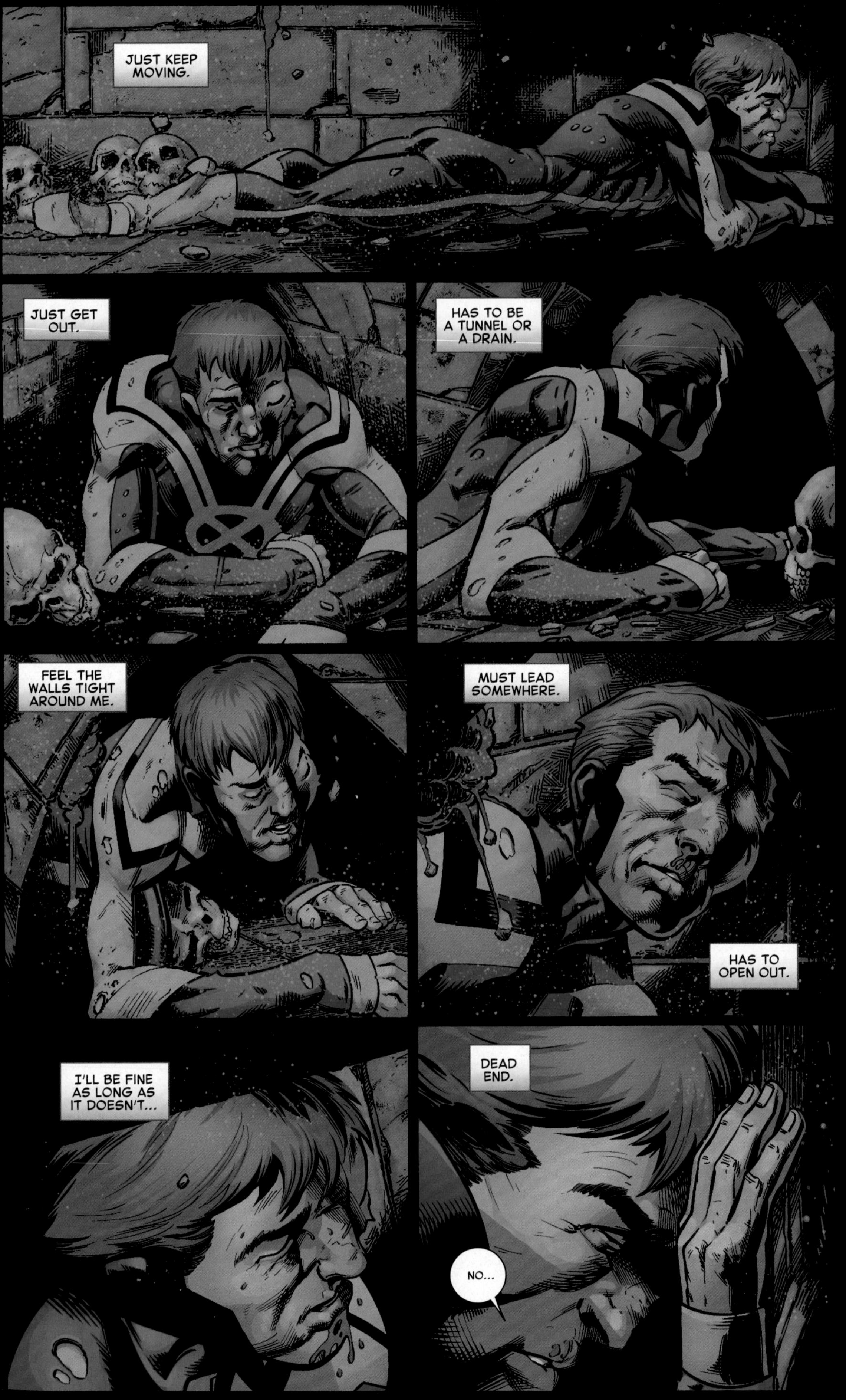
JUST KEEP MOVING.
JUST GET OUT.
HAS TO BE A TUNNEL OR A DRAIN.
FEEL THE WALLS TIGHT AROUND ME.
MUST LEAD SOMEWHERE.
HAS TO OPEN OUT.
I'LL BE FINE AS LONG AS IT DOESN'T...
DEAD END.
NO...

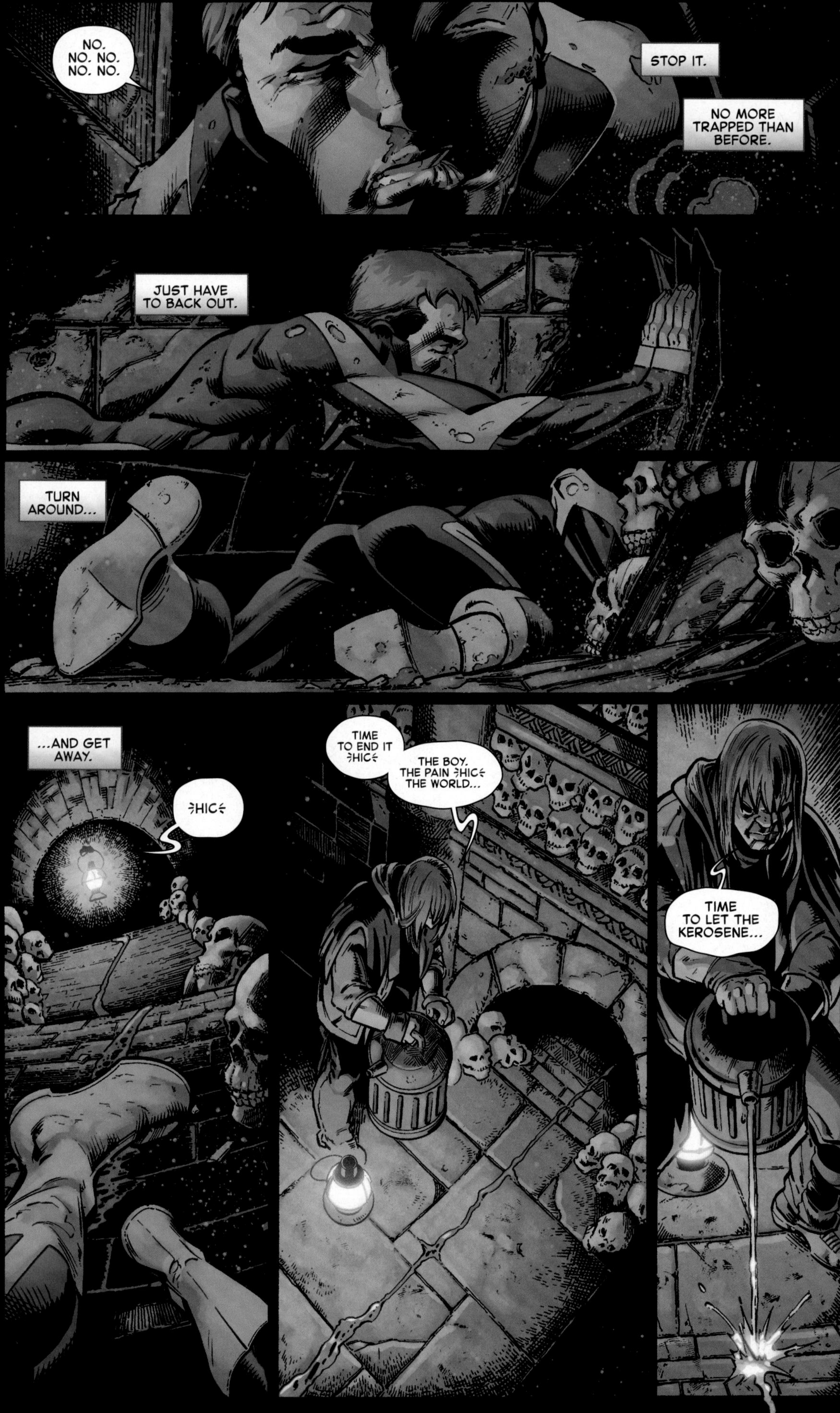
NO. NO. NO. NO. NO.
STOP IT.
NO MORE TRAPPED THAN BEFORE.
JUST HAVE TO BACK OUT.
TURN AROUND...
...AND GET AWAY.
HIC
TIME TO END IT HIC
THE BOY. THE PAIN HIC THE WORLD...
TIME TO LET THE KEROSENE...

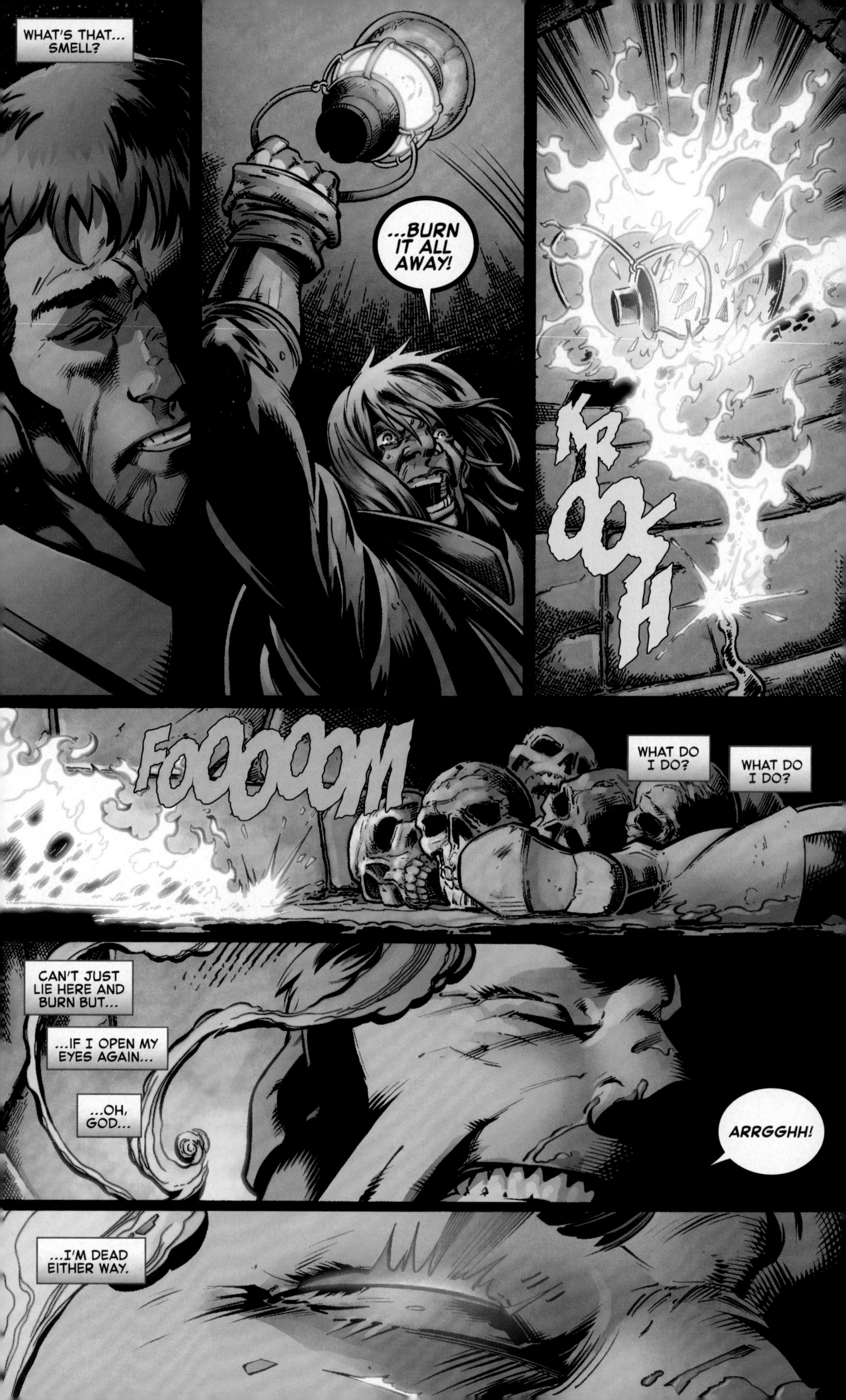
WHAT'S THAT... SMELL?
...BURN IT ALL AWAY!
KRSSH
FOOOOOM
WHAT DO I DO?
WHAT DO I DO?
CAN'T JUST LIE HERE AND BURN BUT...
...IF I OPEN MY EYES AGAIN...
...OH, GOD...
ARRGGHH!
...I'M DEAD EITHER WAY.

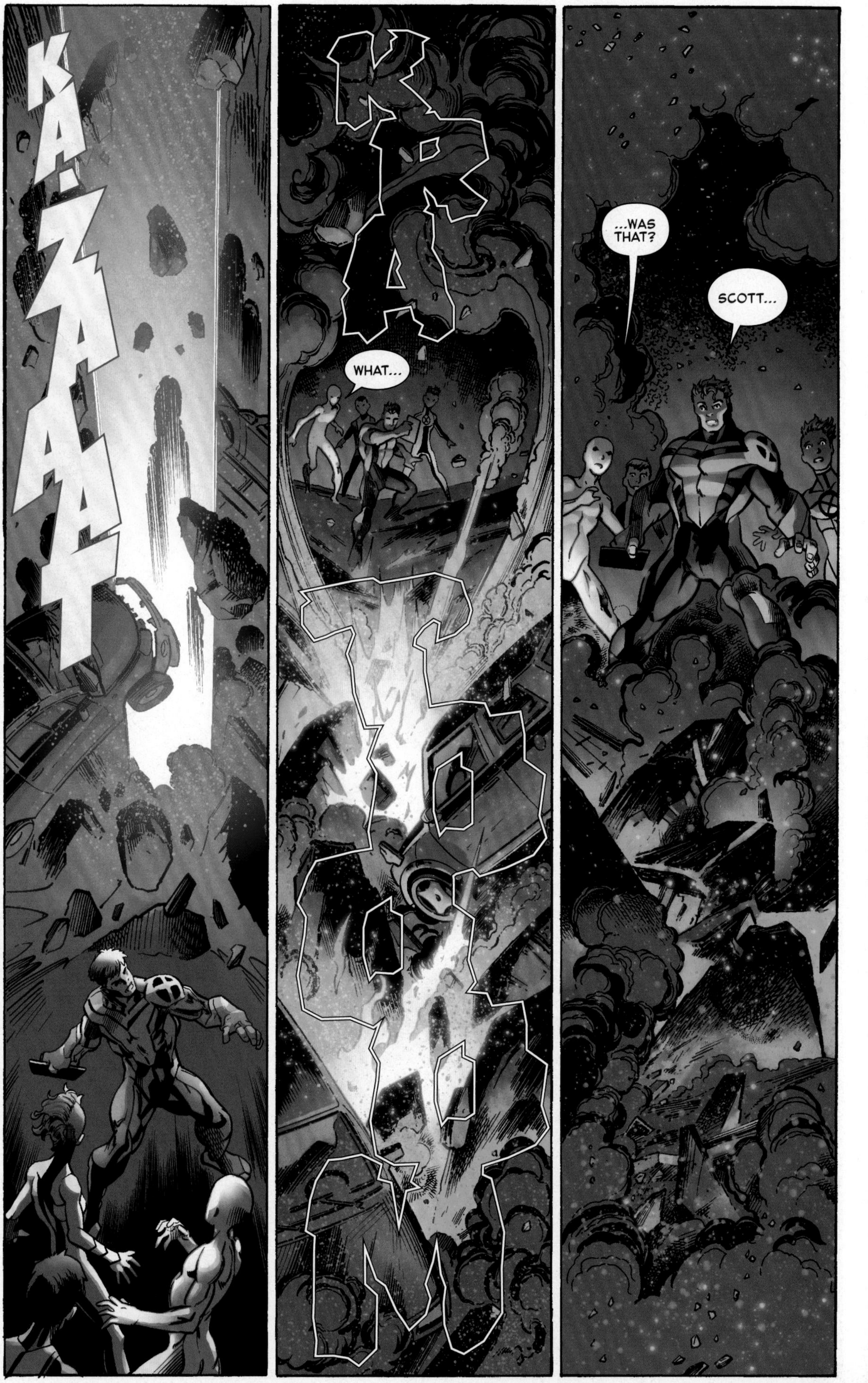
WHAT...
...WAS THAT?
SCOTT...

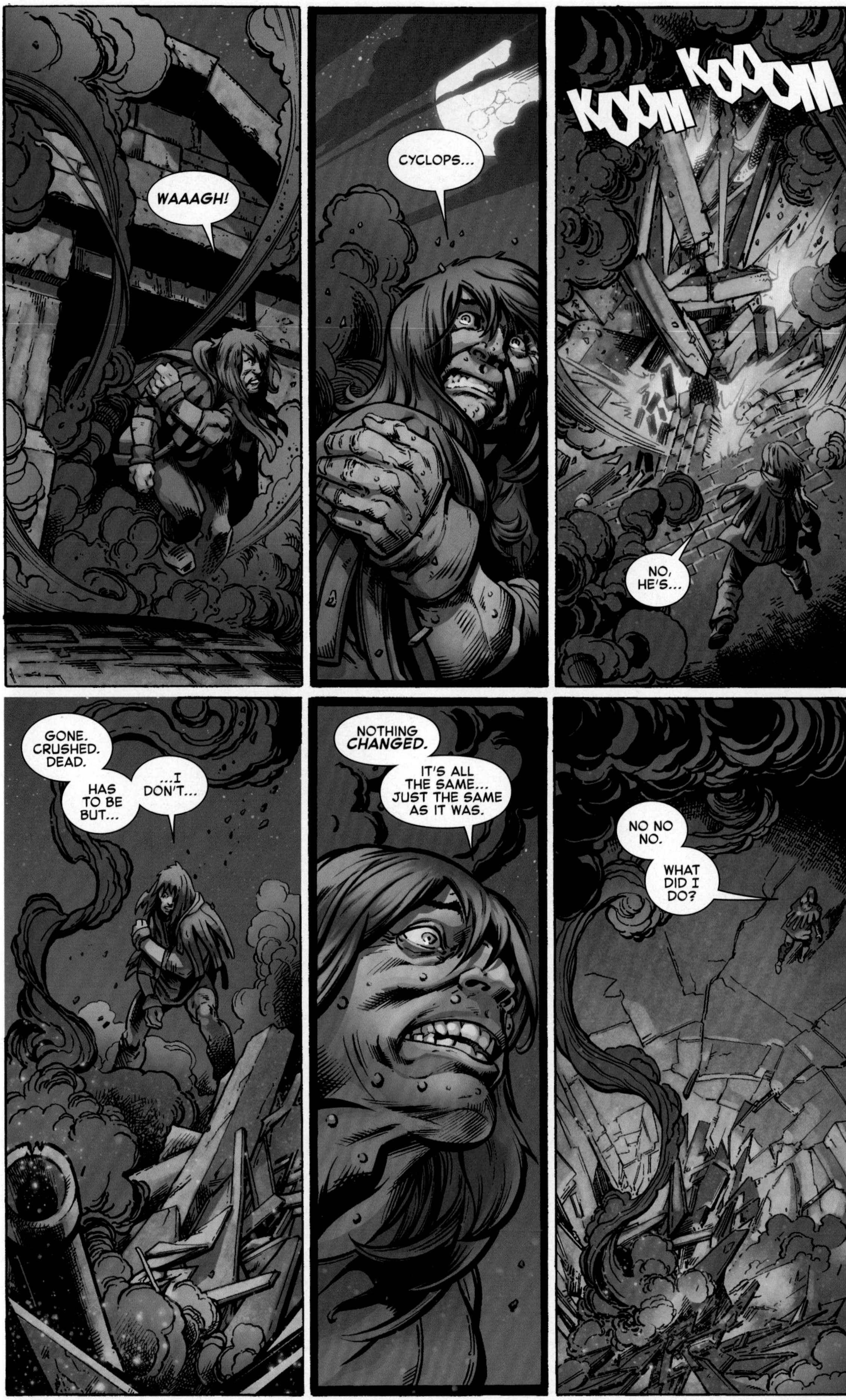
WAAAGH!
CYCLOPS...
KOOM KOOOM
NO, HE'S...
GONE. CRUSHED. DEAD.
HAS TO BE BUT...
...I DON'T...
NOTHING CHANGED.
IT'S ALL THE SAME... JUST THE SAME AS IT WAS.
NO NO NO.
WHAT DID I DO?

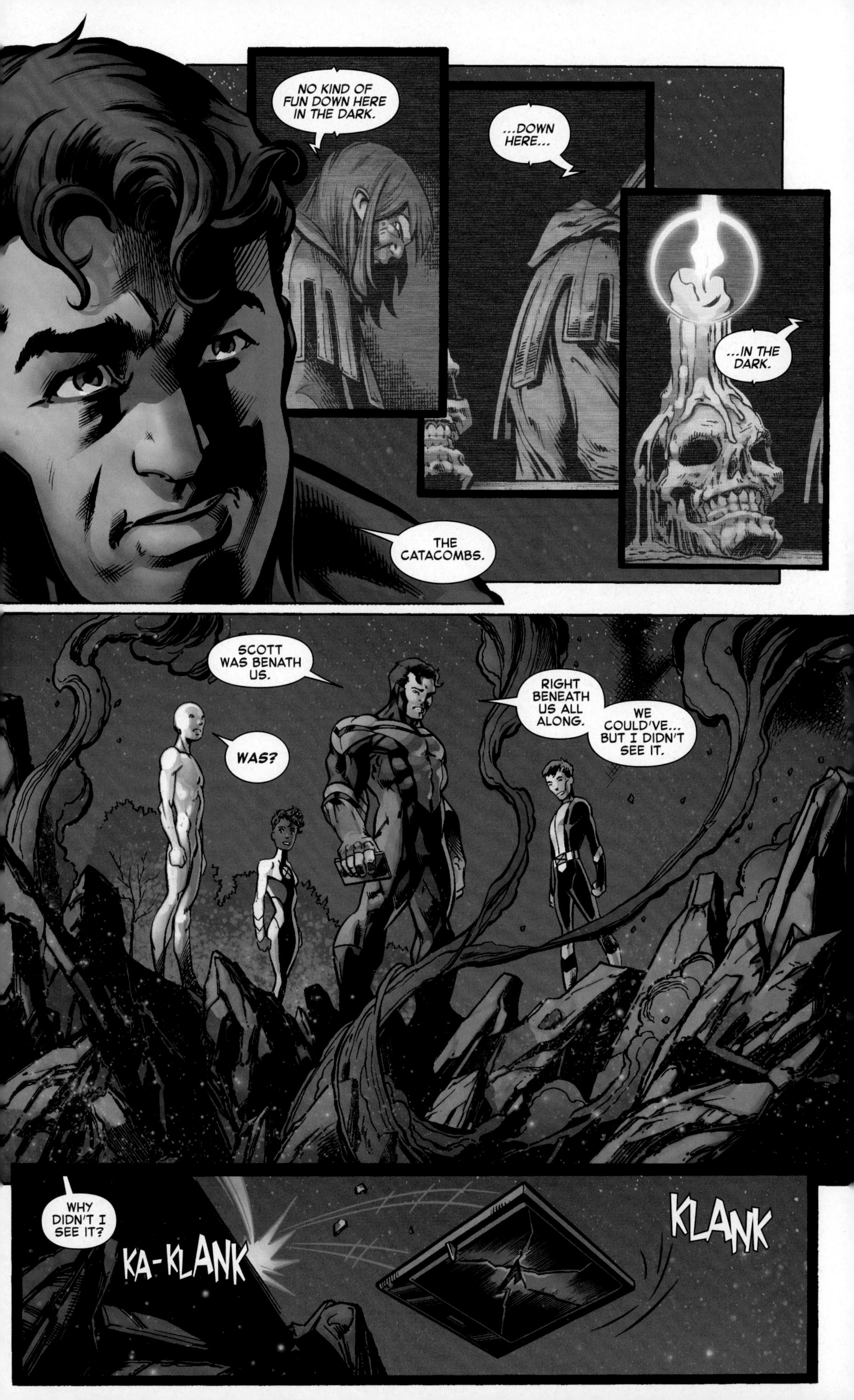
NO KIND OF FUN DOWN HERE IN THE DARK.
...DOWN HERE...
...IN THE DARK.
THE CATACOMBS.
SCOTT WAS BENATH US.
RIGHT BENEATH US ALL ALONG.
WE COULD'VE... BUT I DIDN'T SEE IT.
WAS?
WHY DIDN'T I SEE IT?
KA-KLANK
KLANK

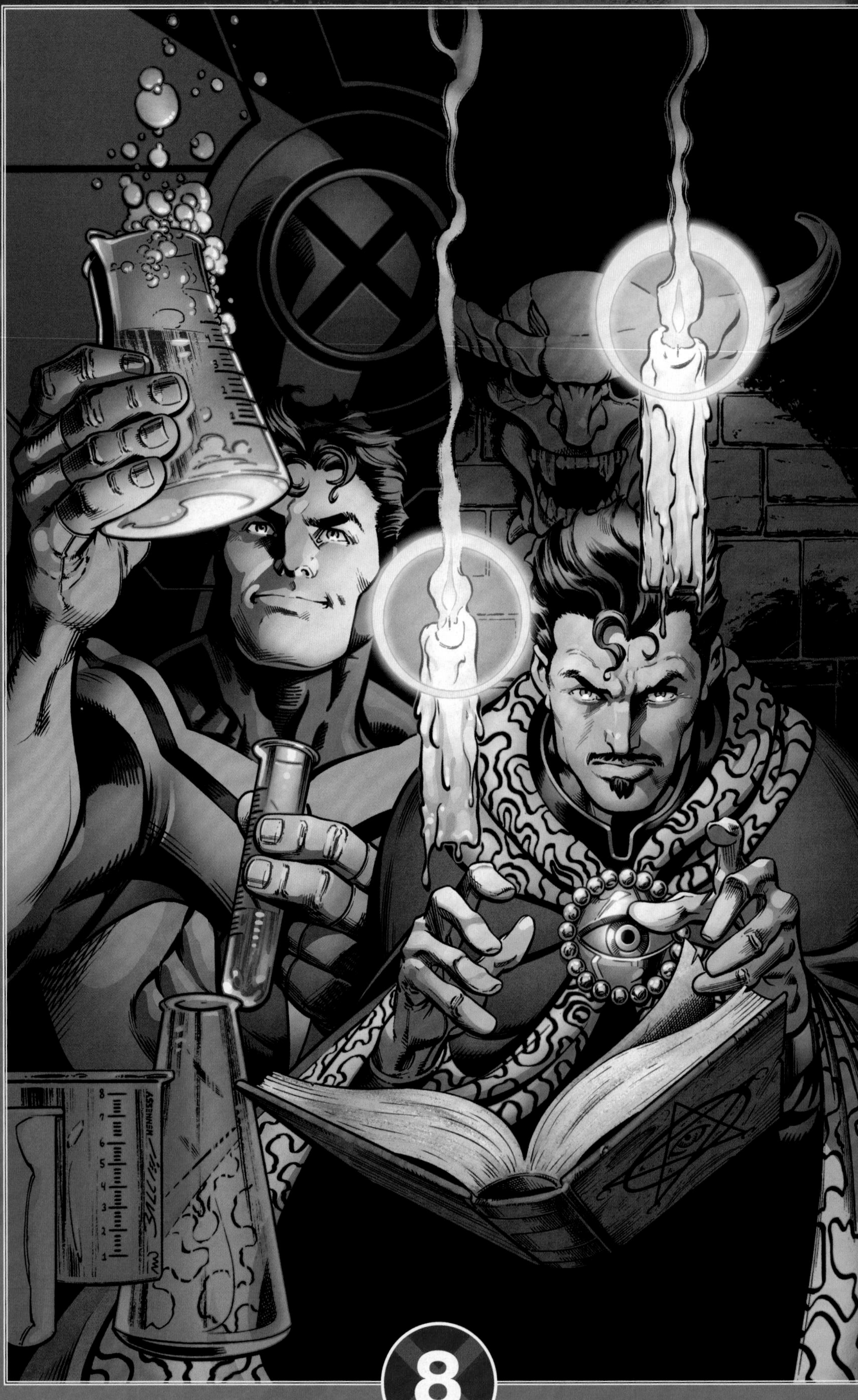

8

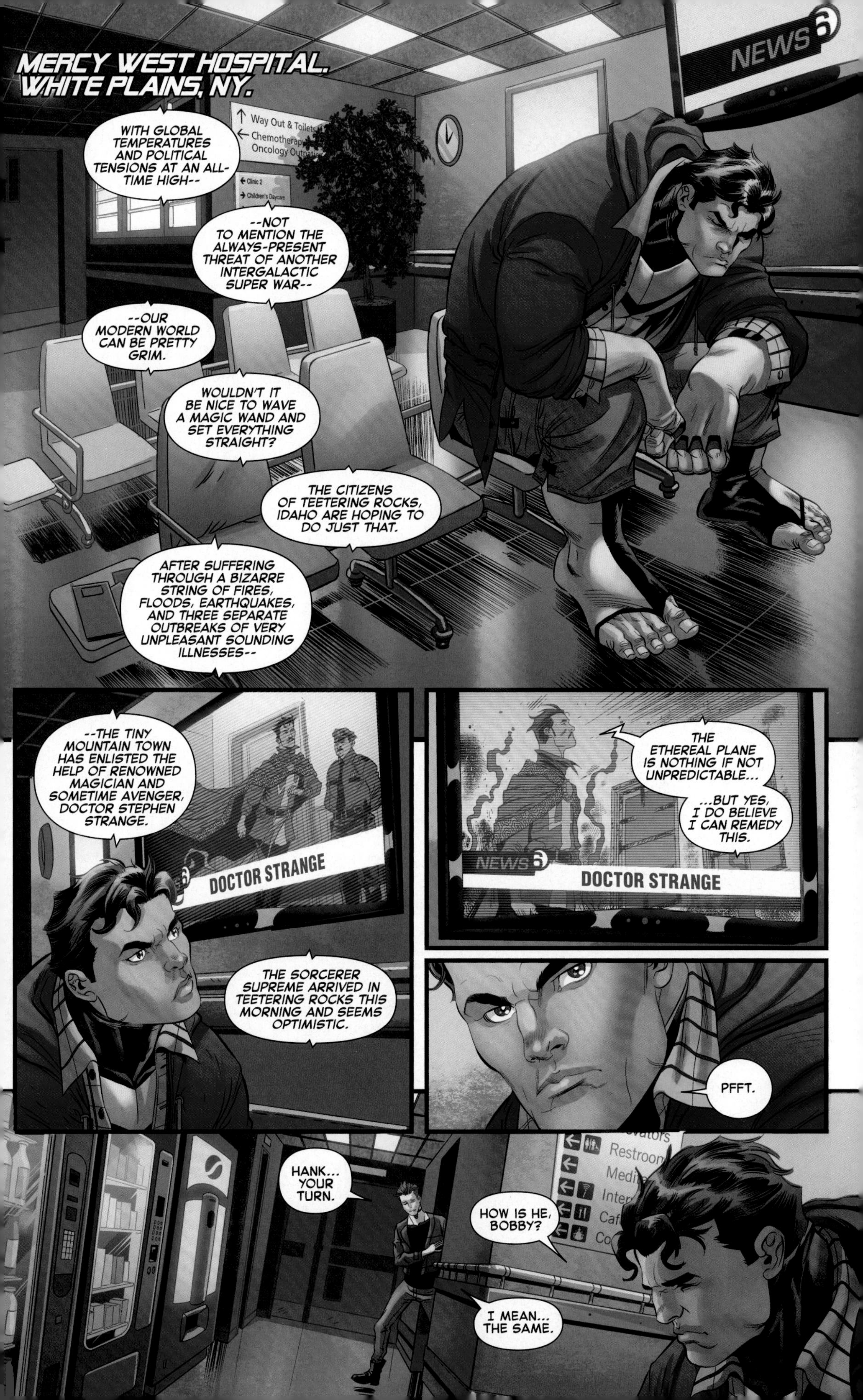

MERCY WEST HOSPITAL. WHITE PLAINS, NY.
NEWS 6
Way Out & Toilets
Chemotherapy
Oncology Outpatients
Clinic 2
Children's Daycare
WITH GLOBAL TEMPERATURES AND POLITICAL TENSIONS AT AN ALL-TIME HIGH--
--NOT TO MENTION THE ALWAYS-PRESENT THREAT OF ANOTHER INTERGALACTIC SUPER WAR--
--OUR MODERN WORLD CAN BE PRETTY GRIM.
WOULDN'T IT BE NICE TO WAVE A MAGIC WAND AND SET EVERYTHING STRAIGHT?
THE CITIZENS OF TEETERING ROCKS, IDAHO ARE HOPING TO DO JUST THAT.
AFTER SUFFERING THROUGH A BIZARRE STRING OF FIRES, FLOODS, EARTHQUAKES, AND THREE SEPARATE OUTBREAKS OF VERY UNPLEASANT SOUNDING ILLNESSES--
--THE TINY MOUNTAIN TOWN HAS ENLISTED THE HELP OF RENOWNED MAGICIAN AND SOMETIME AVENGER, DOCTOR STEPHEN STRANGE.
DOCTOR STRANGE
THE SORCERER SUPREME ARRIVED IN TEETERING ROCKS THIS MORNING AND SEEMS OPTIMISTIC.
THE ETHEREAL PLANE IS NOTHING IF NOT UNPREDICTABLE...
...BUT YES, I DO BELIEVE I CAN REMEDY THIS.
NEWS 6
DOCTOR STRANGE
PFFT.
HANK... YOUR TURN.
Restroom
HOW IS HE, BOBBY?
I MEAN... THE SAME.

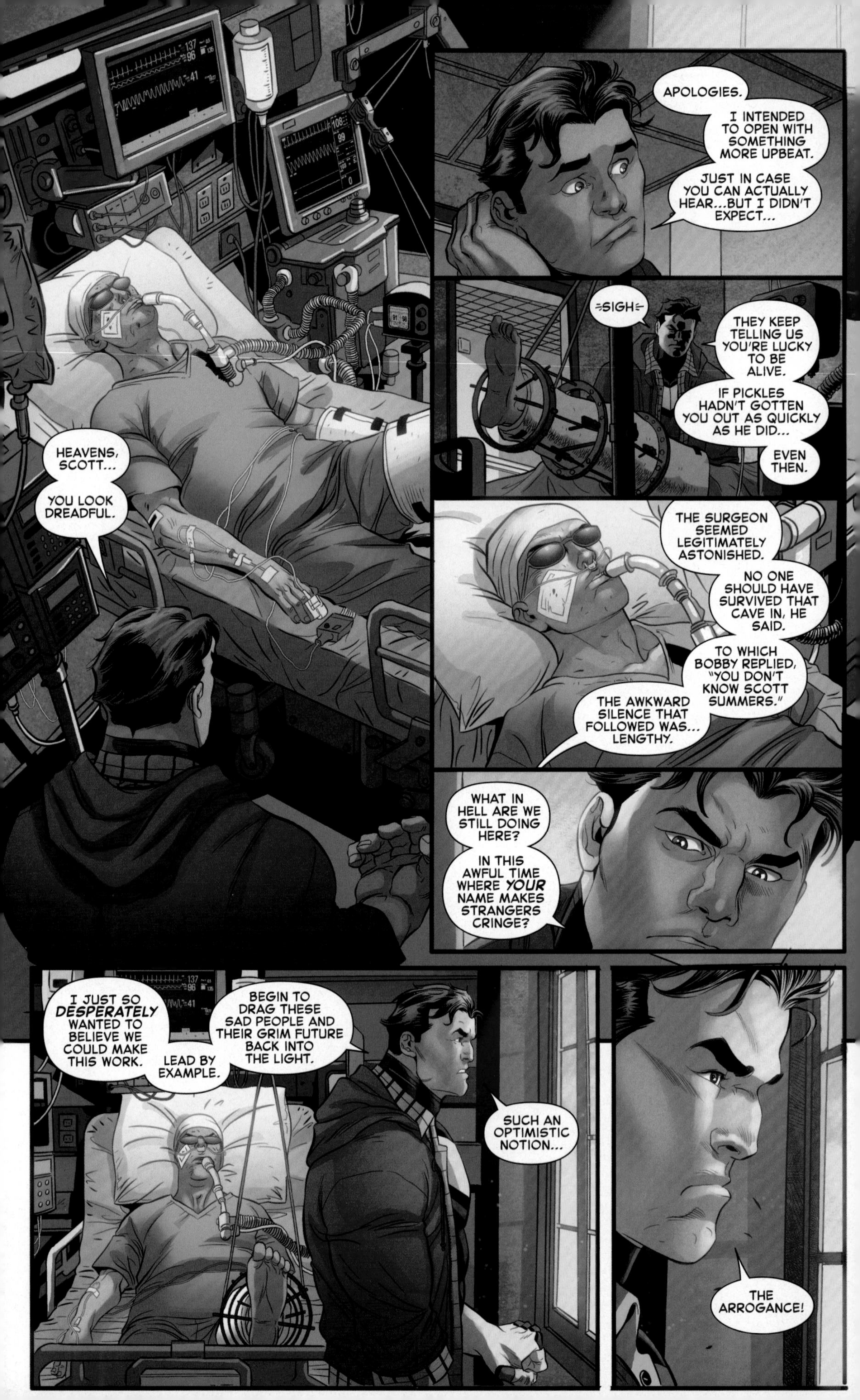
HEAVENS, SCOTT...
YOU LOOK DREADFUL.
APOLOGIES.
I INTENDED TO OPEN WITH SOMETHING MORE UPBEAT.
JUST IN CASE YOU CAN ACTUALLY HEAR...BUT I DIDN'T EXPECT...
≈SIGH≈
THEY KEEP TELLING US YOU'RE LUCKY TO BE ALIVE.
IF PICKLES HADN'T GOTTEN YOU OUT AS QUICKLY AS HE DID...
EVEN THEN.
THE SURGEON SEEMED LEGITIMATELY ASTONISHED.
NO ONE SHOULD HAVE SURVIVED THAT CAVE IN, HE SAID.
TO WHICH BOBBY REPLIED, "YOU DON'T KNOW SCOTT SUMMERS."
THE AWKWARD SILENCE THAT FOLLOWED WAS... LENGTHY.
WHAT IN HELL ARE WE STILL DOING HERE?
IN THIS AWFUL TIME WHERE *YOUR* NAME MAKES STRANGERS CRINGE?
I JUST SO ***DESPERATELY*** WANTED TO BELIEVE WE COULD MAKE THIS WORK.
LEAD BY EXAMPLE.
BEGIN TO DRAG THESE SAD PEOPLE AND THEIR GRIM FUTURE BACK INTO THE LIGHT.
SUCH AN OPTIMISTIC NOTION...
THE ARROGANCE!

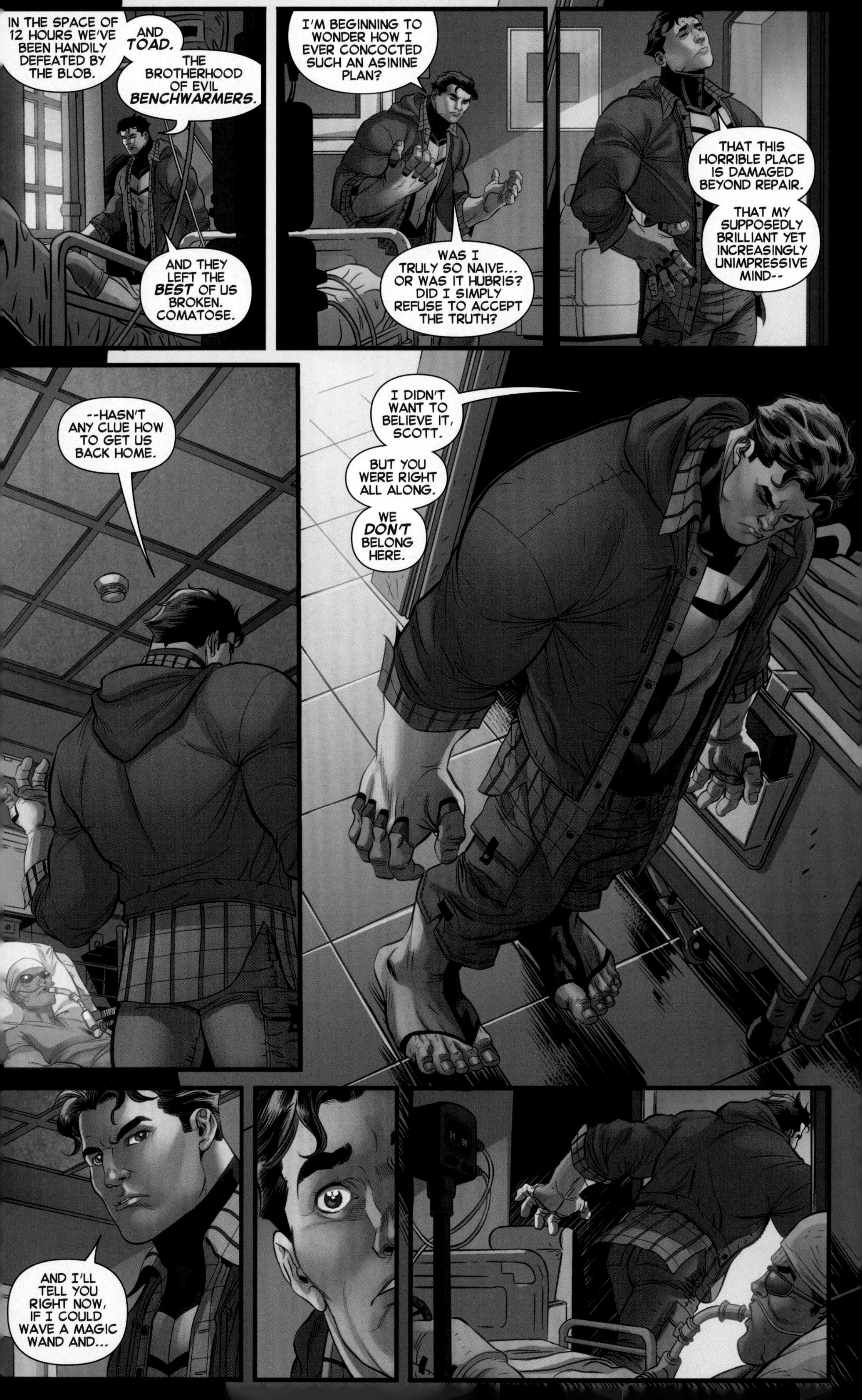
IN THE SPACE OF 12 HOURS WE'VE BEEN HANDILY DEFEATED BY THE BLOB.
AND TOAD.
THE BROTHERHOOD OF EVIL BENCHWARMERS.
AND THEY LEFT THE BEST OF US BROKEN. COMATOSE.
I'M BEGINNING TO WONDER HOW I EVER CONCOCTED SUCH AN ASININE PLAN?
WAS I TRULY SO NAIVE... OR WAS IT HUBRIS? DID I SIMPLY REFUSE TO ACCEPT THE TRUTH?
THAT THIS HORRIBLE PLACE IS DAMAGED BEYOND REPAIR.
THAT MY SUPPOSEDLY BRILLIANT YET INCREASINGLY UNIMPRESSIVE MIND--
--HASN'T ANY CLUE HOW TO GET US BACK HOME.
I DIDN'T WANT TO BELIEVE IT, SCOTT.
BUT YOU WERE RIGHT ALL ALONG.
WE DON'T BELONG HERE.
AND I'LL TELL YOU RIGHT NOW, IF I COULD WAVE A MAGIC WAND AND...

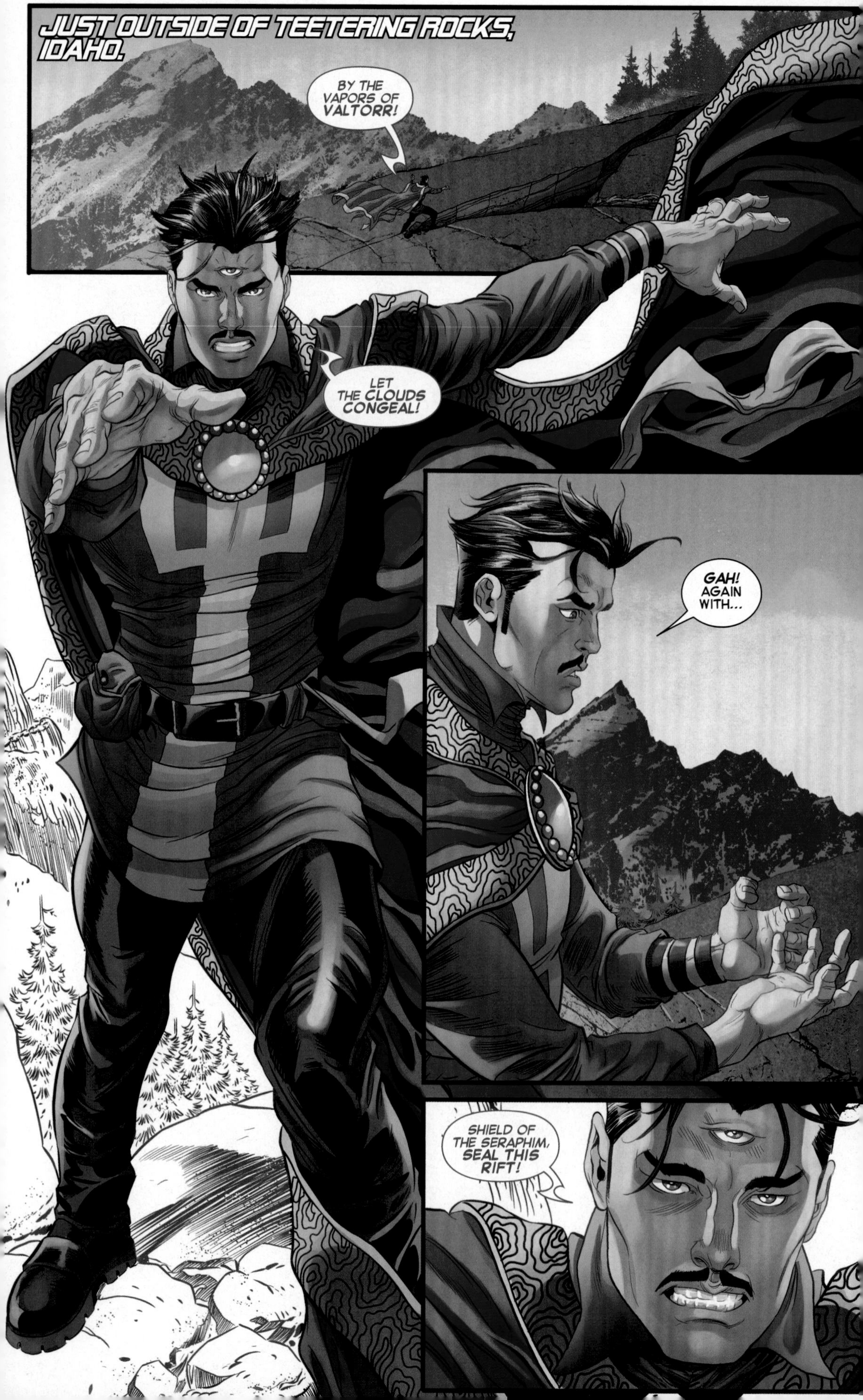
JUST OUTSIDE OF TEETERING ROCKS, IDAHO.
BY THE VAPORS OF VALTORR!
LET THE CLOUDS CONGEAL!
GAH! AGAIN WITH...
SHIELD OF THE SERAPHIM, SEAL THIS RIFT!

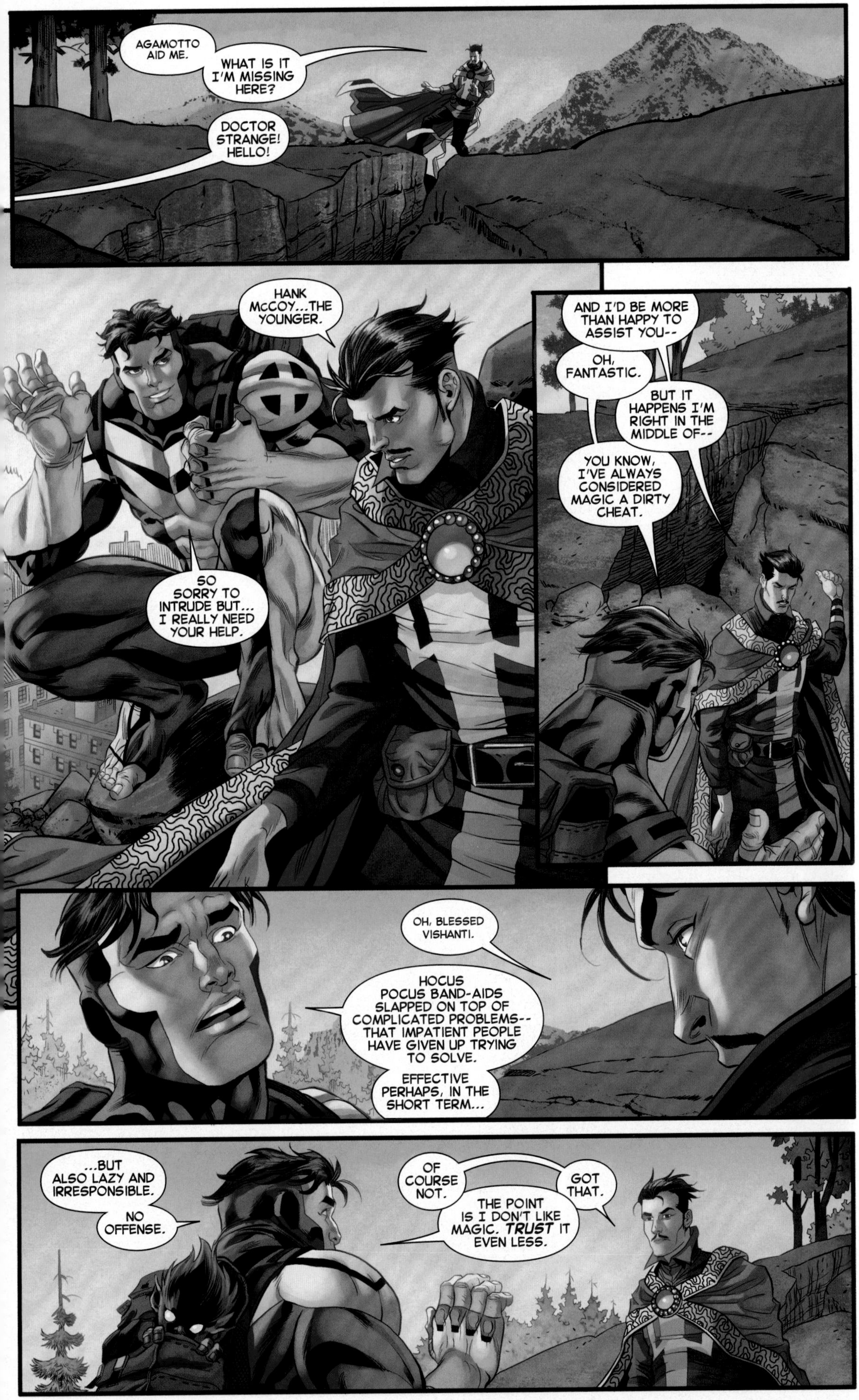
AGAMOTTO AID ME.
WHAT IS IT I'M MISSING HERE?
DOCTOR STRANGE! HELLO!
HANK McCOY...THE YOUNGER.
SO SORRY TO INTRUDE BUT... I REALLY NEED YOUR HELP.
AND I'D BE MORE THAN HAPPY TO ASSIST YOU--
OH, FANTASTIC.
BUT IT HAPPENS I'M RIGHT IN THE MIDDLE OF--
YOU KNOW, I'VE ALWAYS CONSIDERED MAGIC A DIRTY CHEAT.
OH, BLESSED VISHANTI.
HOCUS POCUS BAND-AIDS SLAPPED ON TOP OF COMPLICATED PROBLEMS--THAT IMPATIENT PEOPLE HAVE GIVEN UP TRYING TO SOLVE.
EFFECTIVE PERHAPS, IN THE SHORT TERM...
...BUT ALSO LAZY AND IRRESPONSIBLE.
NO OFFENSE.
OF COURSE NOT.
GOT THAT.
THE POINT IS I DON'T LIKE MAGIC. TRUST IT EVEN LESS.

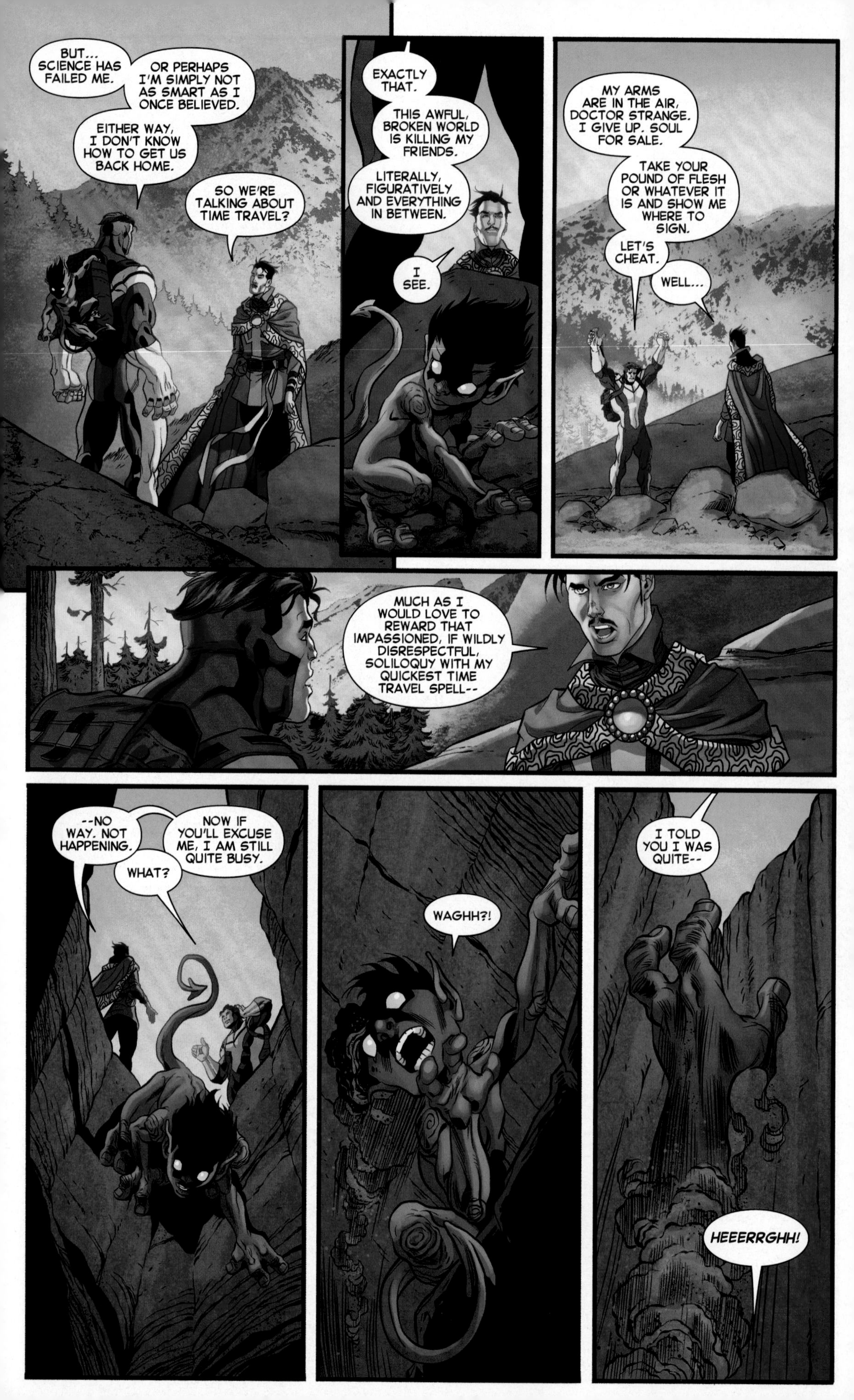
BUT... SCIENCE HAS FAILED ME.
OR PERHAPS I'M SIMPLY NOT AS SMART AS I ONCE BELIEVED.
EITHER WAY, I DON'T KNOW HOW TO GET US BACK HOME.
SO WE'RE TALKING ABOUT TIME TRAVEL?
EXACTLY THAT.
THIS AWFUL, BROKEN WORLD IS KILLING MY FRIENDS.
LITERALLY, FIGURATIVELY AND EVERYTHING IN BETWEEN.
I SEE.
MY ARMS ARE IN THE AIR, DOCTOR STRANGE. I GIVE UP. SOUL FOR SALE.
TAKE YOUR POUND OF FLESH OR WHATEVER IT IS AND SHOW ME WHERE TO SIGN.
LET'S CHEAT.
WELL...
MUCH AS I WOULD LOVE TO REWARD THAT IMPASSIONED, IF WILDLY DISRESPECTFUL, SOLILOQUY WITH MY QUICKEST TIME TRAVEL SPELL--
--NO WAY. NOT HAPPENING.
WHAT?
NOW IF YOU'LL EXCUSE ME, I AM STILL QUITE BUSY.
WAGHH?!
I TOLD YOU I WAS QUITE--
HEEERRGHH!

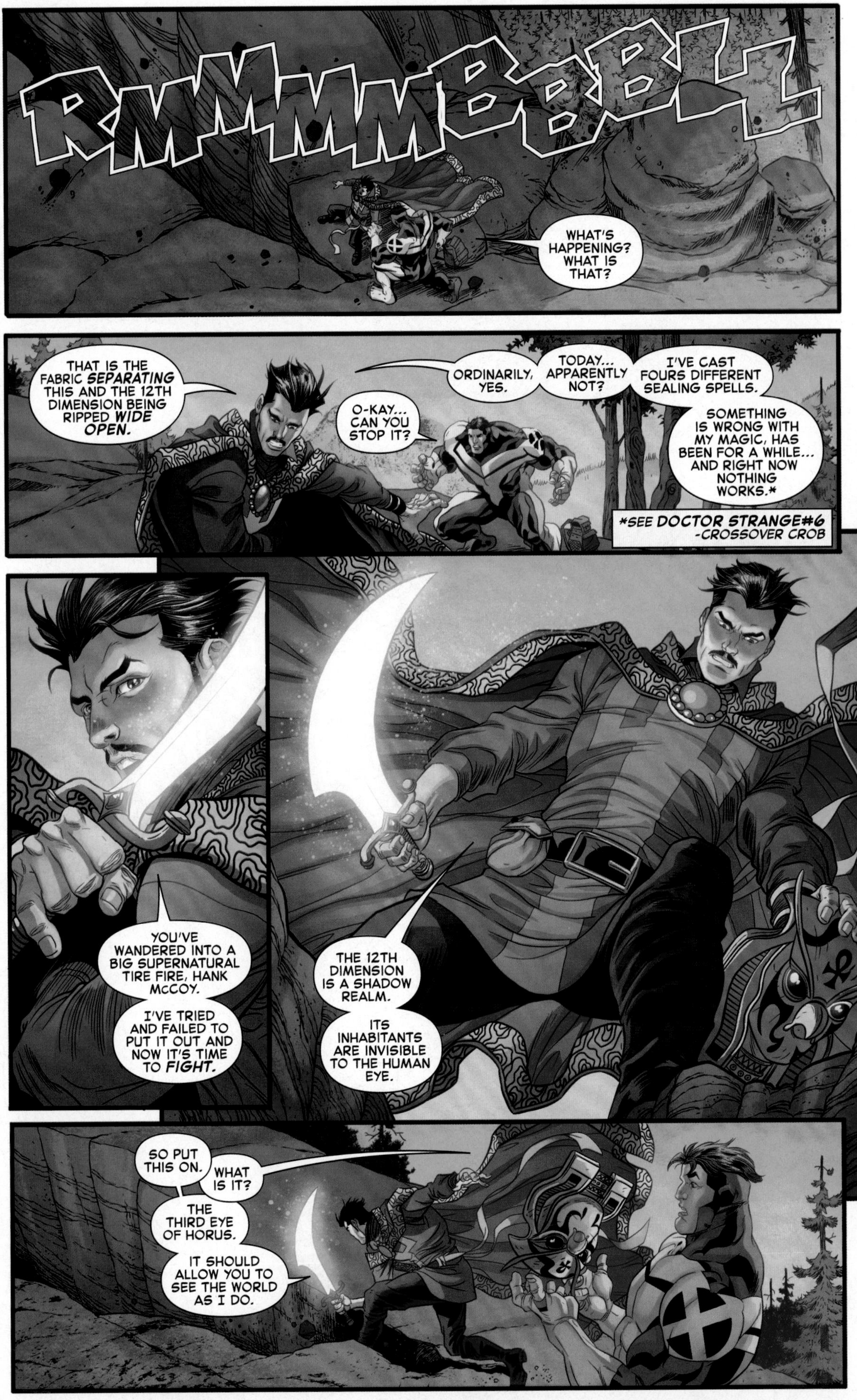
RMMMMBBLL
WHAT'S HAPPENING? WHAT IS THAT?
THAT IS THE FABRIC SEPARATING THIS AND THE 12TH DIMENSION BEING RIPPED WIDE OPEN.
O-KAY... CAN YOU STOP IT?
ORDINARILY, YES.
TODAY... APPARENTLY NOT?
I'VE CAST FOURS DIFFERENT SEALING SPELLS.
SOMETHING IS WRONG WITH MY MAGIC, HAS BEEN FOR A WHILE... AND RIGHT NOW NOTHING WORKS.*
*SEE DOCTOR STRANGE#6 -CROSSOVER CROB
YOU'VE WANDERED INTO A BIG SUPERNATURAL TIRE FIRE, HANK McCOY.
I'VE TRIED AND FAILED TO PUT IT OUT AND NOW IT'S TIME TO FIGHT.
THE 12TH DIMENSION IS A SHADOW REALM.
ITS INHABITANTS ARE INVISIBLE TO THE HUMAN EYE.
SO PUT THIS ON.
WHAT IS IT?
THE THIRD EYE OF HORUS.
IT SHOULD ALLOW YOU TO SEE THE WORLD AS I DO.

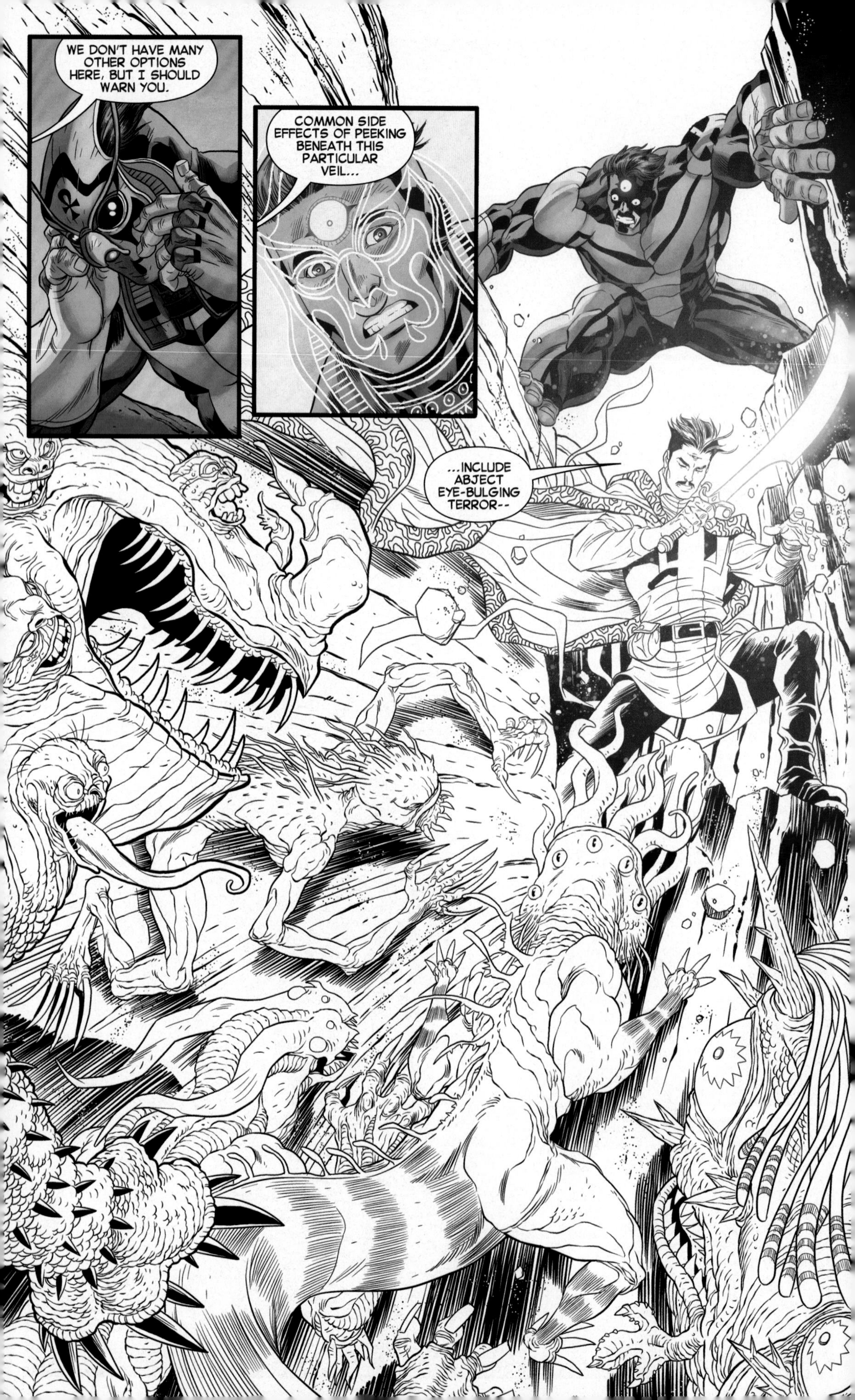
WE DON'T HAVE MANY OTHER OPTIONS HERE, BUT I SHOULD WARN YOU.
COMMON SIDE EFFECTS OF PEEKING BENEATH THIS PARTICULAR VEIL...
...INCLUDE ABJECT EYE-BULGING TERROR--

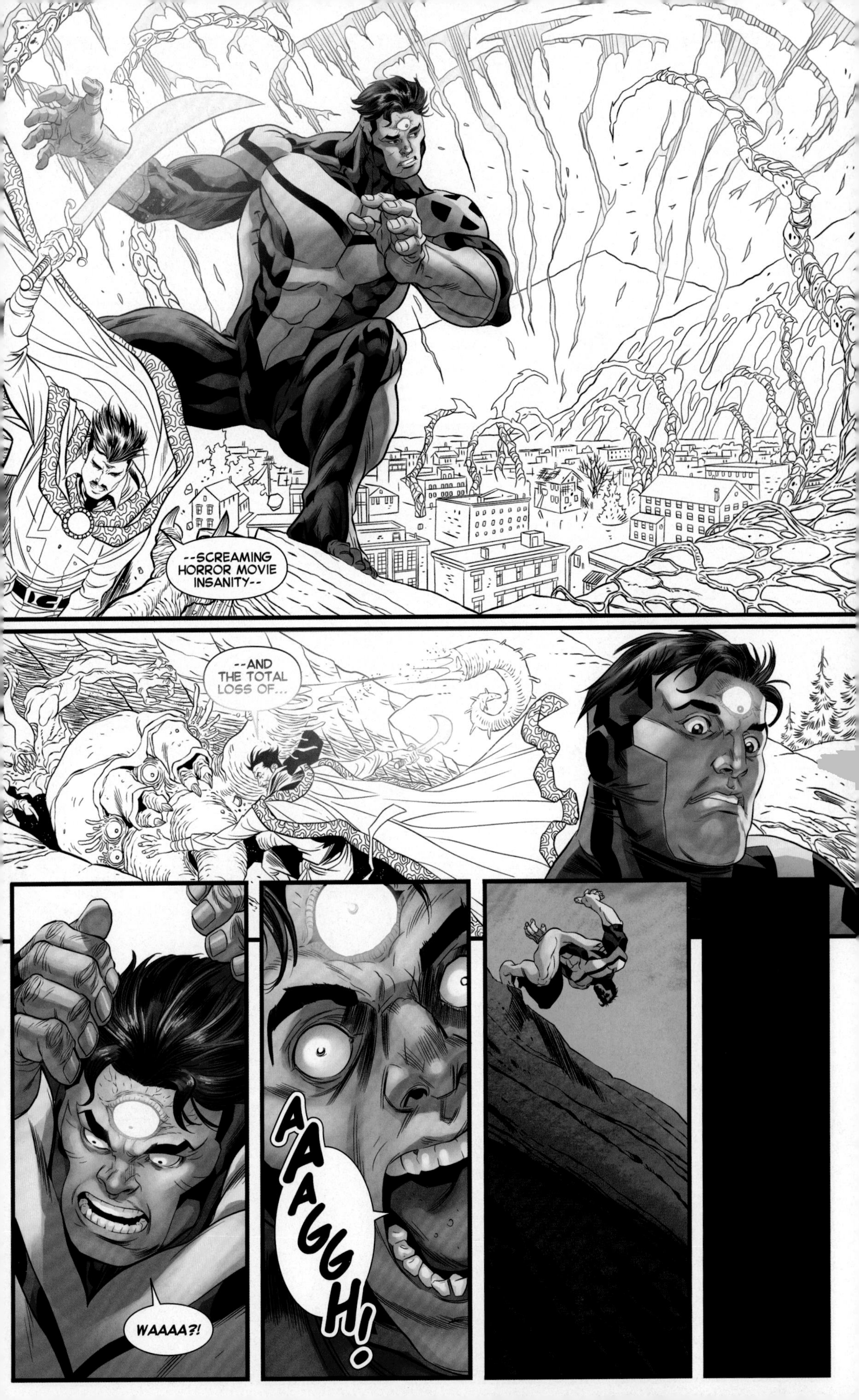
--SCREAMING HORROR MOVIE INSANITY--
--AND THE TOTAL LOSS OF...
WAAAA?!
AAAGGH!

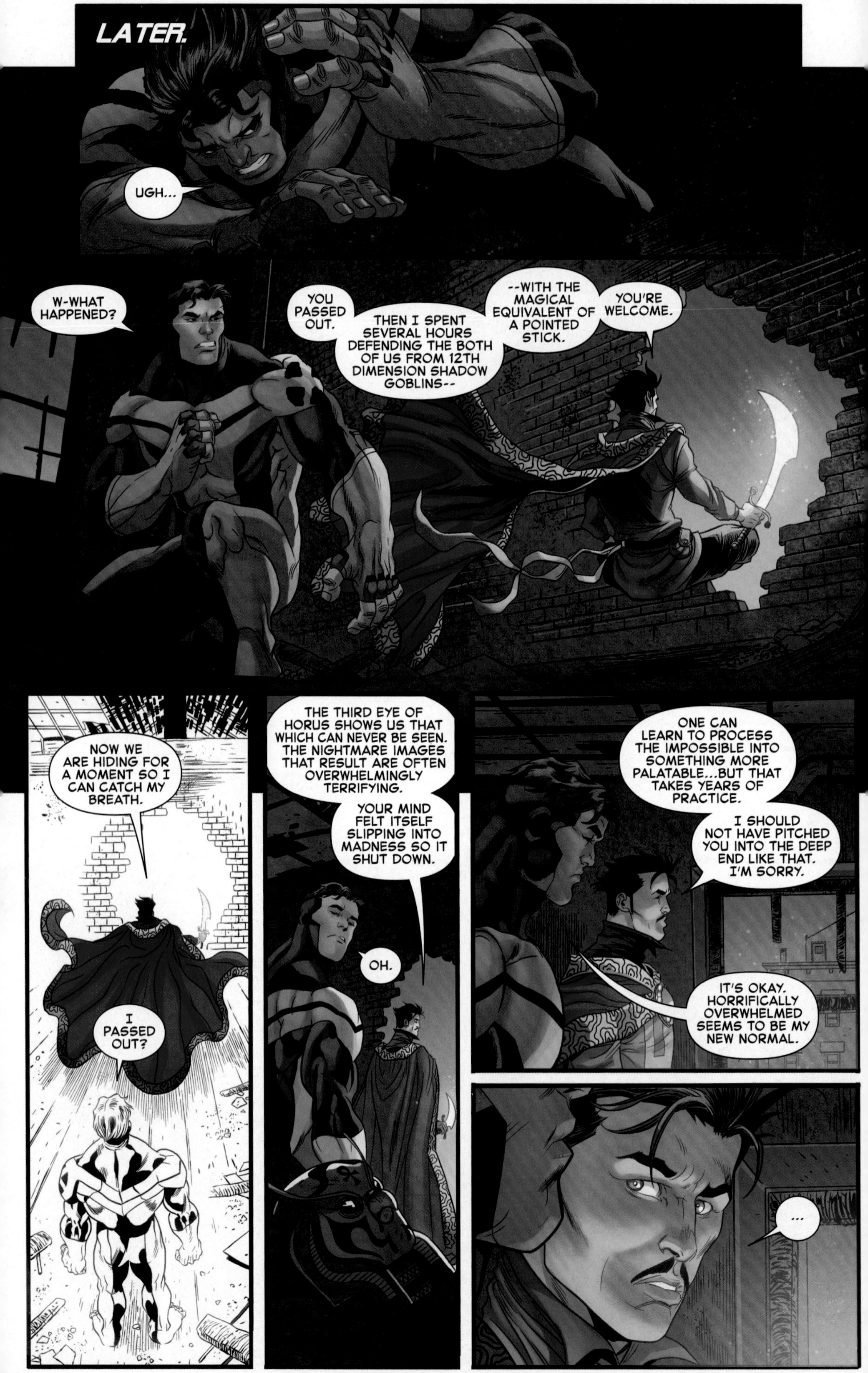
LATER.
UGH...
W-WHAT HAPPENED?
YOU PASSED OUT.
THEN I SPENT SEVERAL HOURS DEFENDING THE BOTH OF US FROM 12TH DIMENSION SHADOW GOBLINS--
--WITH THE MAGICAL EQUIVALENT OF A POINTED STICK.
YOU'RE WELCOME.
NOW WE ARE HIDING FOR A MOMENT SO I CAN CATCH MY BREATH.
I PASSED OUT?
THE THIRD EYE OF HORUS SHOWS US THAT WHICH CAN NEVER BE SEEN. THE NIGHTMARE IMAGES THAT RESULT ARE OFTEN OVERWHELMINGLY TERRIFYING.
YOUR MIND FELT ITSELF SLIPPING INTO MADNESS SO IT SHUT DOWN.
OH.
ONE CAN LEARN TO PROCESS THE IMPOSSIBLE INTO SOMETHING MORE PALATABLE...BUT THAT TAKES YEARS OF PRACTICE.
I SHOULD NOT HAVE PITCHED YOU INTO THE DEEP END LIKE THAT. I'M SORRY.
IT'S OKAY. HORRIFICALLY OVERWHELMED SEEMS TO BE MY NEW NORMAL.
...

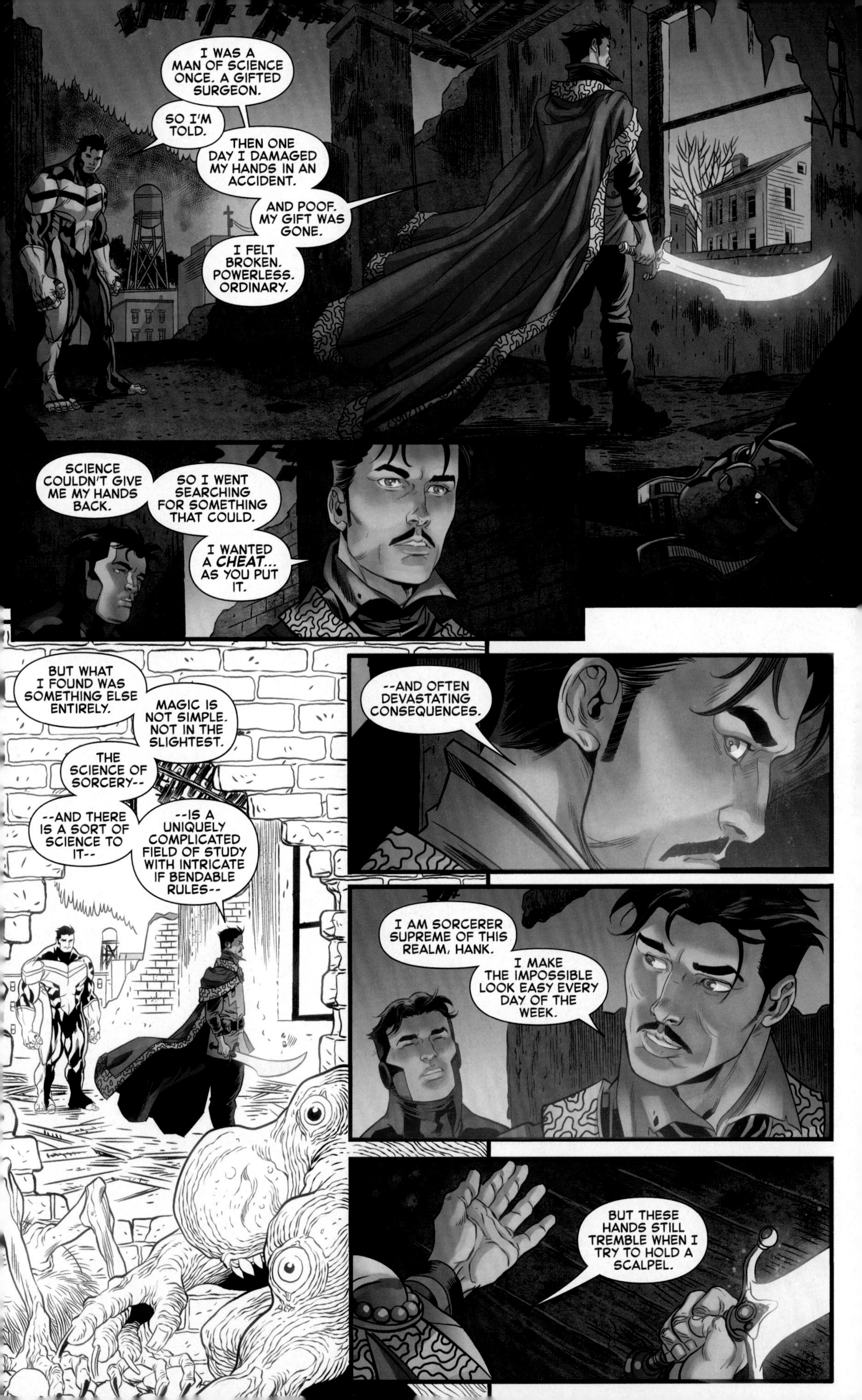
I WAS A MAN OF SCIENCE ONCE. A GIFTED SURGEON.
SO I'M TOLD.
THEN ONE DAY I DAMAGED MY HANDS IN AN ACCIDENT.
AND POOF. MY GIFT WAS GONE.
I FELT BROKEN. POWERLESS. ORDINARY.
SCIENCE COULDN'T GIVE ME MY HANDS BACK.
SO I WENT SEARCHING FOR SOMETHING THAT COULD.
I WANTED A *CHEAT*... AS YOU PUT IT.
BUT WHAT I FOUND WAS SOMETHING ELSE ENTIRELY.
MAGIC IS NOT SIMPLE. NOT IN THE SLIGHTEST.
THE SCIENCE OF SORCERY--
--AND THERE IS A SORT OF SCIENCE TO IT--
--IS A UNIQUELY COMPLICATED FIELD OF STUDY WITH INTRICATE IF BENDABLE RULES--
--AND OFTEN DEVASTATING CONSEQUENCES.
I AM SORCERER SUPREME OF THIS REALM, HANK.
I MAKE THE IMPOSSIBLE LOOK EASY EVERY DAY OF THE WEEK.
BUT THESE HANDS STILL TREMBLE WHEN I TRY TO HOLD A SCALPEL.

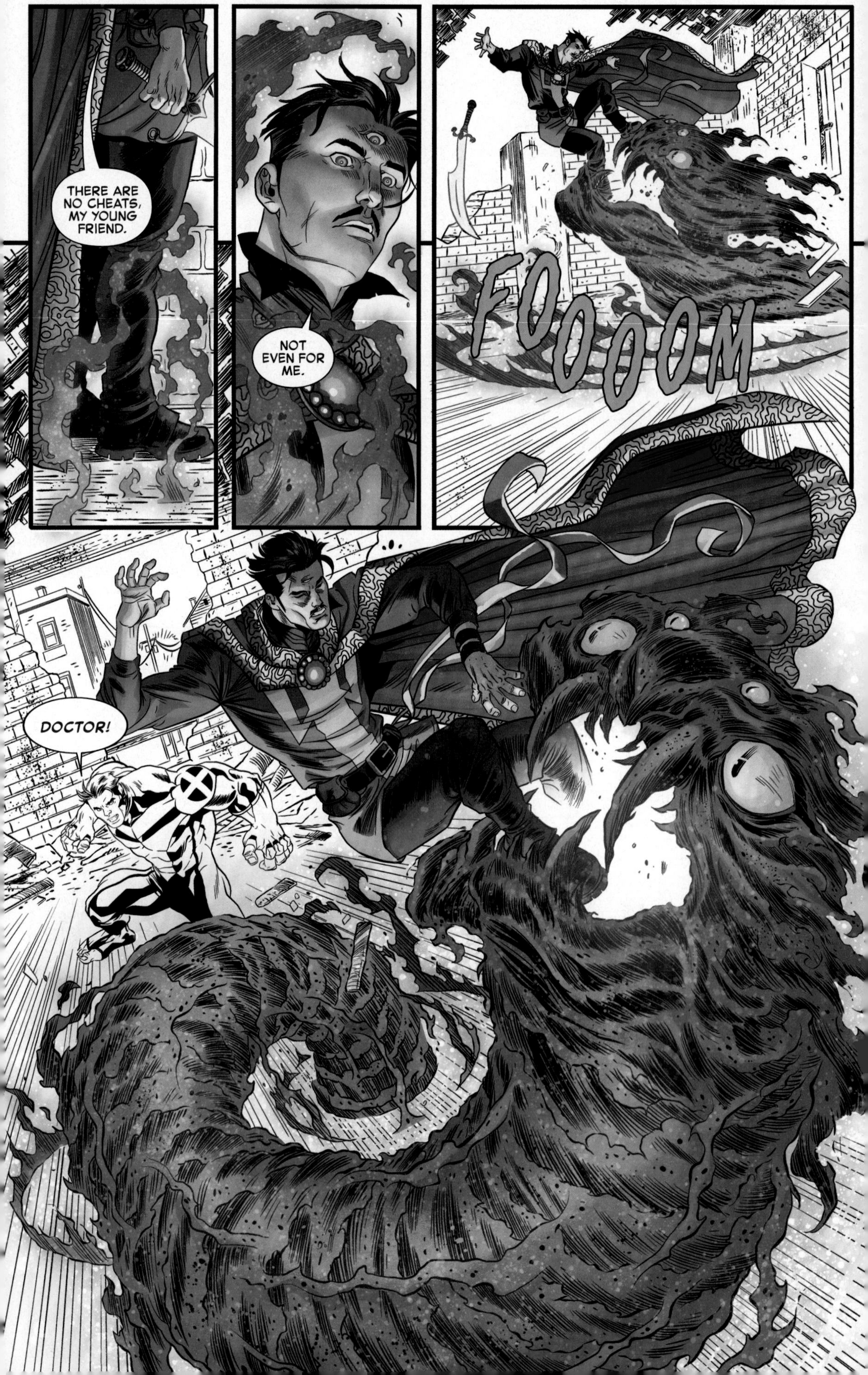
THERE ARE NO CHEATS, MY YOUNG FRIEND.
NOT EVEN FOR ME.
FOOOOM
DOCTOR!

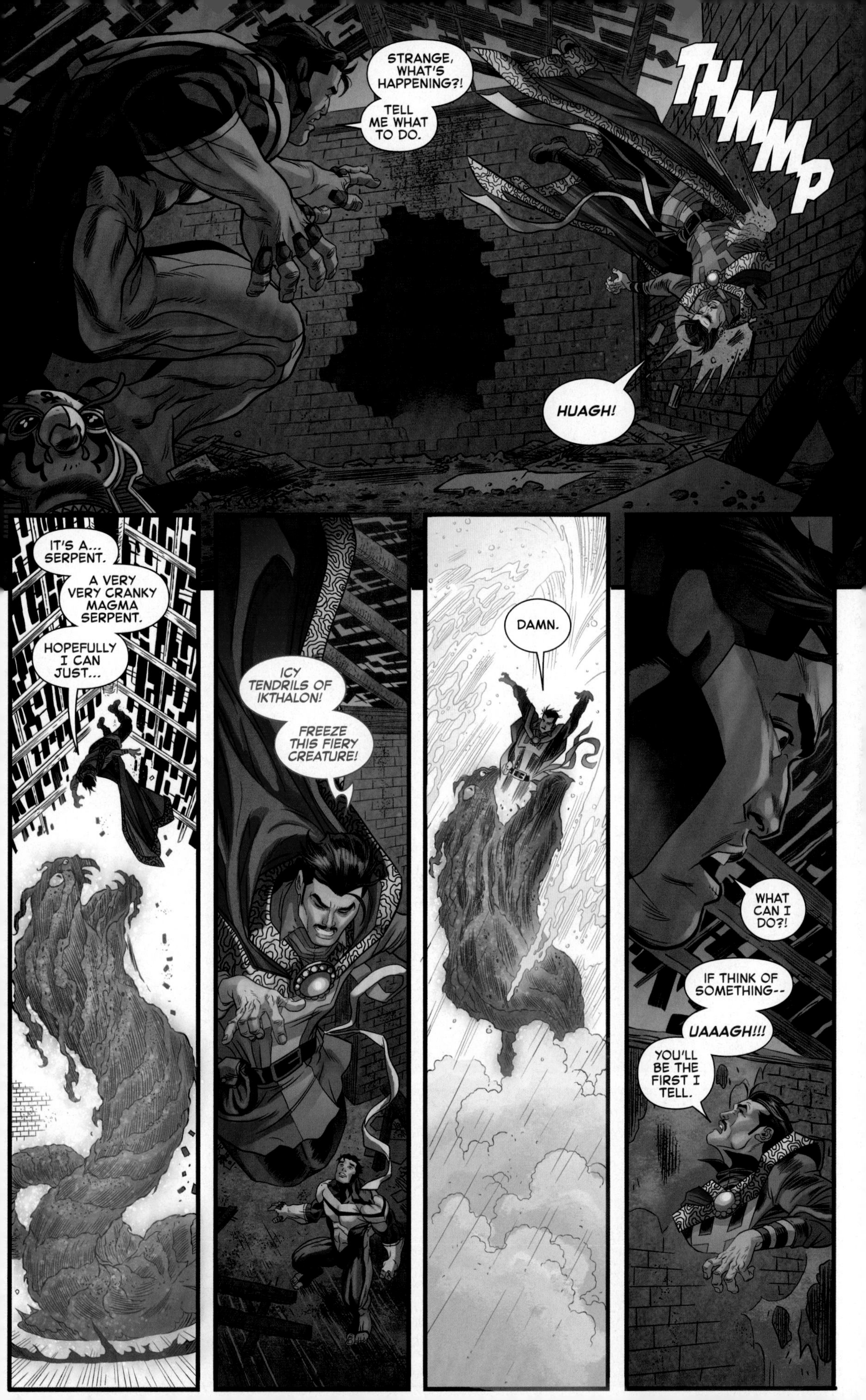
STRANGE, WHAT'S HAPPENING?!
TELL ME WHAT TO DO.
THMMMP
HUAGH!
IT'S A... SERPENT.
A VERY VERY CRANKY MAGMA SERPENT.
HOPEFULLY I CAN JUST...
ICY TENDRILS OF IKTHALON!
FREEZE THIS FIERY CREATURE!
DAMN.
WHAT CAN I DO?!
IF THINK OF SOMETHING--
UAAAGH!!!
YOU'LL BE THE FIRST I TELL.

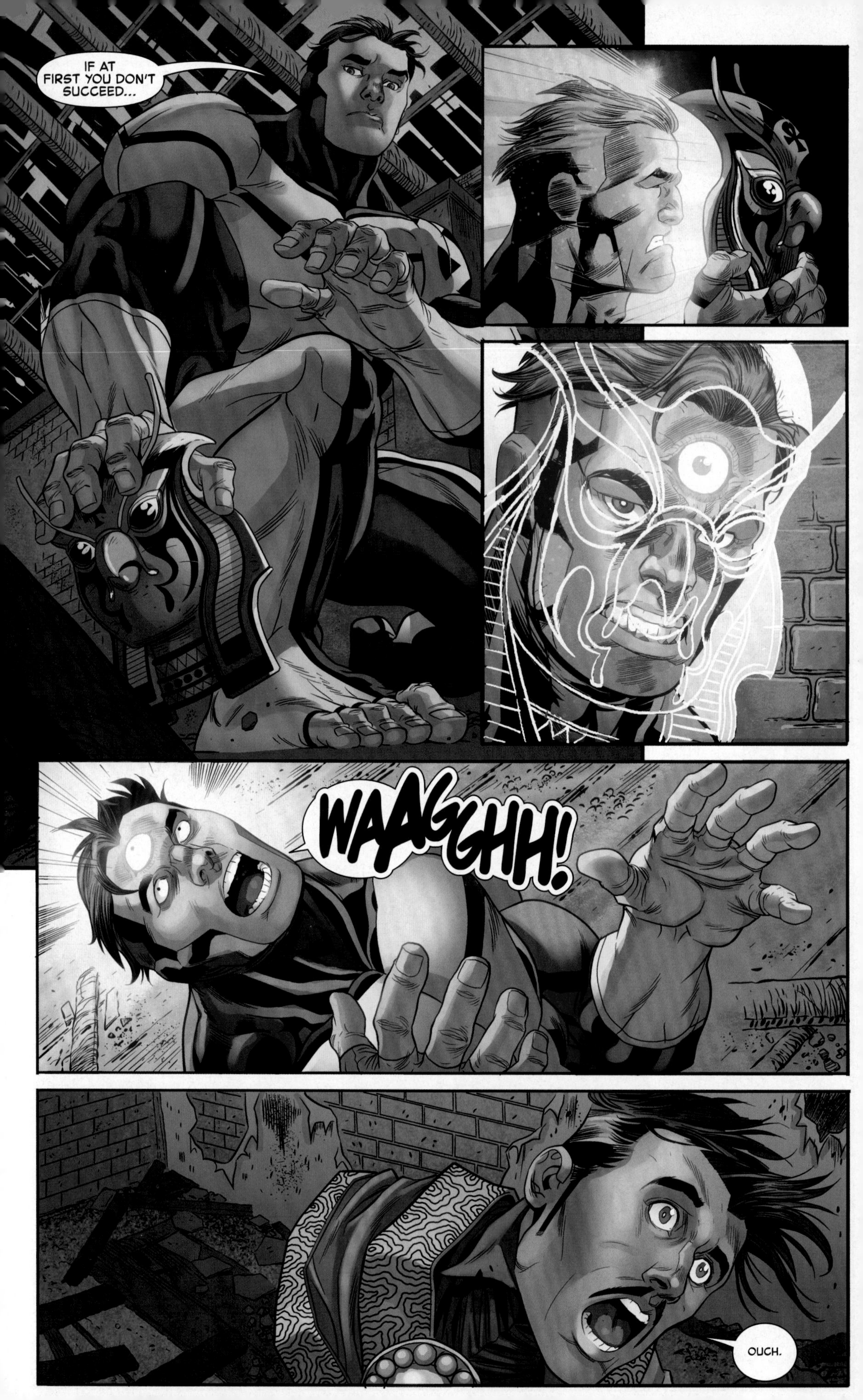
IF AT FIRST YOU DON'T SUCCEED...
WAAGGHH!
OUCH.

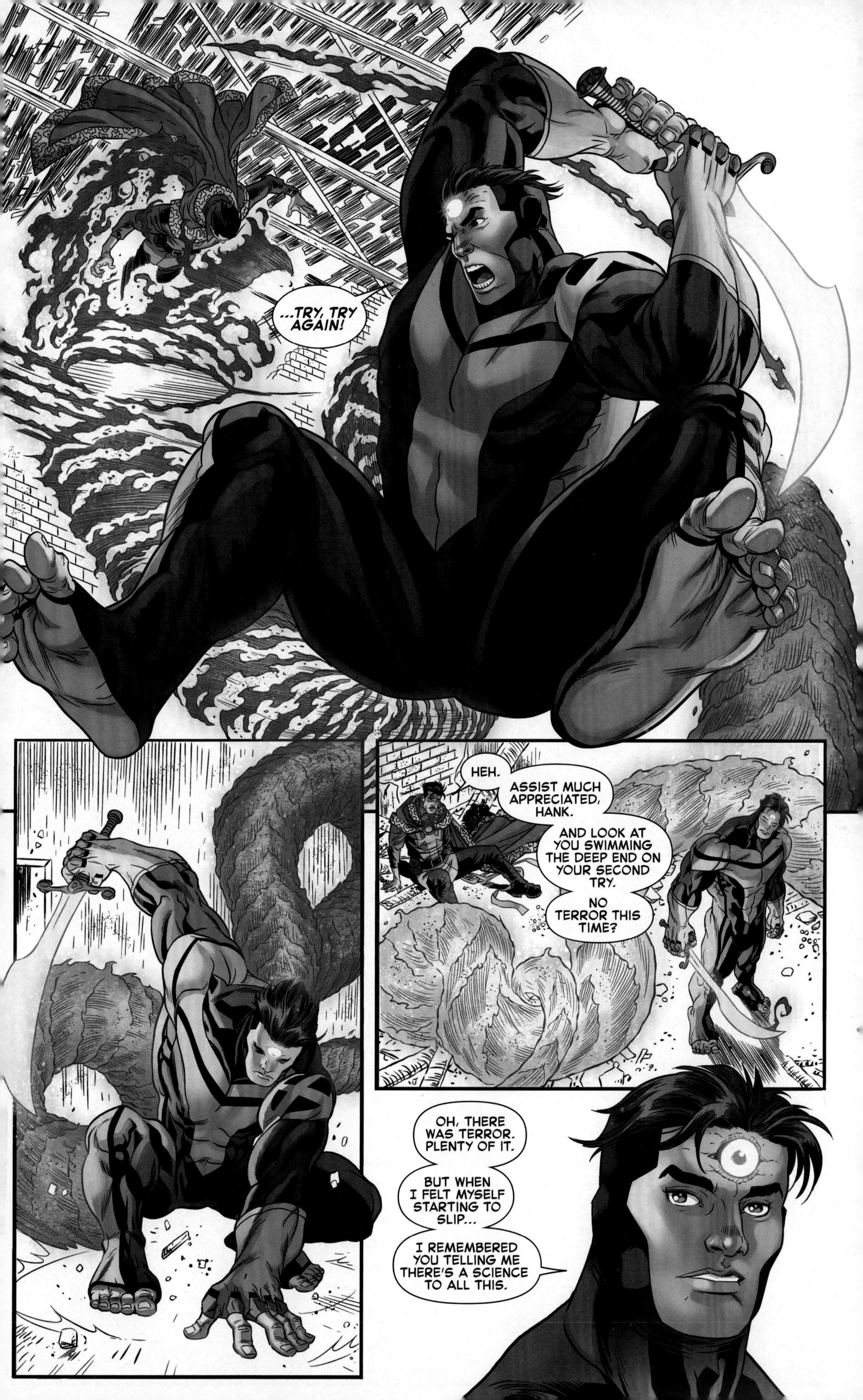
...TRY, TRY AGAIN!
HEH.
ASSIST MUCH APPRECIATED, HANK.
AND LOOK AT YOU SWIMMING THE DEEP END ON YOUR SECOND TRY.
NO TERROR THIS TIME?
OH, THERE WAS TERROR. PLENTY OF IT.
BUT WHEN I FELT MYSELF STARTING TO SLIP...
I REMEMBERED YOU TELLING ME THERE'S A SCIENCE TO ALL THIS.

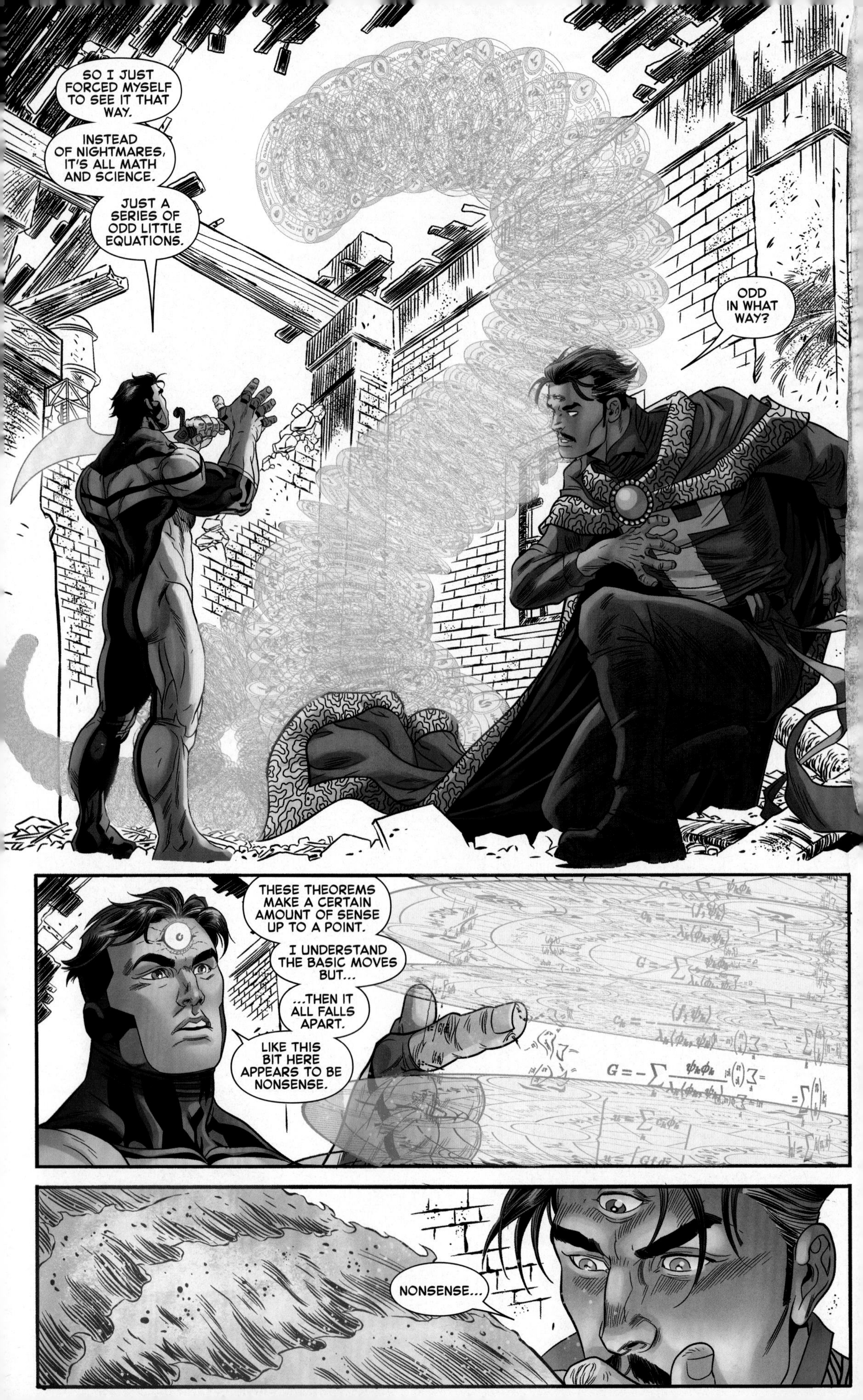
SO I JUST FORCED MYSELF TO SEE IT THAT WAY.
INSTEAD OF NIGHTMARES, IT'S ALL MATH AND SCIENCE.
JUST A SERIES OF ODD LITTLE EQUATIONS.
ODD IN WHAT WAY?
THESE THEOREMS MAKE A CERTAIN AMOUNT OF SENSE UP TO A POINT.
I UNDERSTAND THE BASIC MOVES BUT...
...THEN IT ALL FALLS APART.
LIKE THIS BIT HERE APPEARS TO BE NONSENSE.
NONSENSE...

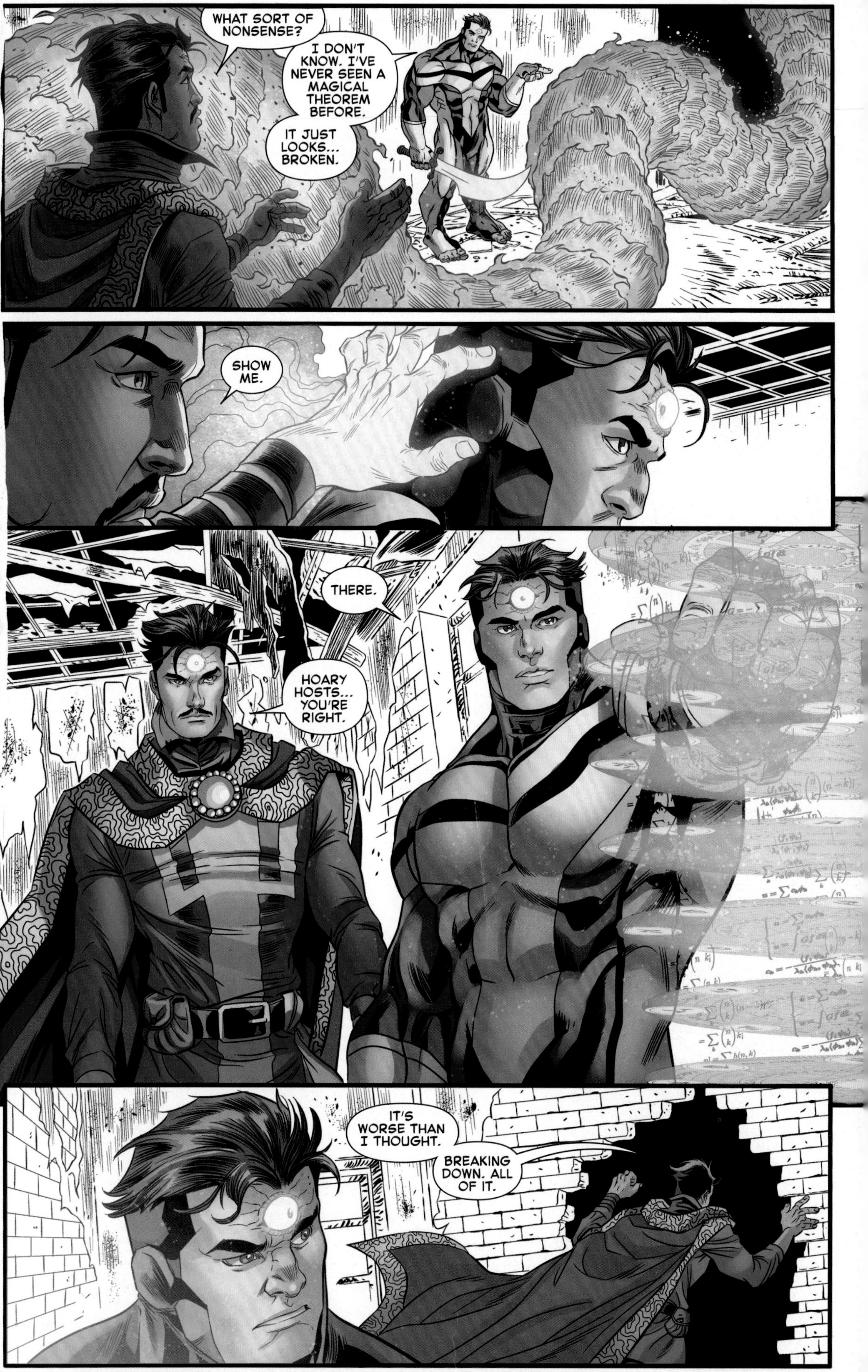
WHAT SORT OF NONSENSE?
I DON'T KNOW. I'VE NEVER SEEN A MAGICAL THEOREM BEFORE.
IT JUST LOOKS... BROKEN.
SHOW ME.
THERE.
HOARY HOSTS... YOU'RE RIGHT.
IT'S WORSE THAN I THOUGHT.
BREAKING DOWN. ALL OF IT.

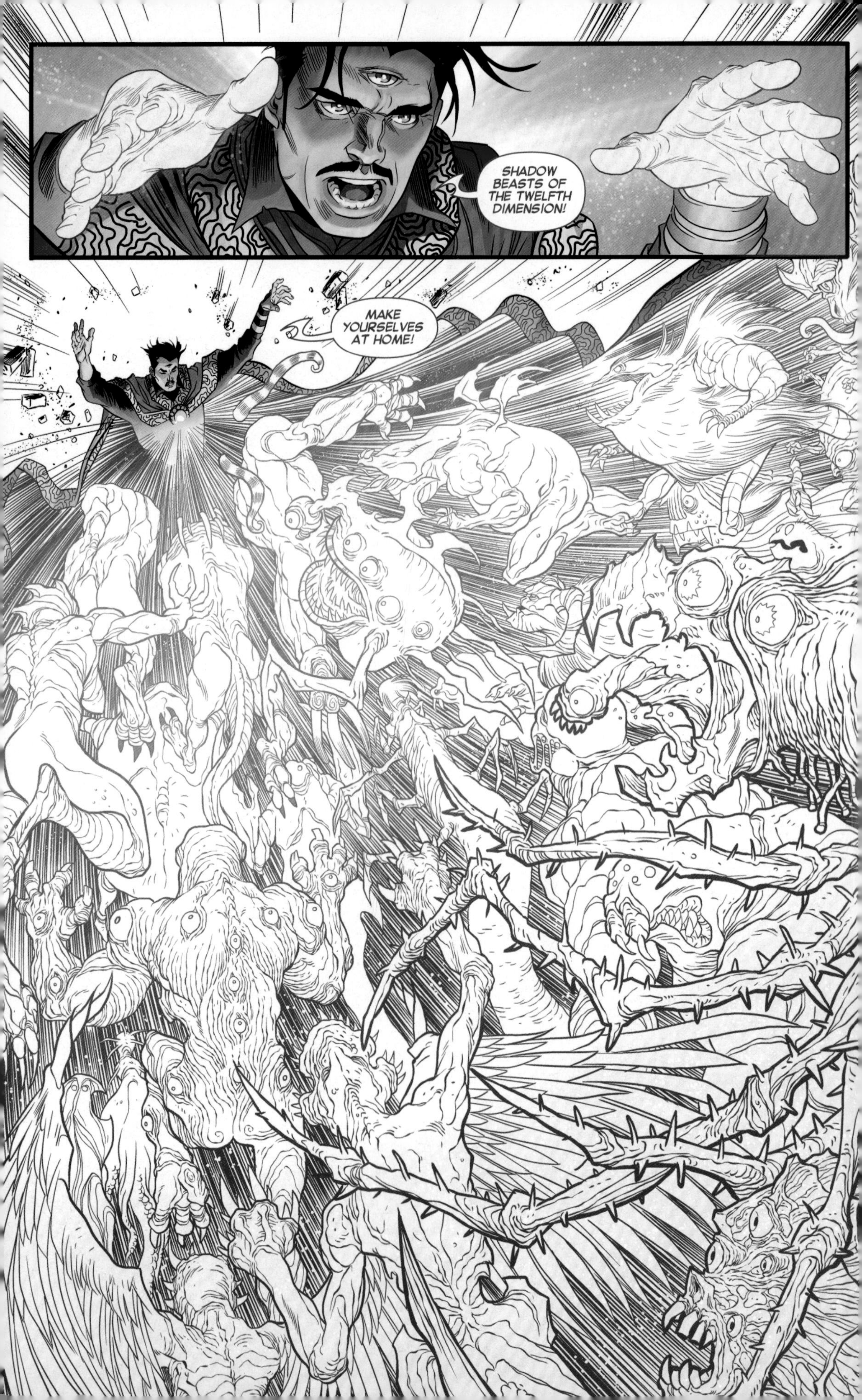
SHADOW BEASTS OF THE TWELFTH DIMENSION!
MAKE YOURSELVES AT HOME!

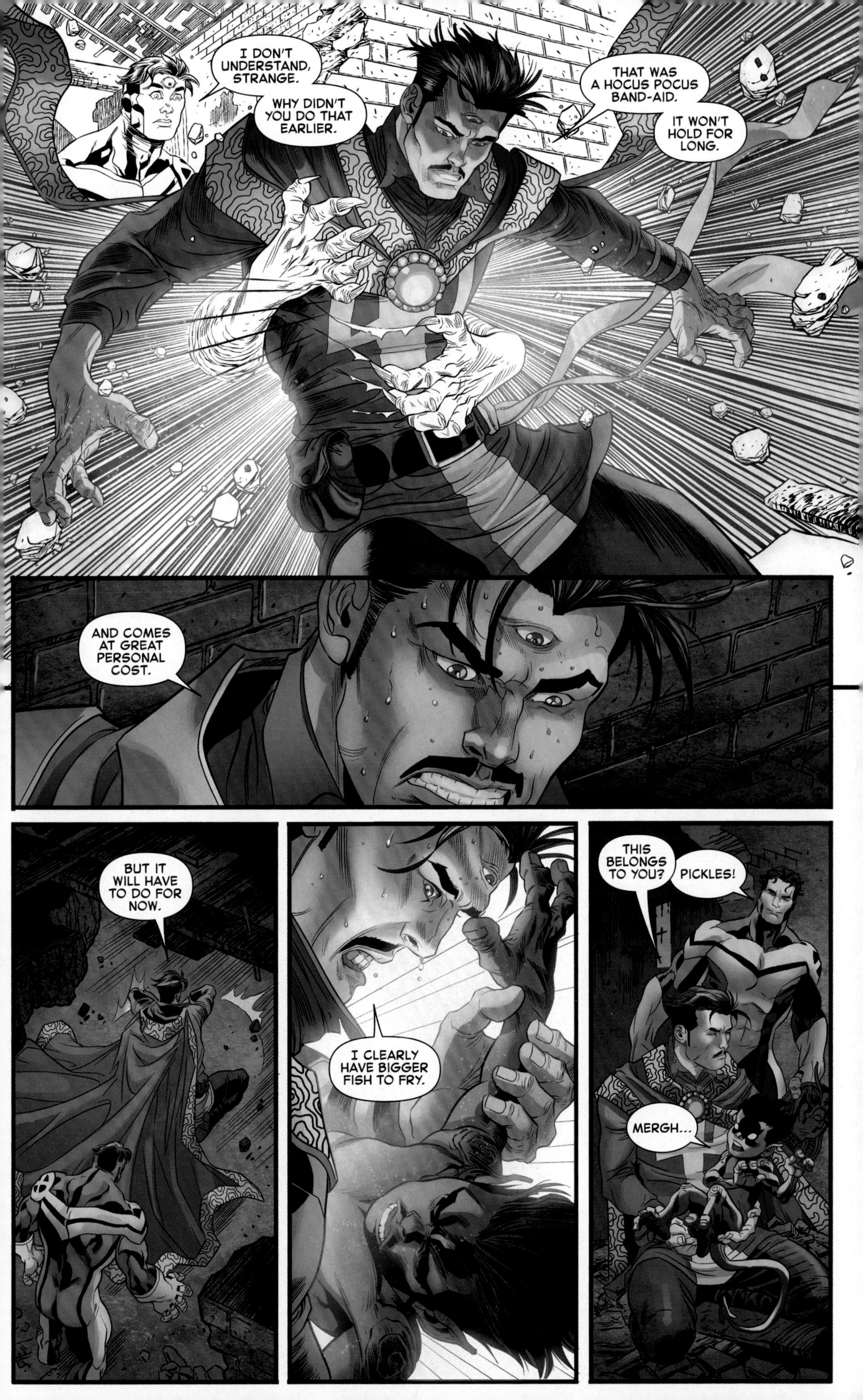
I DON'T UNDERSTAND, STRANGE.
WHY DIDN'T YOU DO THAT EARLIER.
THAT WAS A HOCUS POCUS BAND-AID.
IT WON'T HOLD FOR LONG.
AND COMES AT GREAT PERSONAL COST.
BUT IT WILL HAVE TO DO FOR NOW.
I CLEARLY HAVE BIGGER FISH TO FRY.
THIS BELONGS TO YOU?
PICKLES!
MERGH...

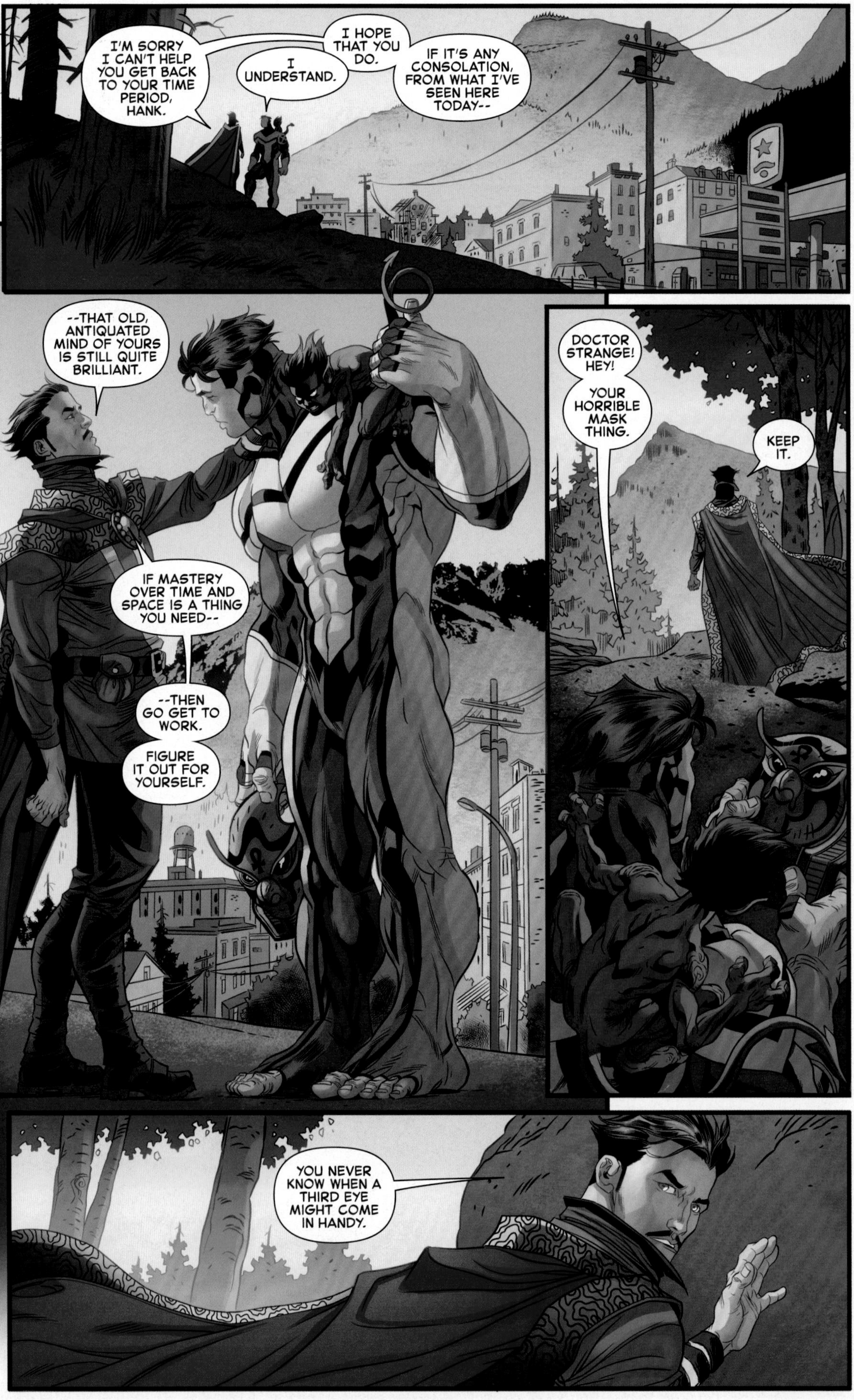
I'M SORRY I CAN'T HELP YOU GET BACK TO YOUR TIME PERIOD, HANK.
I UNDERSTAND.
I HOPE THAT YOU DO.
IF IT'S ANY CONSOLATION, FROM WHAT I'VE SEEN HERE TODAY--
--THAT OLD, ANTIQUATED MIND OF YOURS IS STILL QUITE BRILLIANT.
IF MASTERY OVER TIME AND SPACE IS A THING YOU NEED--
--THEN GO GET TO WORK.
FIGURE IT OUT FOR YOURSELF.
DOCTOR STRANGE! HEY!
YOUR HORRIBLE MASK THING.
KEEP IT.
YOU NEVER KNOW WHEN A THIRD EYE MIGHT COME IN HANDY.

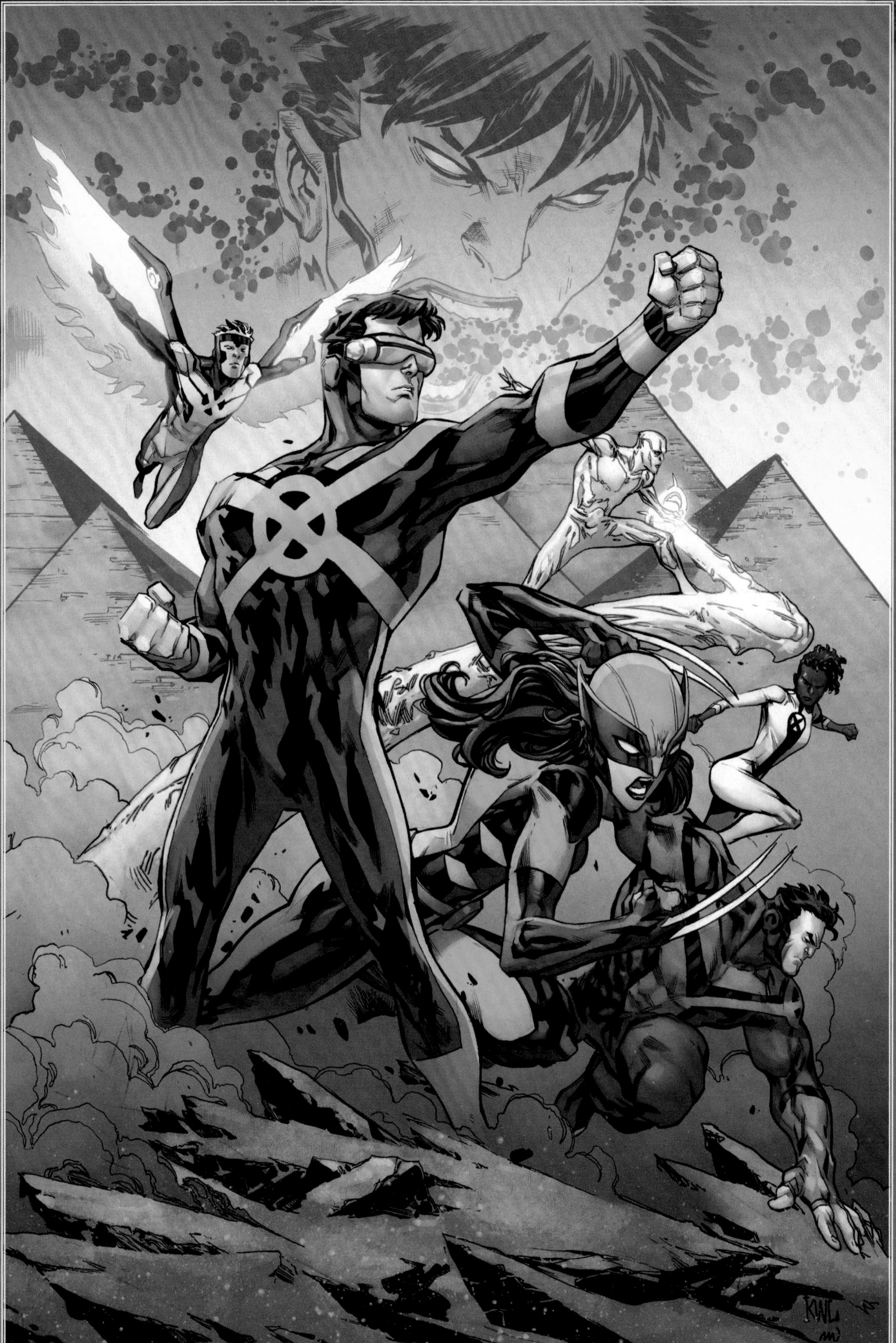

#9 VARIANT BY **KEN LASHLEY** & **NOLAN WOODARD**

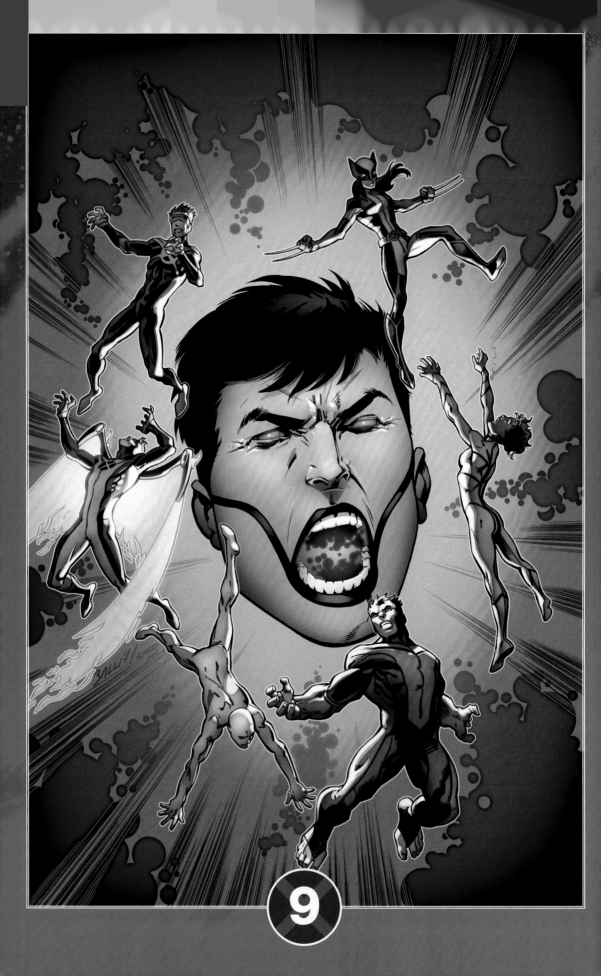

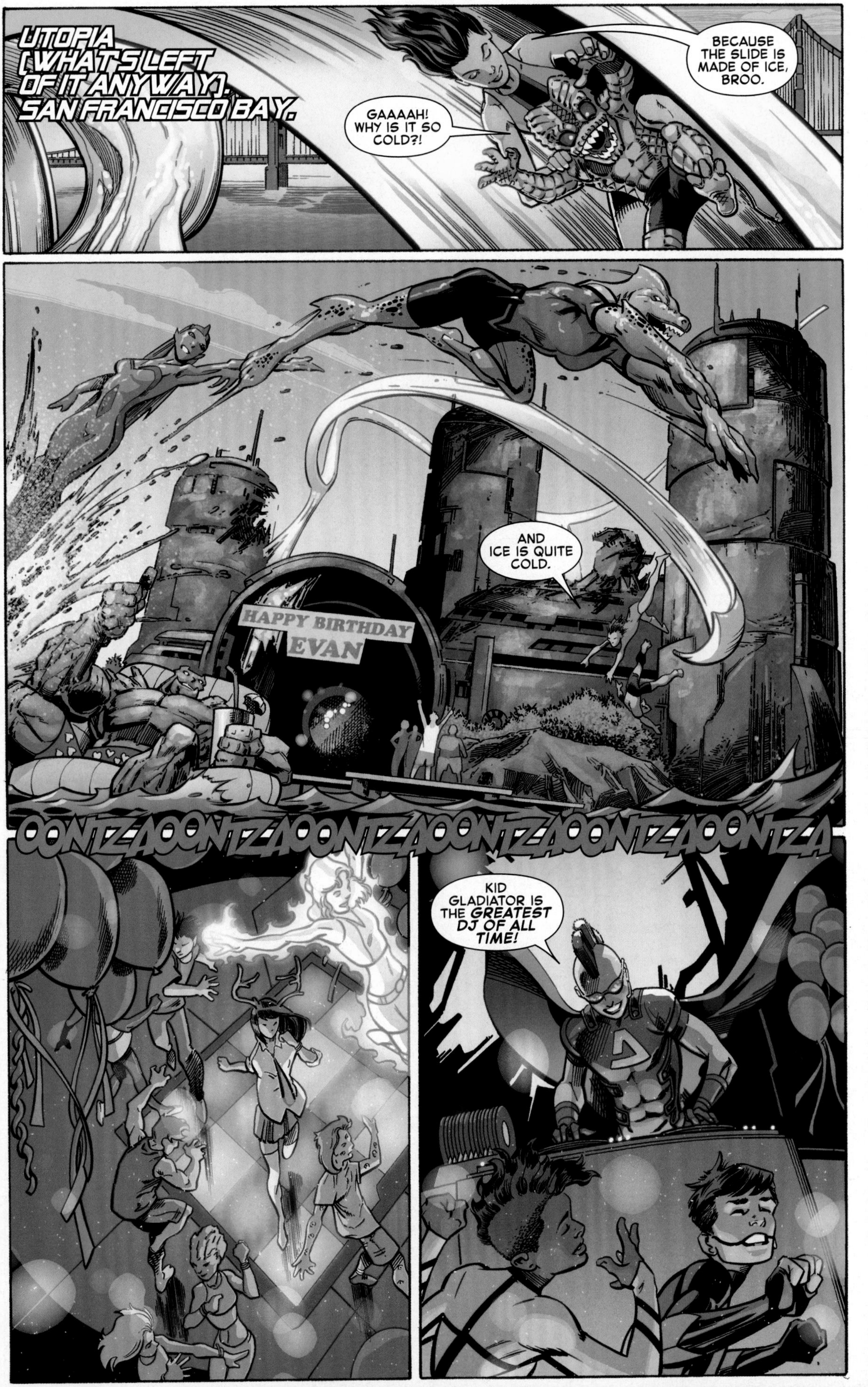
UTOPIA (WHAT'S LEFT OF IT ANYWAY). SAN FRANCISCO BAY.
GAAAAH! WHY IS IT SO COLD?!
BECAUSE THE SLIDE IS MADE OF ICE, BROO.
AND ICE IS QUITE COLD.
HAPPY BIRTHDAY EVAN
OONTZAOONTZAOONTZAOONTZAOONTZAOONTZA
KID GLADIATOR IS THE GREATEST DJ OF ALL TIME!

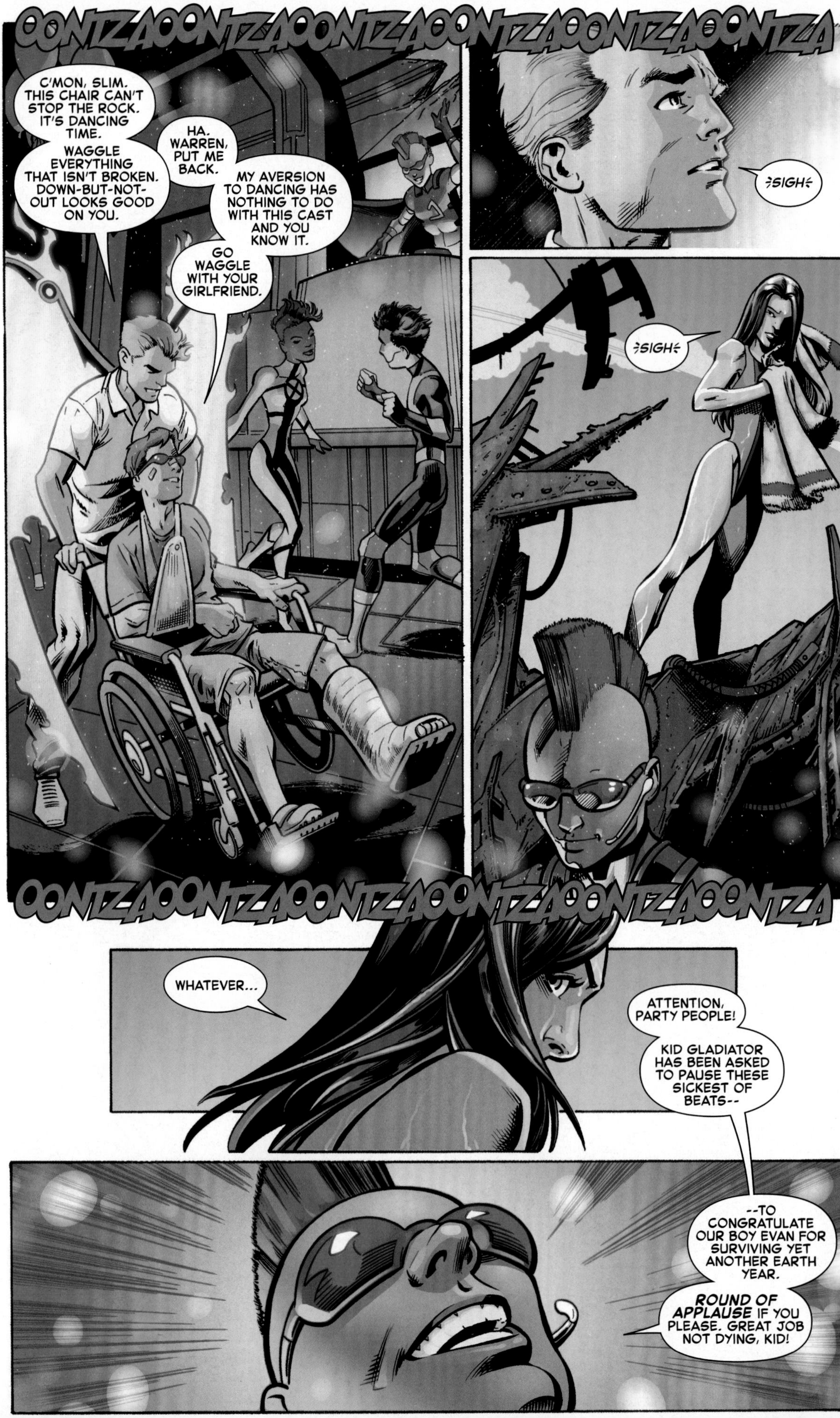
OONTZAOONTZAOONTZAOONTZAOONTZAOONTZA
C'MON, SLIM. THIS CHAIR CAN'T STOP THE ROCK. IT'S DANCING TIME.
WAGGLE EVERYTHING THAT ISN'T BROKEN. DOWN-BUT-NOT-OUT LOOKS GOOD ON YOU.
HA. WARREN, PUT ME BACK.
MY AVERSION TO DANCING HAS NOTHING TO DO WITH THIS CAST AND YOU KNOW IT.
GO WAGGLE WITH YOUR GIRLFRIEND.
SIGH
SIGH
OONTZAOONTZAOONTZAOONTZAOONTZAOONTZA
WHATEVER...
ATTENTION, PARTY PEOPLE!
KID GLADIATOR HAS BEEN ASKED TO PAUSE THESE SICKEST OF BEATS--
--TO CONGRATULATE OUR BOY EVAN FOR SURVIVING YET ANOTHER EARTH YEAR.
ROUND OF APPLAUSE IF YOU PLEASE. GREAT JOB NOT DYING, KID!

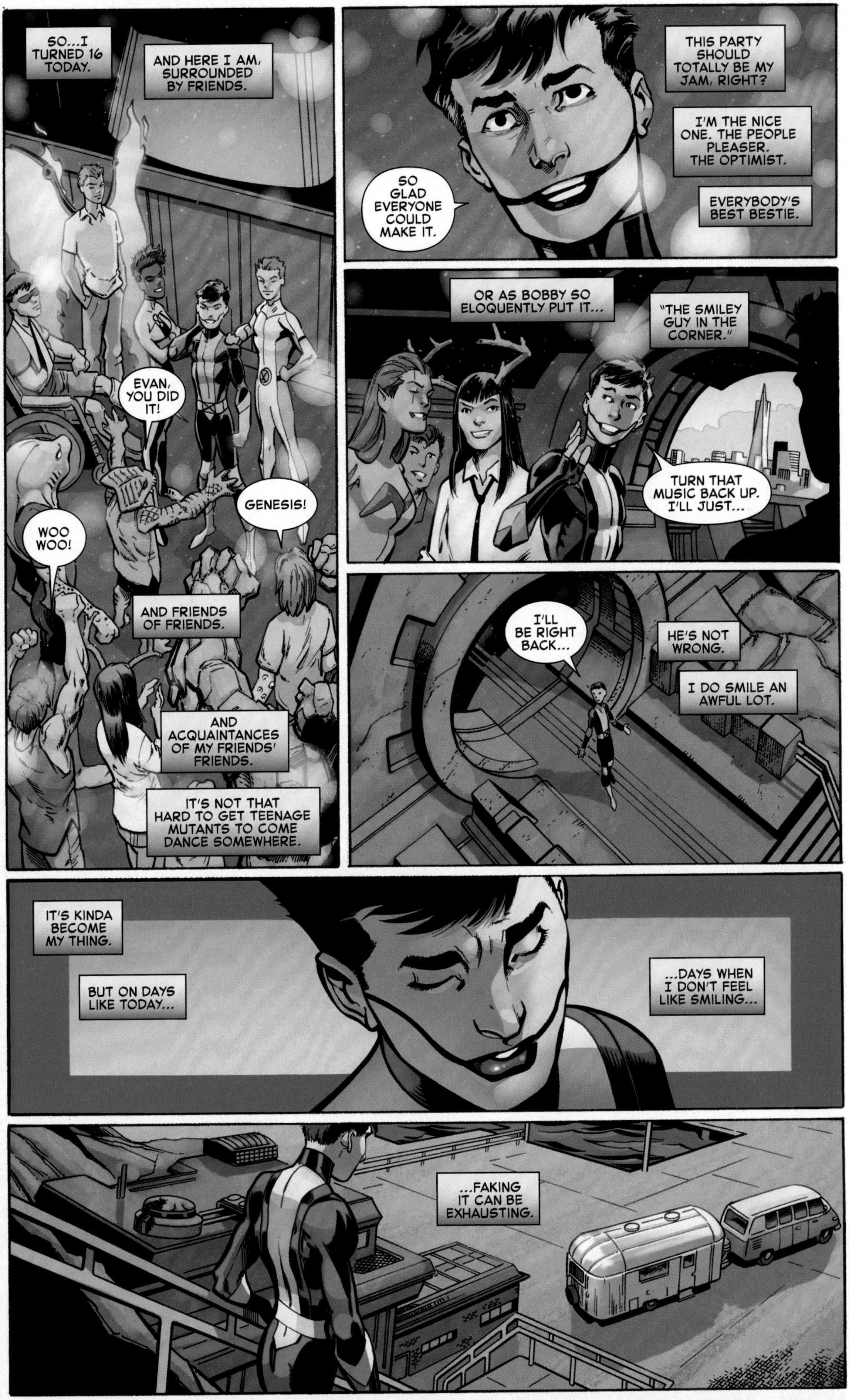
SO...I TURNED 16 TODAY.
AND HERE I AM, SURROUNDED BY FRIENDS.
EVAN, YOU DID IT!
GENESIS!
WOO WOO!
AND FRIENDS OF FRIENDS.
AND ACQUAINTANCES OF MY FRIENDS' FRIENDS.
IT'S NOT THAT HARD TO GET TEENAGE MUTANTS TO COME DANCE SOMEWHERE.
THIS PARTY SHOULD TOTALLY BE MY JAM, RIGHT?
I'M THE NICE ONE. THE PEOPLE PLEASER. THE OPTIMIST.
EVERYBODY'S BEST BESTIE.
SO GLAD EVERYONE COULD MAKE IT.
OR AS BOBBY SO ELOQUENTLY PUT IT...
"THE SMILEY GUY IN THE CORNER."
TURN THAT MUSIC BACK UP. I'LL JUST...
I'LL BE RIGHT BACK...
HE'S NOT WRONG.
I DO SMILE AN AWFUL LOT.
IT'S KINDA BECOME MY THING.
BUT ON DAYS LIKE TODAY...
...DAYS WHEN I DON'T FEEL LIKE SMILING...
...FAKING IT CAN BE EXHAUSTING.

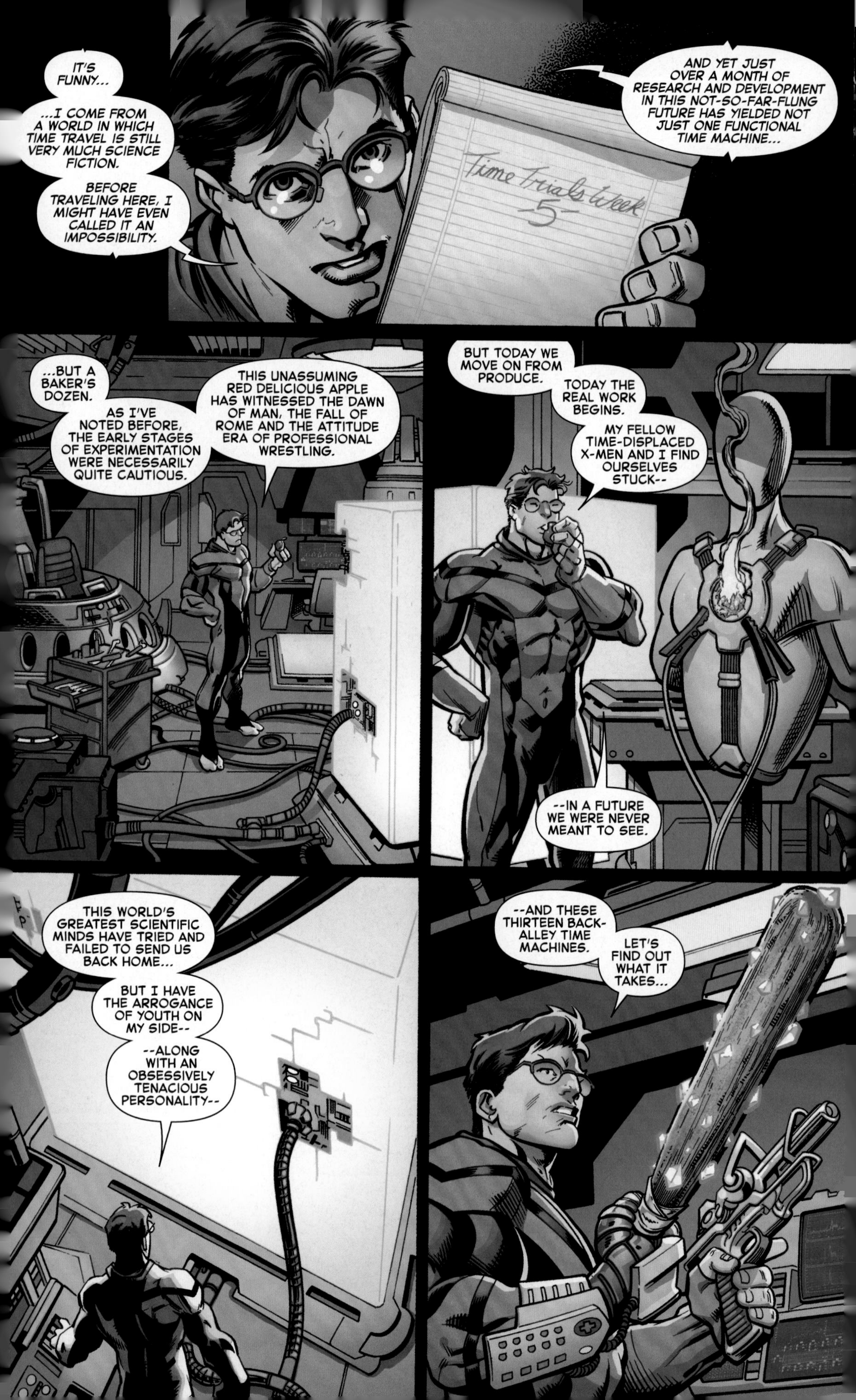
IT'S FUNNY...
...I COME FROM A WORLD IN WHICH TIME TRAVEL IS STILL VERY MUCH SCIENCE FICTION.
BEFORE TRAVELING HERE, I MIGHT HAVE EVEN CALLED IT AN IMPOSSIBILITY.
Time Trials Week -5-
AND YET JUST OVER A MONTH OF RESEARCH AND DEVELOPMENT IN THIS NOT-SO-FAR-FLUNG FUTURE HAS YIELDED NOT JUST ONE FUNCTIONAL TIME MACHINE...
...BUT A BAKER'S DOZEN.
AS I'VE NOTED BEFORE, THE EARLY STAGES OF EXPERIMENTATION WERE NECESSARILY QUITE CAUTIOUS.
THIS UNASSUMING RED DELICIOUS APPLE HAS WITNESSED THE DAWN OF MAN, THE FALL OF ROME AND THE ATTITUDE ERA OF PROFESSIONAL WRESTLING.
BUT TODAY WE MOVE ON FROM PRODUCE.
TODAY THE REAL WORK BEGINS.
MY FELLOW TIME-DISPLACED X-MEN AND I FIND OURSELVES STUCK--
--IN A FUTURE WE WERE NEVER MEANT TO SEE.
THIS WORLD'S GREATEST SCIENTIFIC MINDS HAVE TRIED AND FAILED TO SEND US BACK HOME...
BUT I HAVE THE ARROGANCE OF YOUTH ON MY SIDE--
--ALONG WITH AN OBSESSIVELY TENACIOUS PERSONALITY--
--AND THESE THIRTEEN BACK-ALLEY TIME MACHINES.
LET'S FIND OUT WHAT IT TAKES...

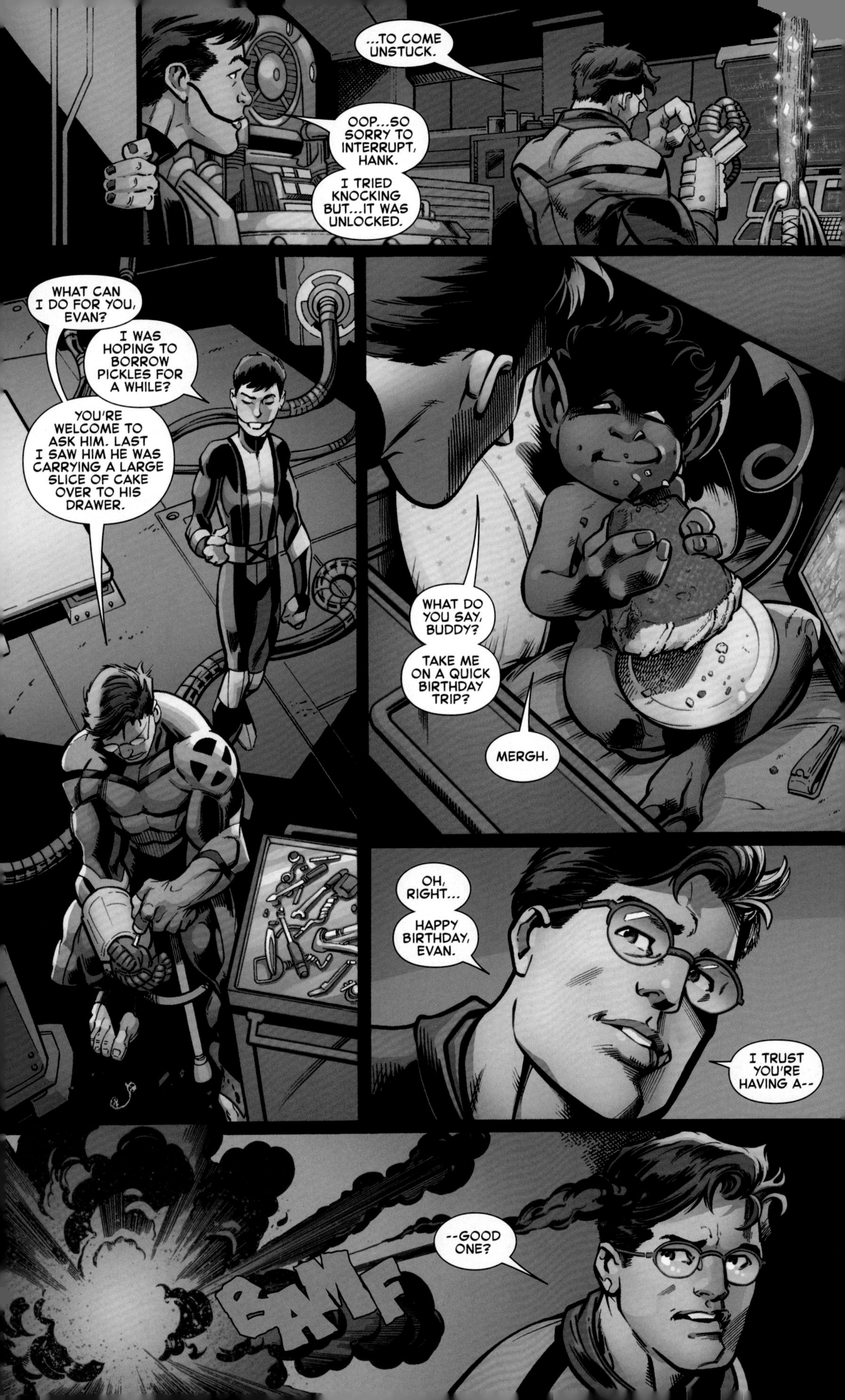
...TO COME UNSTUCK.
OOP...SO SORRY TO INTERRUPT, HANK.
I TRIED KNOCKING BUT...IT WAS UNLOCKED.
WHAT CAN I DO FOR YOU, EVAN?
I WAS HOPING TO BORROW PICKLES FOR A WHILE?
YOU'RE WELCOME TO ASK HIM. LAST I SAW HIM HE WAS CARRYING A LARGE SLICE OF CAKE OVER TO HIS DRAWER.
WHAT DO YOU SAY, BUDDY?
TAKE ME ON A QUICK BIRTHDAY TRIP?
MERGH.
OH, RIGHT...
HAPPY BIRTHDAY, EVAN.
I TRUST YOU'RE HAVING A--
--GOOD ONE?
BAMF

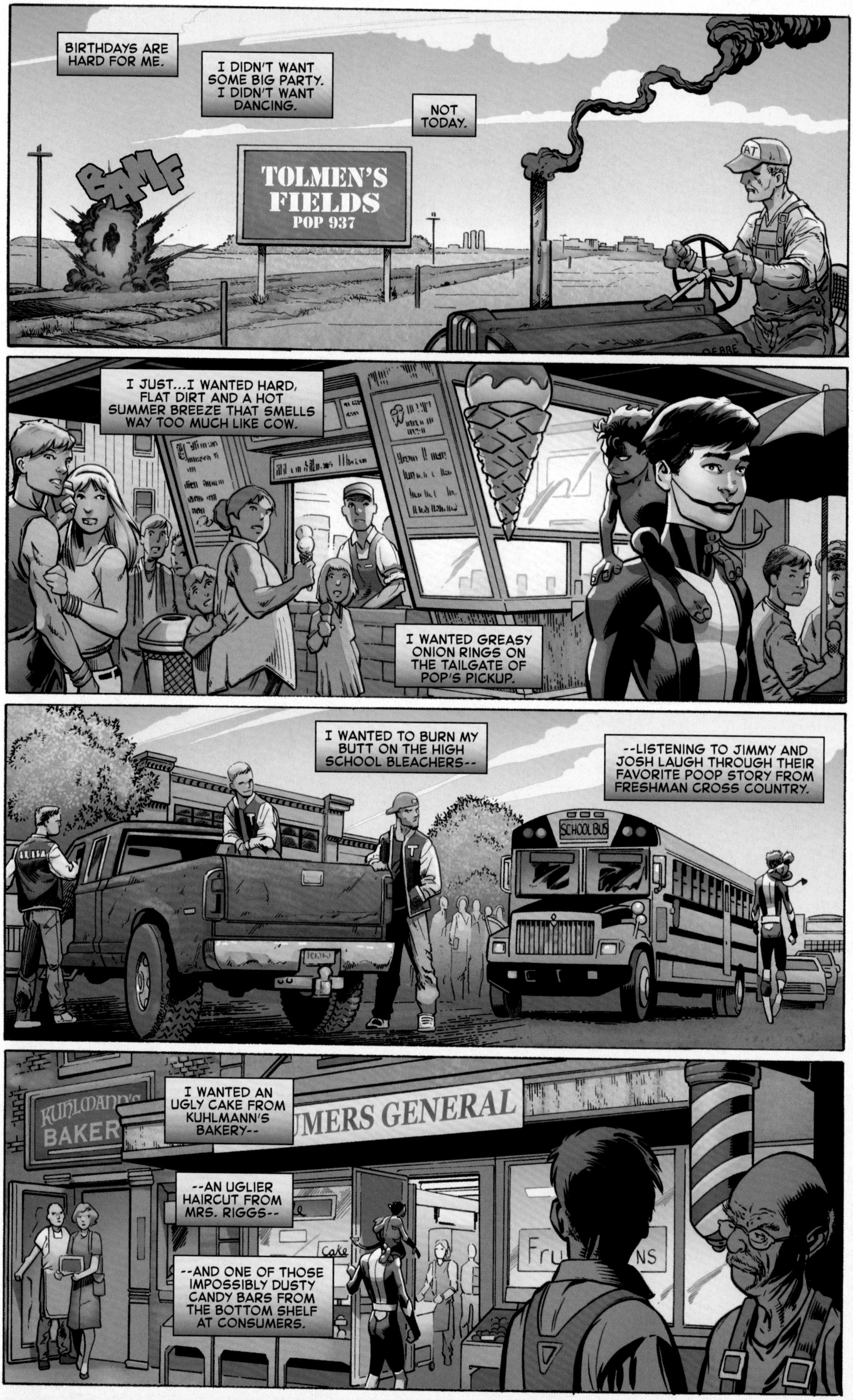

BIRTHDAYS ARE HARD FOR ME.
I DIDN'T WANT SOME BIG PARTY. I DIDN'T WANT DANCING.
NOT TODAY.
BAMF
TOLMEN'S FIELDS POP 937
I JUST...I WANTED HARD, FLAT DIRT AND A HOT SUMMER BREEZE THAT SMELLS WAY TOO MUCH LIKE COW.
I WANTED GREASY ONION RINGS ON THE TAILGATE OF POP'S PICKUP.
I WANTED TO BURN MY BUTT ON THE HIGH SCHOOL BLEACHERS--
--LISTENING TO JIMMY AND JOSH LAUGH THROUGH THEIR FAVORITE POOP STORY FROM FRESHMAN CROSS COUNTRY.
SCHOOL BUS
KUHLMANN'S BAKER
I WANTED AN UGLY CAKE FROM KUHLMANN'S BAKERY--
UMERS GENERAL
--AN UGLIER HAIRCUT FROM MRS. RIGGS--
--AND ONE OF THOSE IMPOSSIBLY DUSTY CANDY BARS FROM THE BOTTOM SHELF AT CONSUMERS.

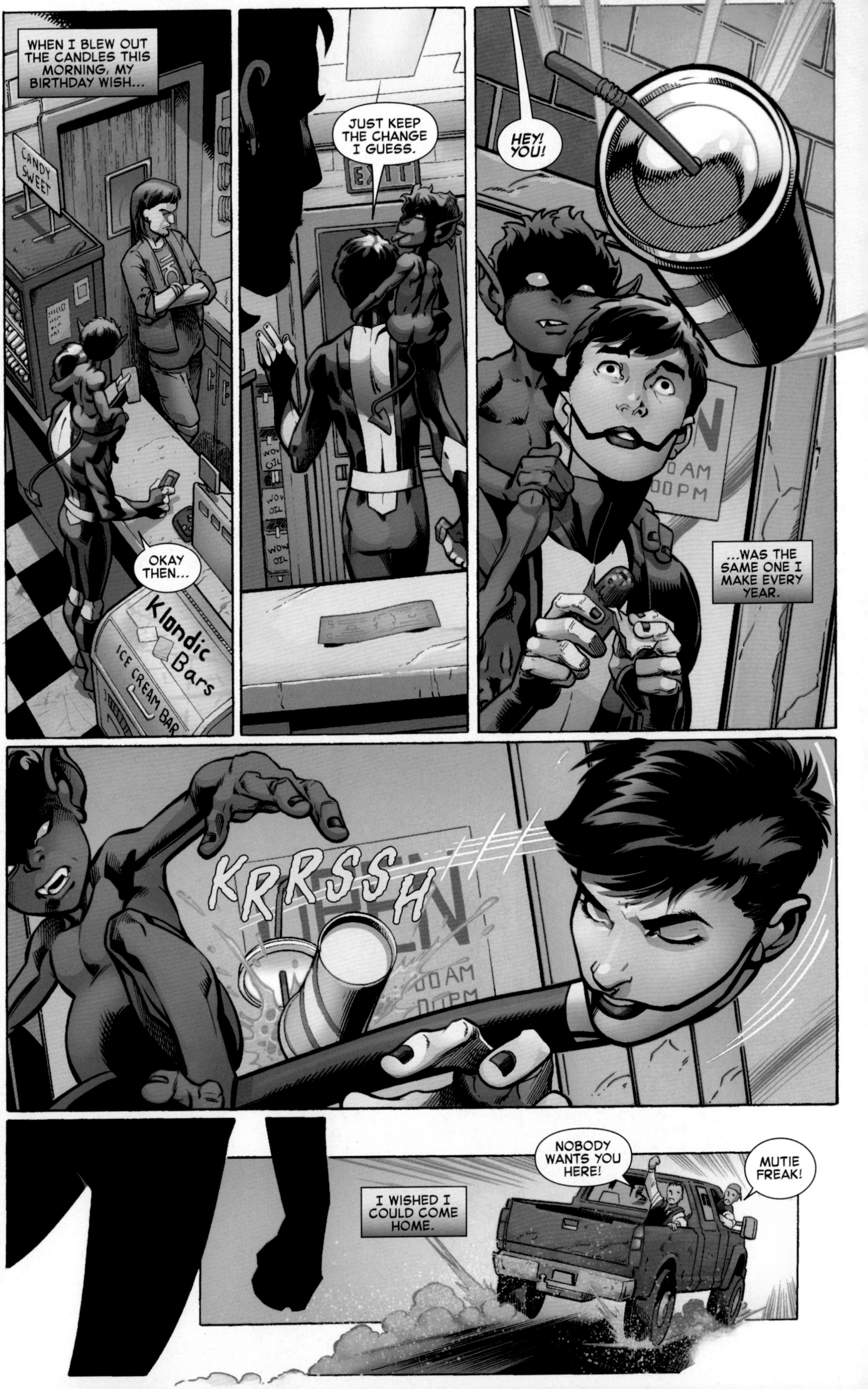
WHEN I BLEW OUT THE CANDLES THIS MORNING, MY BIRTHDAY WISH...
CANDY SWEET
OKAY THEN...
Klondic Bars
ICE CREAM BAR
JUST KEEP THE CHANGE I GUESS.
EXIT
WOW OIL
HEY! YOU!
...WAS THE SAME ONE I MAKE EVERY YEAR.
KRRSSH
I WISHED I COULD COME HOME.
NOBODY WANTS YOU HERE!
MUTIE FREAK!

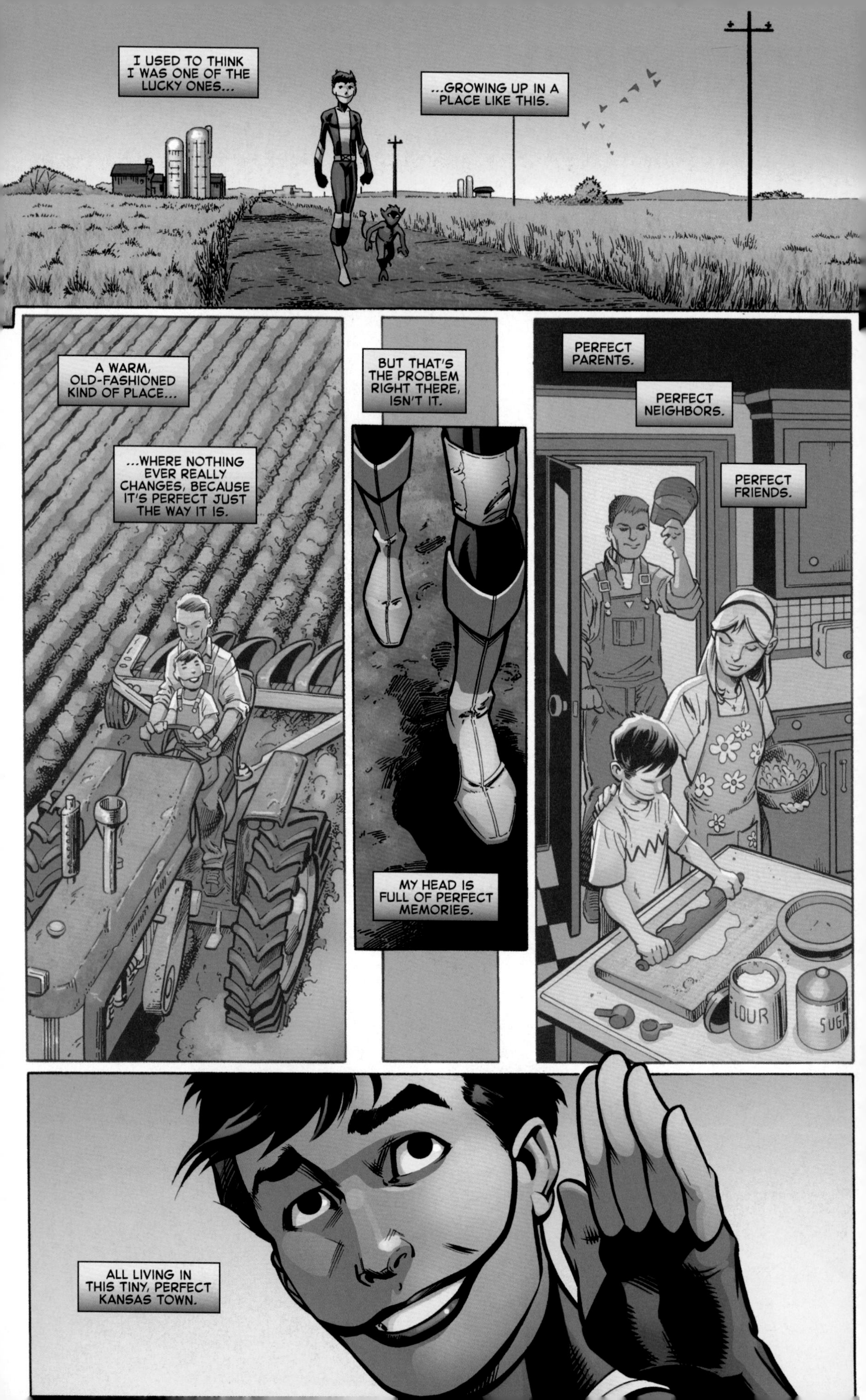
I USED TO THINK I WAS ONE OF THE LUCKY ONES...
...GROWING UP IN A PLACE LIKE THIS.
A WARM, OLD-FASHIONED KIND OF PLACE...
...WHERE NOTHING EVER REALLY CHANGES, BECAUSE IT'S PERFECT JUST THE WAY IT IS.
BUT THAT'S THE PROBLEM RIGHT THERE, ISN'T IT.
MY HEAD IS FULL OF PERFECT MEMORIES.
PERFECT PARENTS.
PERFECT NEIGHBORS.
PERFECT FRIENDS.
FLOUR
ALL LIVING IN THIS TINY, PERFECT KANSAS TOWN.

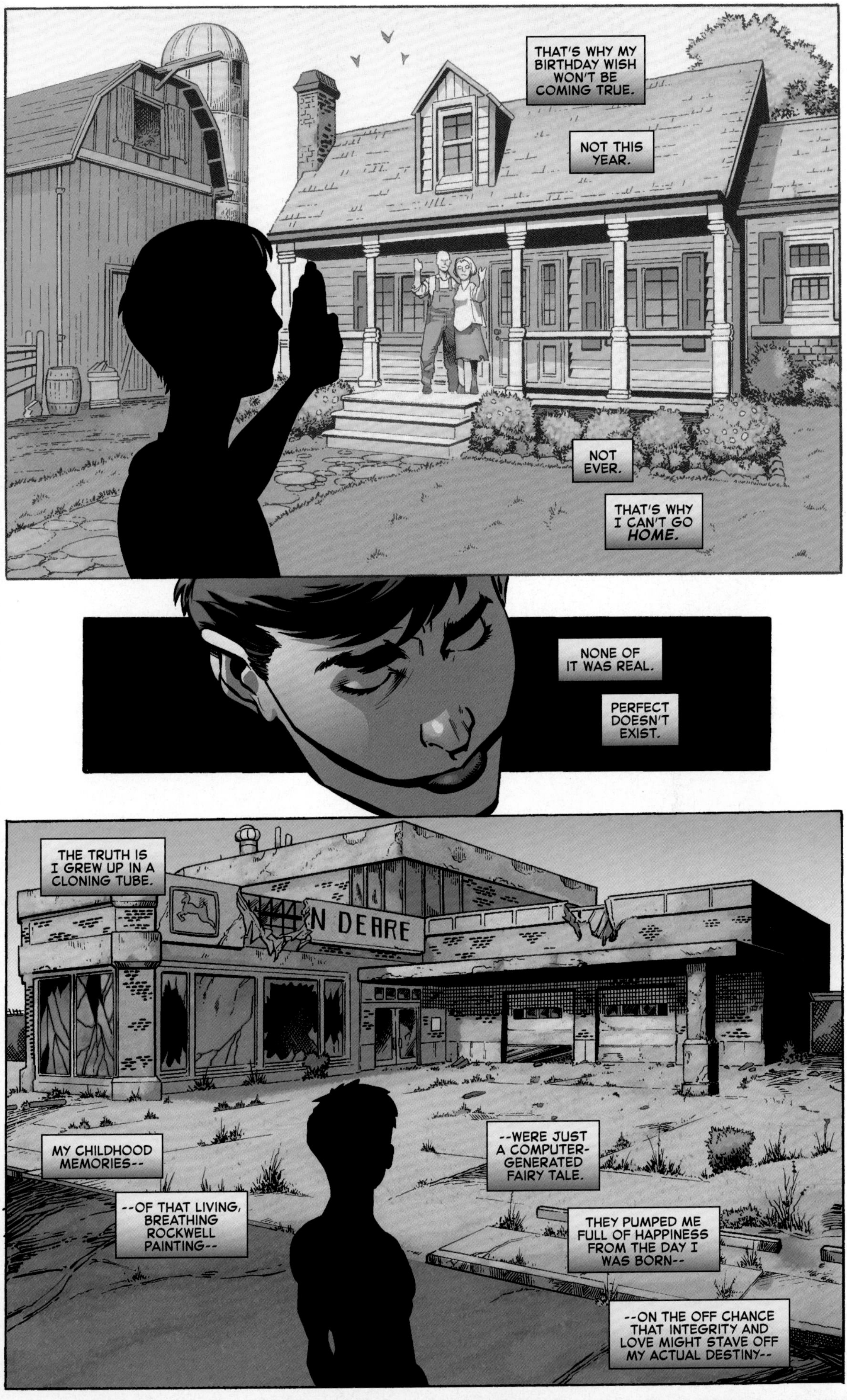

THAT'S WHY MY BIRTHDAY WISH WON'T BE COMING TRUE.
NOT THIS YEAR.
NOT EVER.
THAT'S WHY I CAN'T GO *HOME.*
NONE OF IT WAS REAL.
PERFECT DOESN'T EXIST.
THE TRUTH IS I GREW UP IN A CLONING TUBE.
N DEARE
MY CHILDHOOD MEMORIES--
--OF THAT LIVING, BREATHING ROCKWELL PAINTING--
--WERE JUST A COMPUTER-GENERATED FAIRY TALE.
THEY PUMPED ME FULL OF HAPPINESS FROM THE DAY I WAS BORN--
--ON THE OFF CHANCE THAT INTEGRITY AND LOVE MIGHT STAVE OFF MY ACTUAL DESTINY--

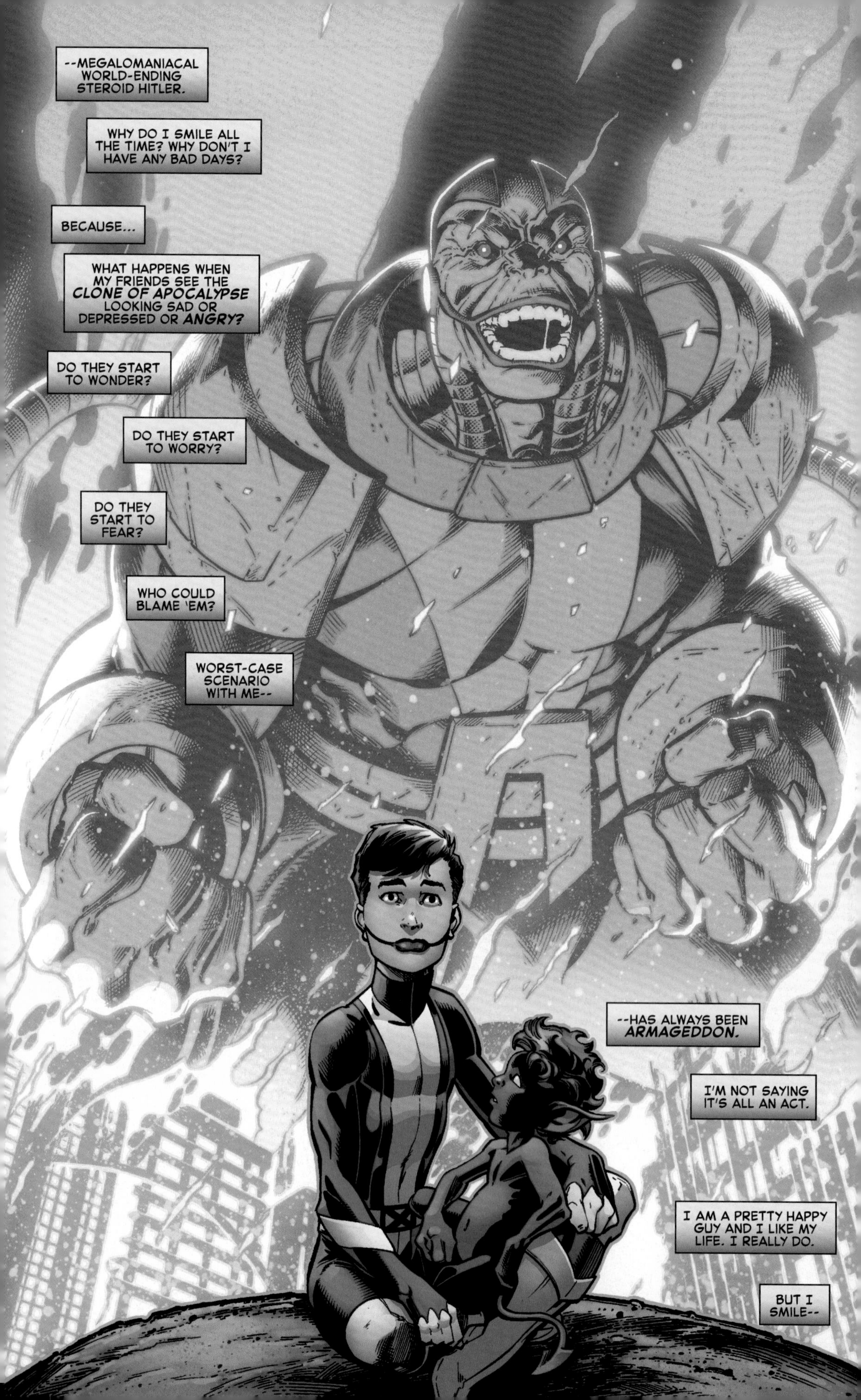
--MEGALOMANIACAL WORLD-ENDING STEROID HITLER.
WHY DO I SMILE ALL THE TIME? WHY DON'T I HAVE ANY BAD DAYS?
BECAUSE...
WHAT HAPPENS WHEN MY FRIENDS SEE THE *CLONE OF APOCALYPSE* LOOKING SAD OR DEPRESSED OR *ANGRY?*
DO THEY START TO WONDER?
DO THEY START TO WORRY?
DO THEY START TO FEAR?
WHO COULD BLAME 'EM?
WORST-CASE SCENARIO WITH ME--
--HAS ALWAYS BEEN *ARMAGEDDON.*
I'M NOT SAYING IT'S ALL AN ACT.
I AM A PRETTY HAPPY GUY AND I LIKE MY LIFE. I REALLY DO.
BUT I SMILE--

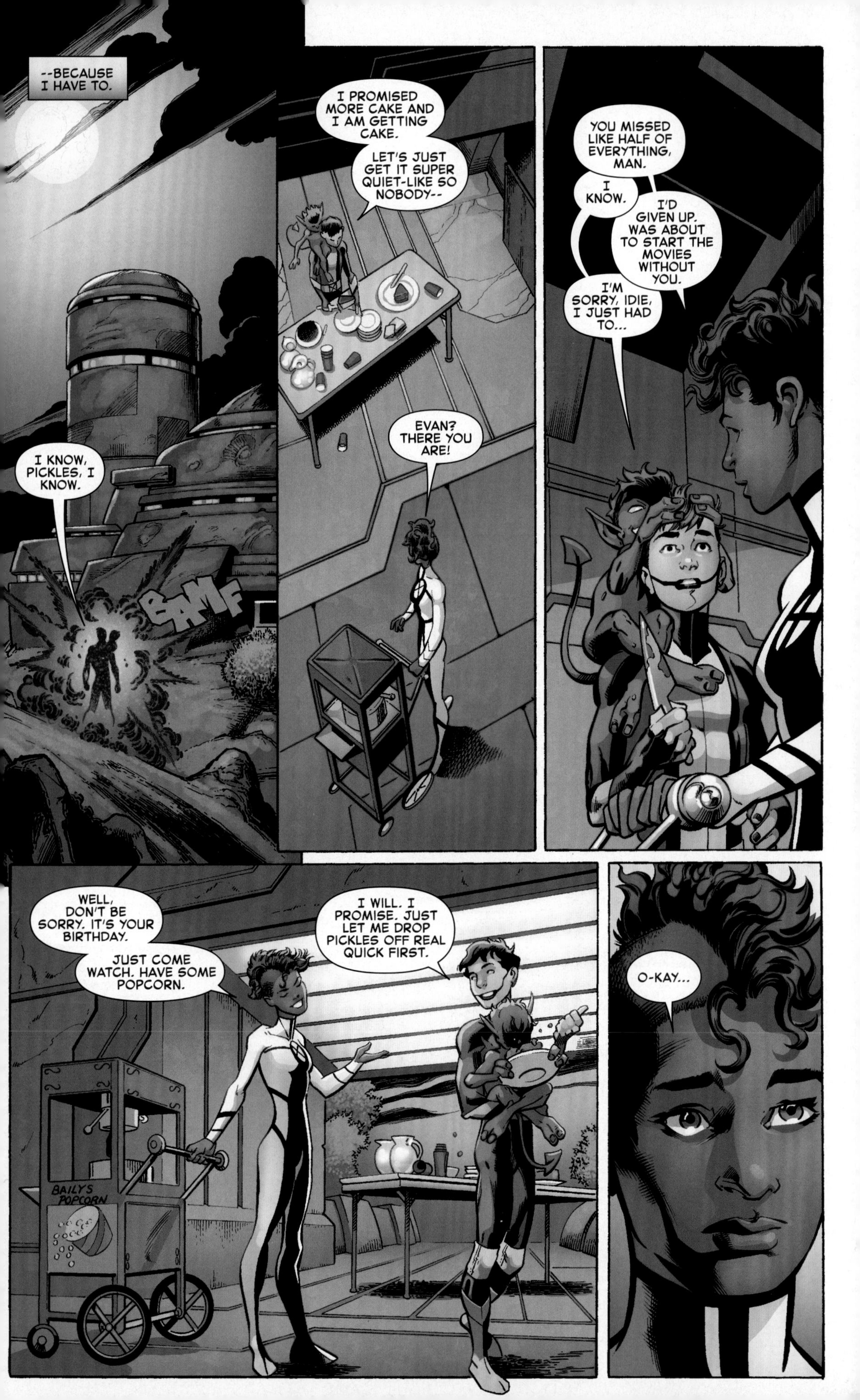
--BECAUSE I HAVE TO.
I KNOW, PICKLES, I KNOW.
BAMF
I PROMISED MORE CAKE AND I AM GETTING CAKE.
LET'S JUST GET IT SUPER QUIET-LIKE SO NOBODY--
EVAN? THERE YOU ARE!
YOU MISSED LIKE HALF OF EVERYTHING, MAN.
I KNOW.
I'D GIVEN UP. WAS ABOUT TO START THE MOVIES WITHOUT YOU.
I'M SORRY, IDIE, I JUST HAD TO...
WELL, DON'T BE SORRY. IT'S YOUR BIRTHDAY.
JUST COME WATCH. HAVE SOME POPCORN.
I WILL. I PROMISE. JUST LET ME DROP PICKLES OFF REAL QUICK FIRST.
BAILY'S POPCORN
O-KAY...

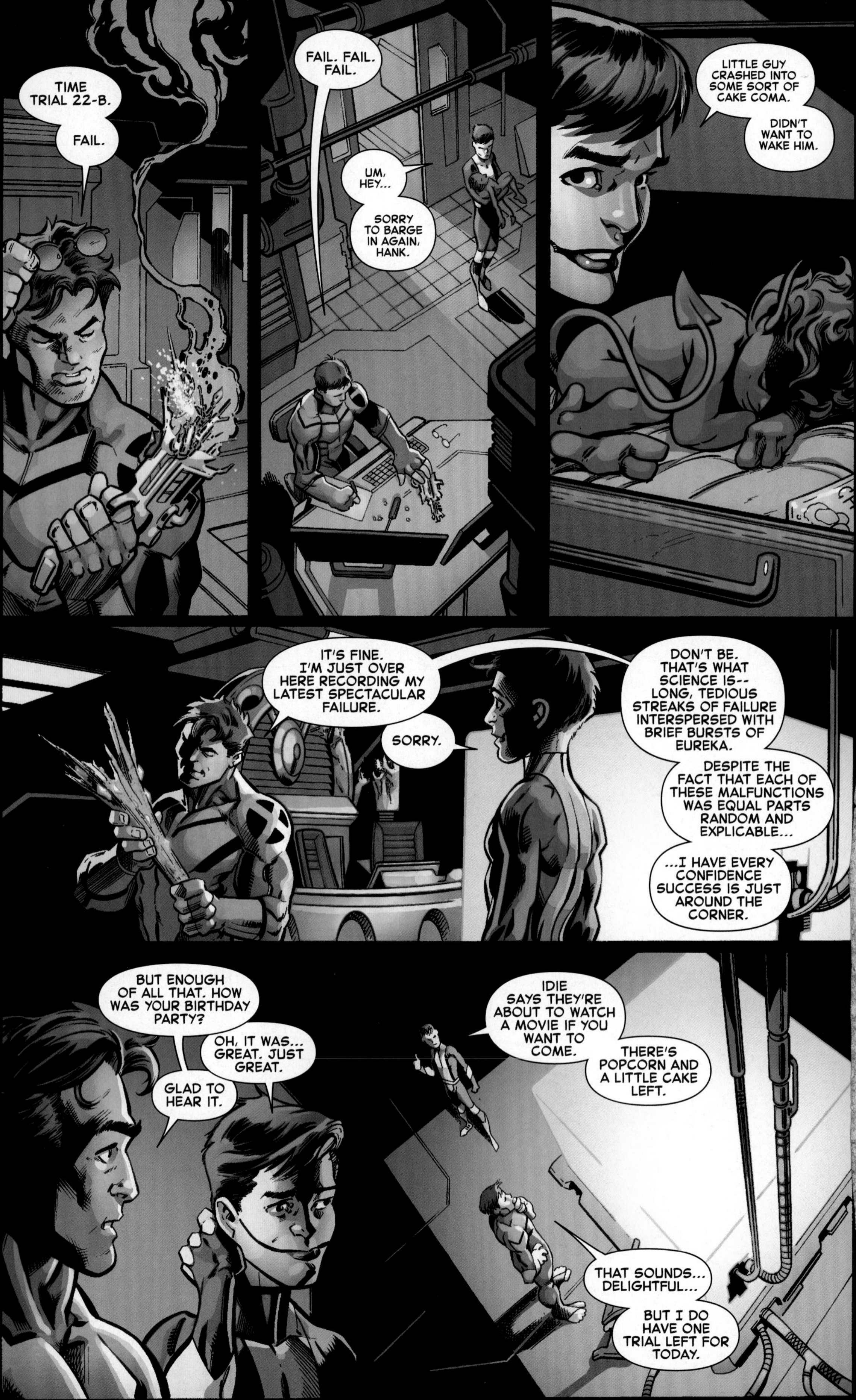
TIME TRIAL 22-B.
FAIL.
FAIL. FAIL. FAIL.
UM, HEY...
SORRY TO BARGE IN AGAIN, HANK.
LITTLE GUY CRASHED INTO SOME SORT OF CAKE COMA.
DIDN'T WANT TO WAKE HIM.
IT'S FINE. I'M JUST OVER HERE RECORDING MY LATEST SPECTACULAR FAILURE.
SORRY.
DON'T BE. THAT'S WHAT SCIENCE IS-- LONG, TEDIOUS STREAKS OF FAILURE INTERSPERSED WITH BRIEF BURSTS OF EUREKA.
DESPITE THE FACT THAT EACH OF THESE MALFUNCTIONS WAS EQUAL PARTS RANDOM AND EXPLICABLE...
...I HAVE EVERY CONFIDENCE SUCCESS IS JUST AROUND THE CORNER.
BUT ENOUGH OF ALL THAT. HOW WAS YOUR BIRTHDAY PARTY?
OH, IT WAS... GREAT. JUST GREAT.
GLAD TO HEAR IT.
IDIE SAYS THEY'RE ABOUT TO WATCH A MOVIE IF YOU WANT TO COME.
THERE'S POPCORN AND A LITTLE CAKE LEFT.
THAT SOUNDS... DELIGHTFUL...
BUT I DO HAVE ONE TRIAL LEFT FOR TODAY.

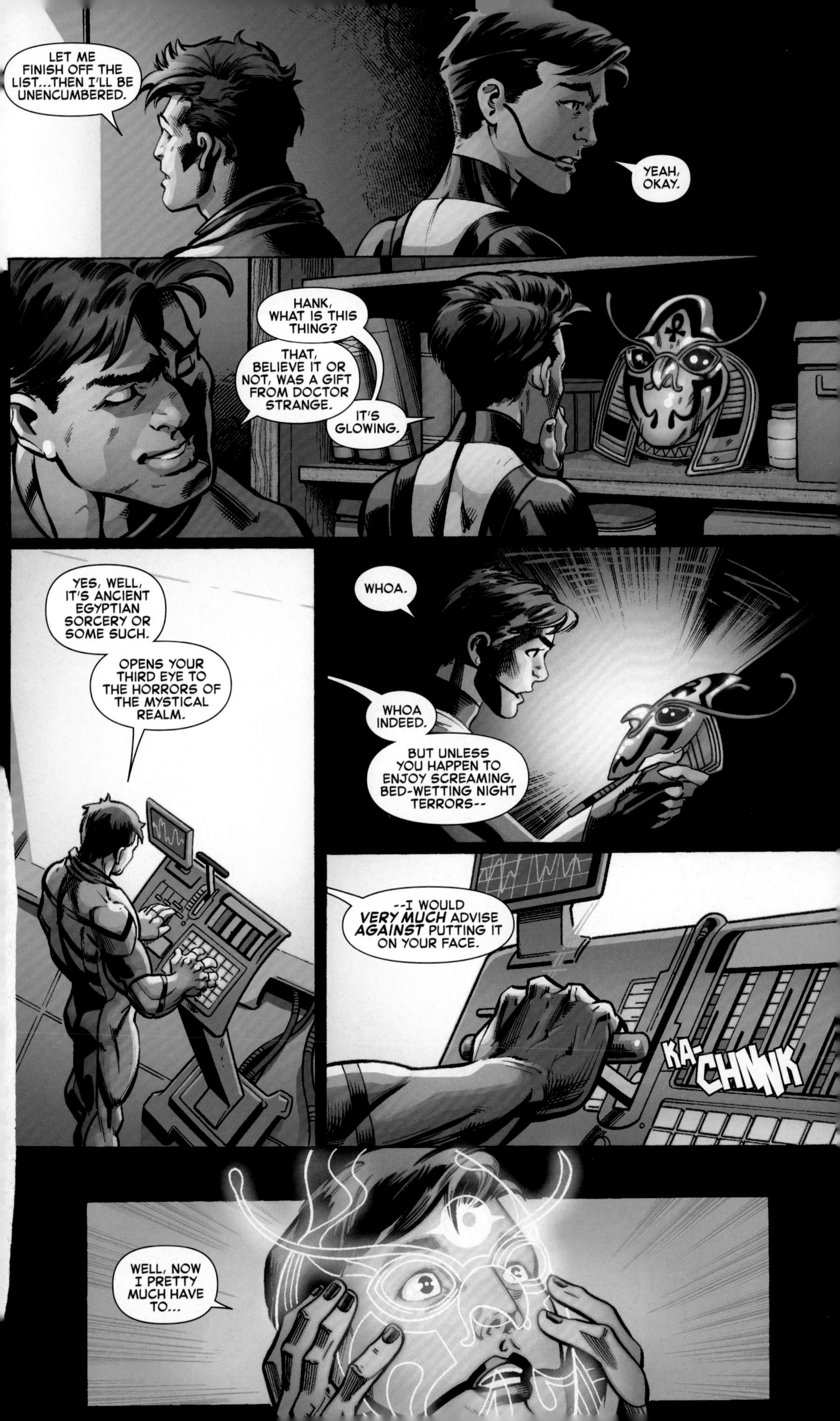
LET ME FINISH OFF THE LIST...THEN I'LL BE UNENCUMBERED.
YEAH, OKAY.
HANK, WHAT IS THIS THING?
THAT, BELIEVE IT OR NOT, WAS A GIFT FROM DOCTOR STRANGE.
IT'S GLOWING.
YES, WELL, IT'S ANCIENT EGYPTIAN SORCERY OR SOME SUCH.
OPENS YOUR THIRD EYE TO THE HORRORS OF THE MYSTICAL REALM.
WHOA.
WHOA INDEED.
BUT UNLESS YOU HAPPEN TO ENJOY SCREAMING, BED-WETTING NIGHT TERRORS--
--I WOULD VERY MUCH ADVISE AGAINST PUTTING IT ON YOUR FACE.
KA-CHNNK
WELL, NOW I PRETTY MUCH HAVE TO...

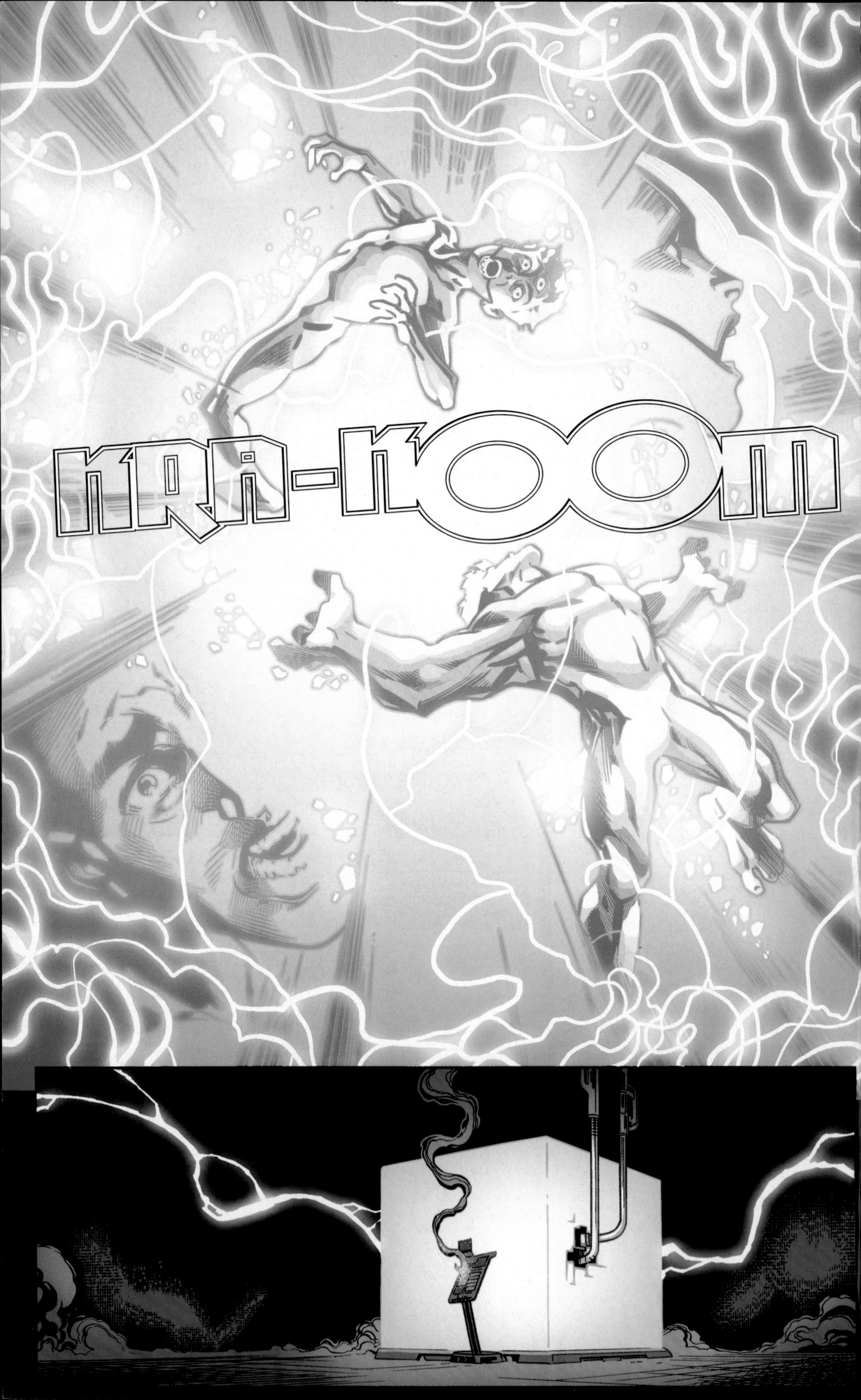
KRA-KOOM

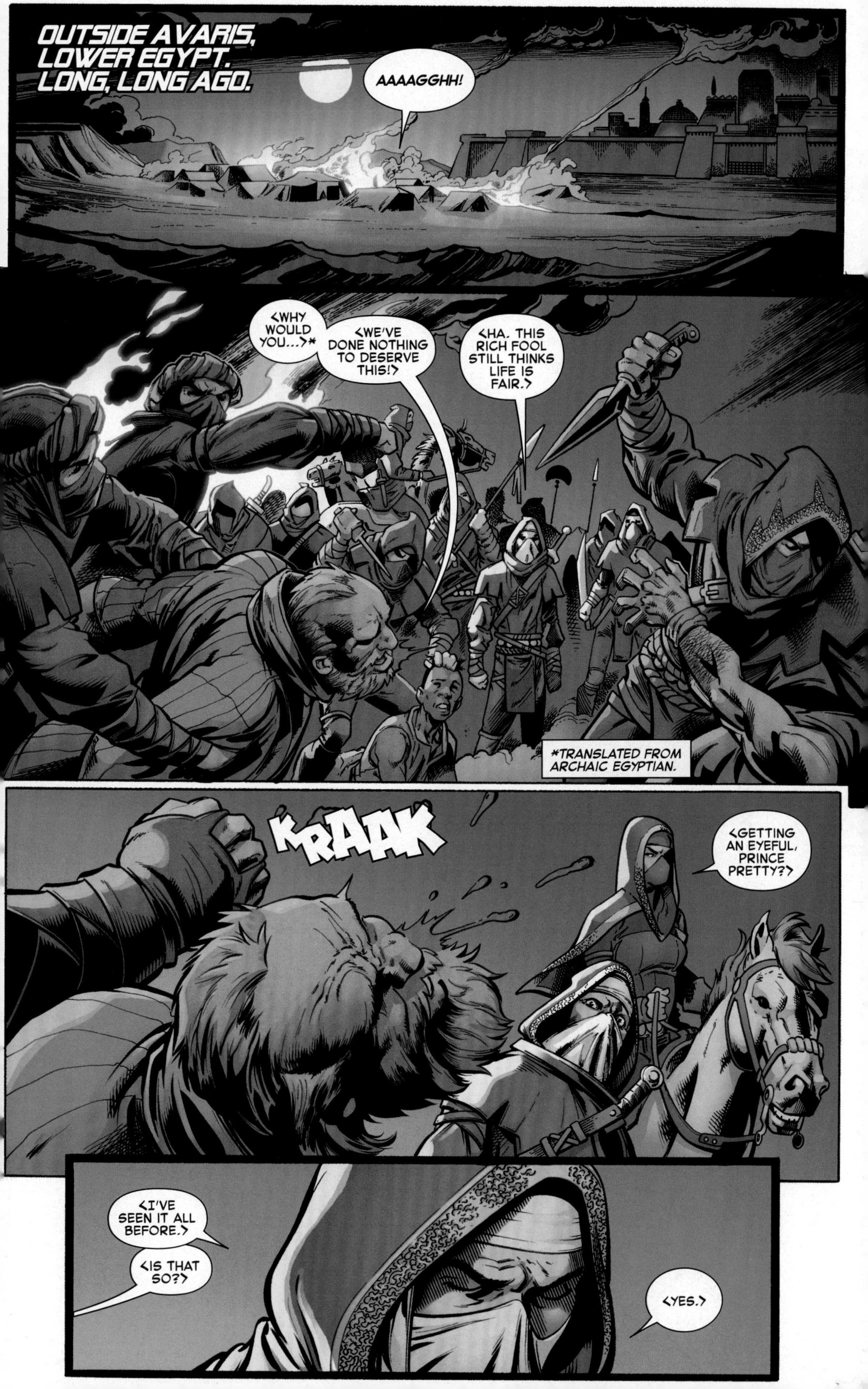
OUTSIDE AVARIS, LOWER EGYPT. LONG, LONG AGO.
AAAAGGHH!
<WHY WOULD YOU...>*
<WE'VE DONE NOTHING TO DESERVE THIS!>
<HA. THIS RICH FOOL STILL THINKS LIFE IS FAIR.>
*TRANSLATED FROM ARCHAIC EGYPTIAN.
KRAAK
<GETTING AN EYEFUL, PRINCE PRETTY?>
<I'VE SEEN IT ALL BEFORE.>
<IS THAT SO?>
<YES.>

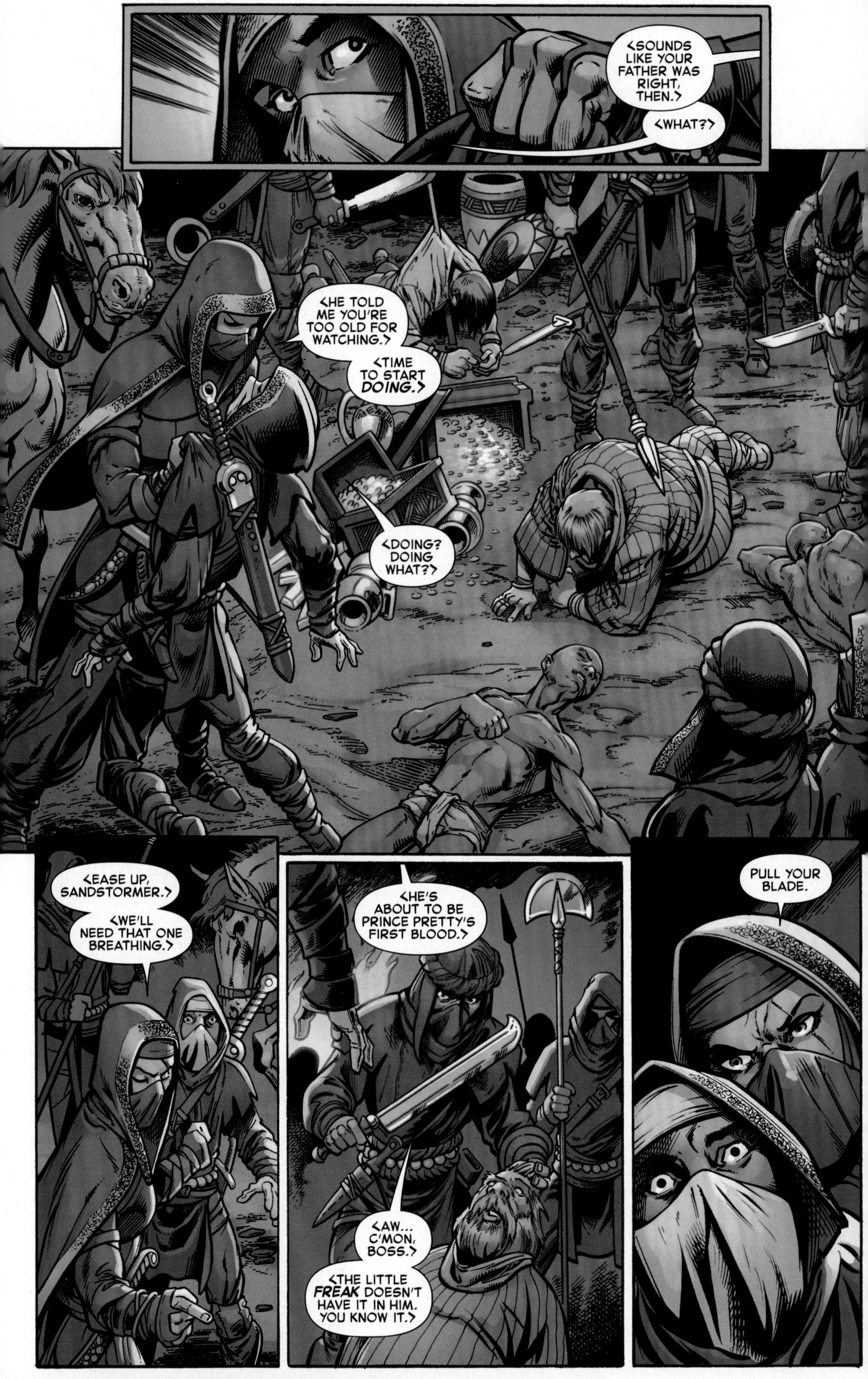
<SOUNDS LIKE YOUR FATHER WAS RIGHT, THEN.>
<WHAT?>
<HE TOLD ME YOU'RE TOO OLD FOR WATCHING.>
<TIME TO START *DOING.*>
<DOING? DOING WHAT?>
<EASE UP, SANDSTORMER.>
<WE'LL NEED THAT ONE BREATHING.>
<HE'S ABOUT TO BE PRINCE PRETTY'S FIRST BLOOD.>
<AW... C'MON, BOSS.>
<THE LITTLE *FREAK* DOESN'T HAVE IT IN HIM. YOU KNOW IT.>
PULL YOUR BLADE.

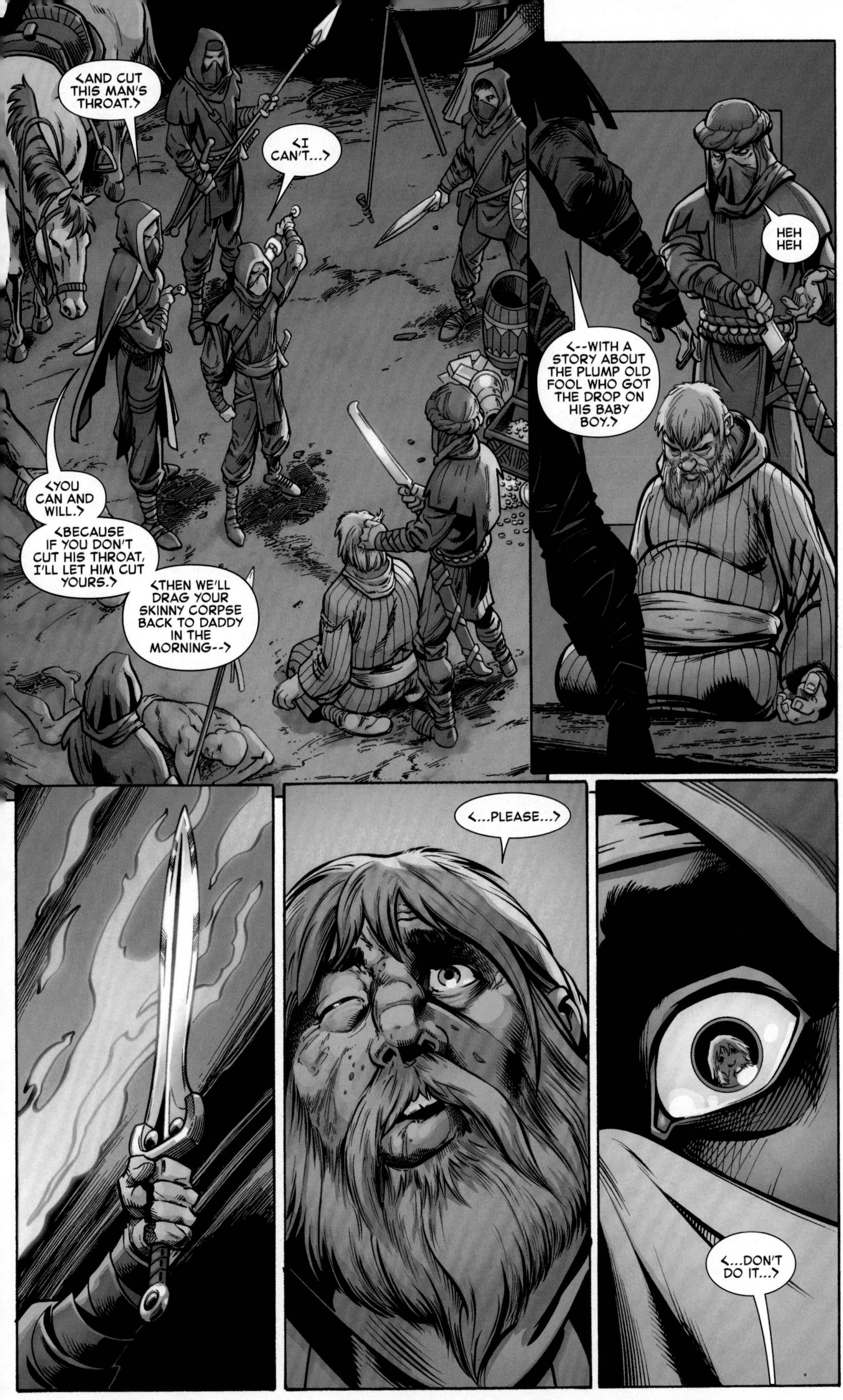
<AND CUT THIS MAN'S THROAT.>
<I CAN'T...>
<YOU CAN AND WILL.>
<BECAUSE IF YOU DON'T CUT HIS THROAT, I'LL LET HIM CUT YOURS.>
<THEN WE'LL DRAG YOUR SKINNY CORPSE BACK TO DADDY IN THE MORNING-->
<--WITH A STORY ABOUT THE PLUMP OLD FOOL WHO GOT THE DROP ON HIS BABY BOY.>
HEH HEH
<...PLEASE...>
<...DON'T DO IT...>

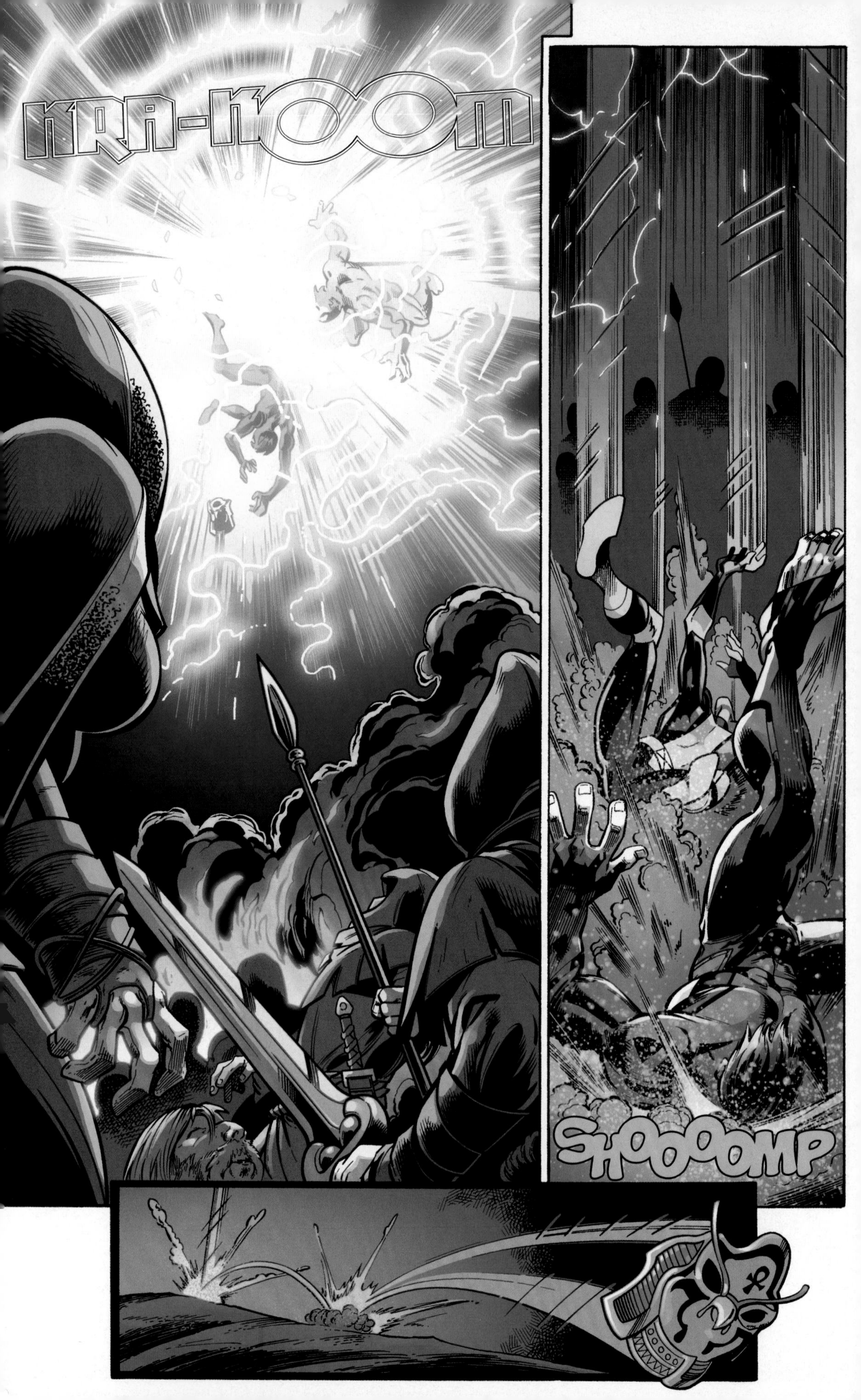
KRA-KOOM
SHOOOOOMP

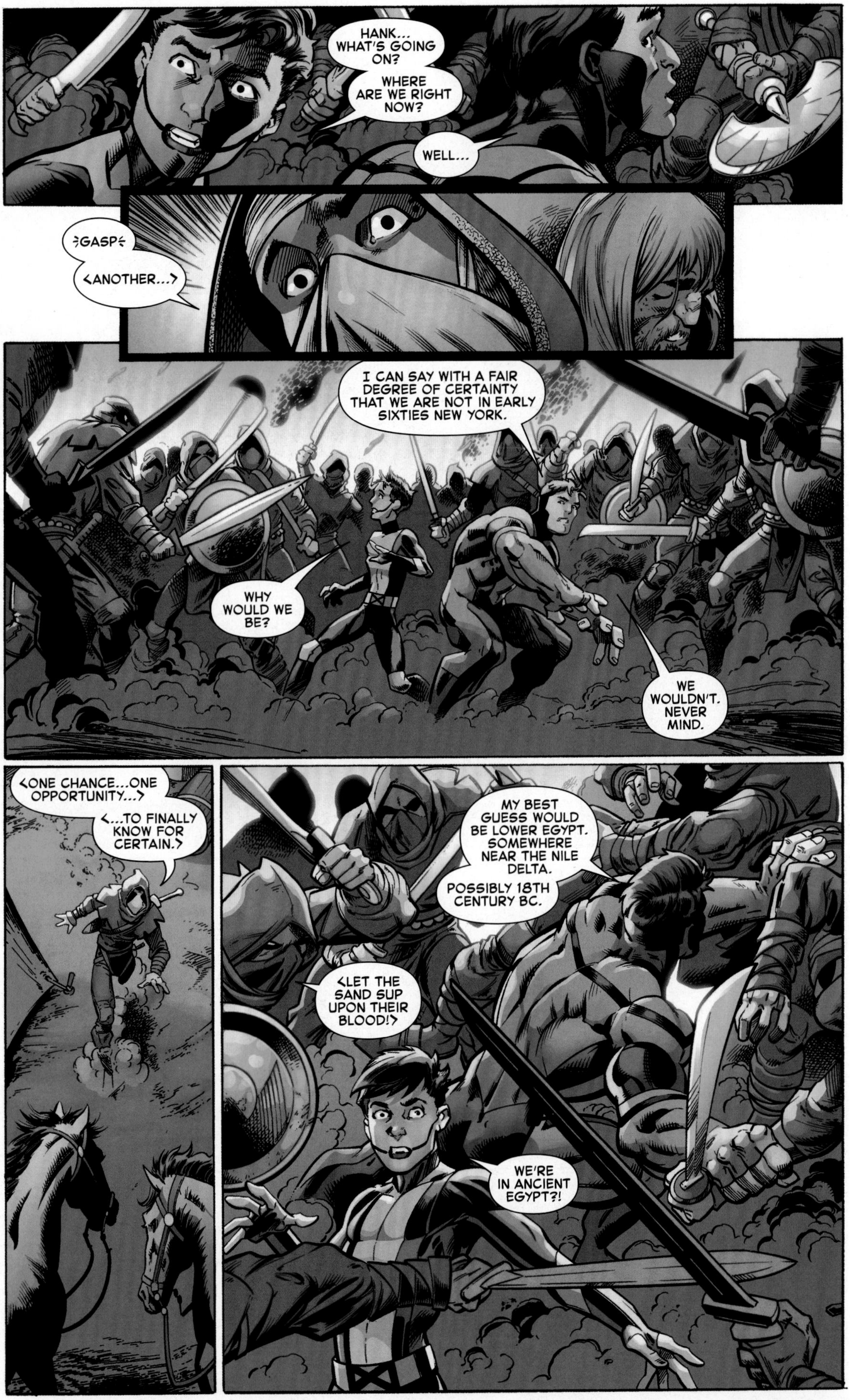
HANK... WHAT'S GOING ON?
WHERE ARE WE RIGHT NOW?
WELL...
GASP
<ANOTHER...>
I CAN SAY WITH A FAIR DEGREE OF CERTAINTY THAT WE ARE NOT IN EARLY SIXTIES NEW YORK.
WHY WOULD WE BE?
WE WOULDN'T. NEVER MIND.
<ONE CHANCE...ONE OPPORTUNITY...>
<...TO FINALLY KNOW FOR CERTAIN.>
MY BEST GUESS WOULD BE LOWER EGYPT. SOMEWHERE NEAR THE NILE DELTA.
POSSIBLY 18TH CENTURY BC.
<LET THE SAND SUP UPON THEIR BLOOD!>
WE'RE IN ANCIENT EGYPT?!

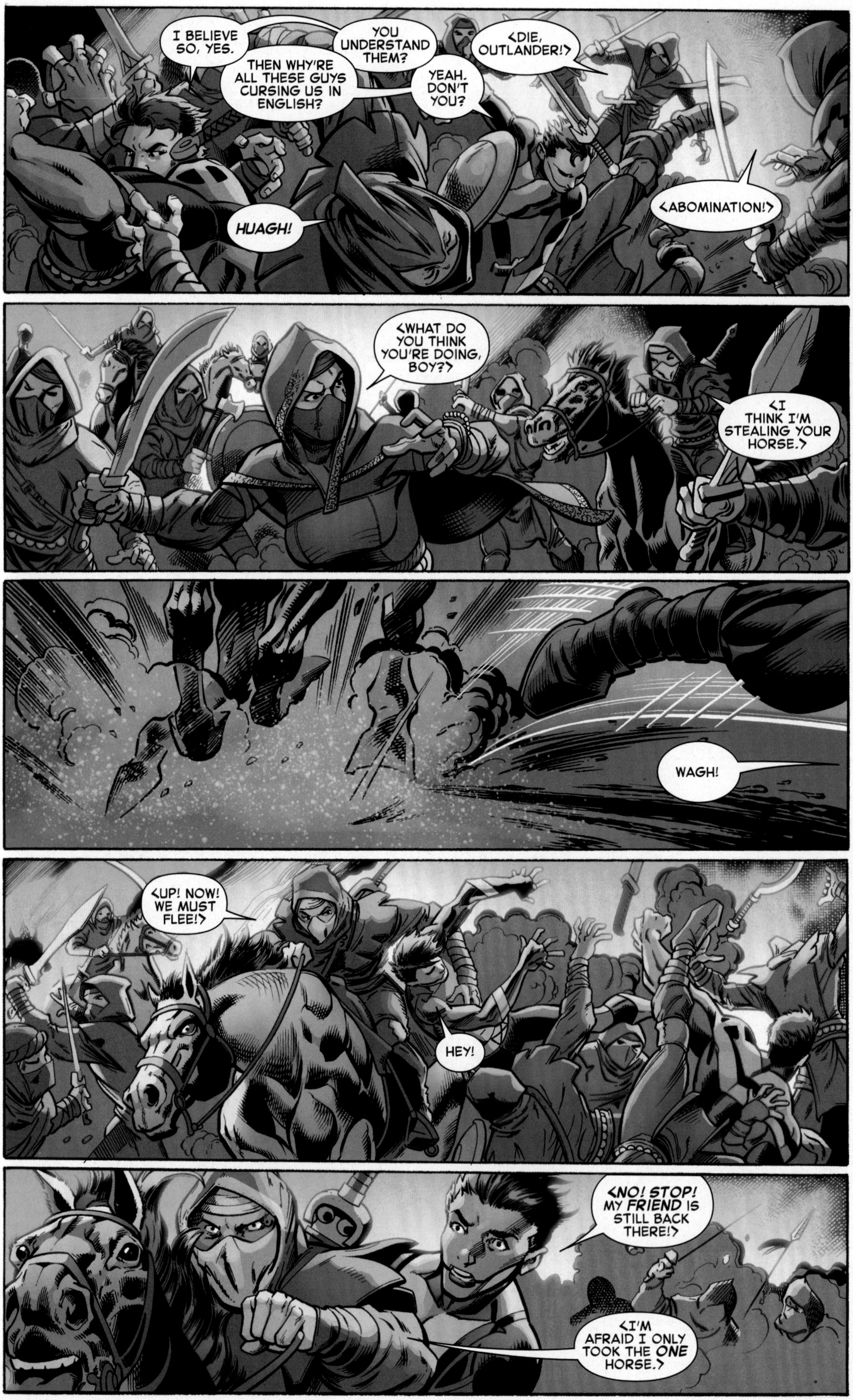
I BELIEVE SO, YES.
YOU UNDERSTAND THEM?
THEN WHY'RE ALL THESE GUYS CURSING US IN ENGLISH?
YEAH. DON'T YOU?
<DIE, OUTLANDER!>
HUAGH!
<ABOMINATION!>
<WHAT DO YOU THINK YOU'RE DOING, BOY?>
<I THINK I'M STEALING YOUR HORSE.>
WAGH!
<UP! NOW! WE MUST FLEE!>
HEY!
<NO! STOP! MY FRIEND IS STILL BACK THERE!>
<I'M AFRAID I ONLY TOOK THE ONE HORSE.>

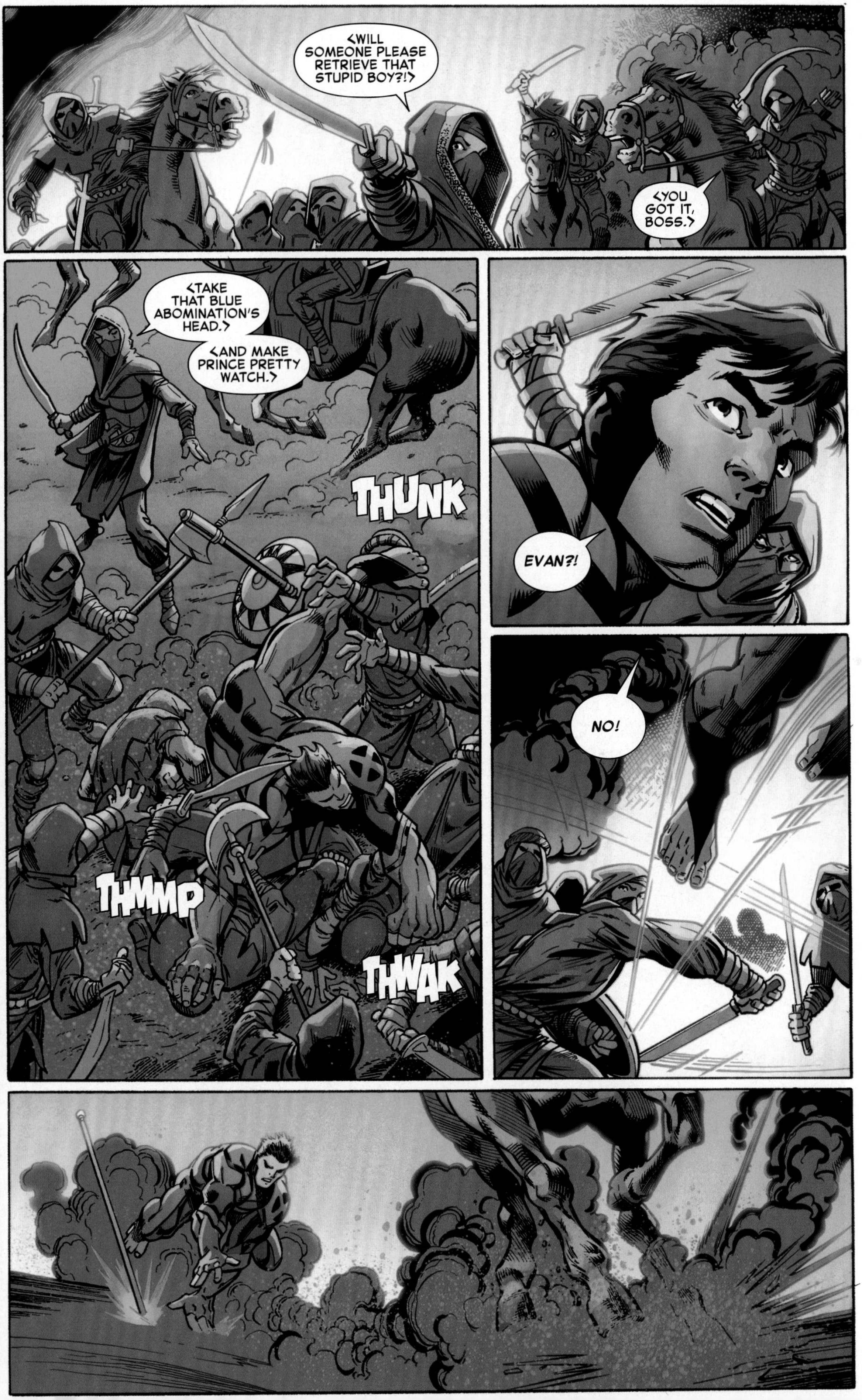
<WILL SOMEONE PLEASE RETRIEVE THAT STUPID BOY?!>
<YOU GOT IT, BOSS.>
<TAKE THAT BLUE ABOMINATION'S HEAD.>
<AND MAKE PRINCE PRETTY WATCH.>
THUNK
THMMP
THWAK
EVAN?!
NO!

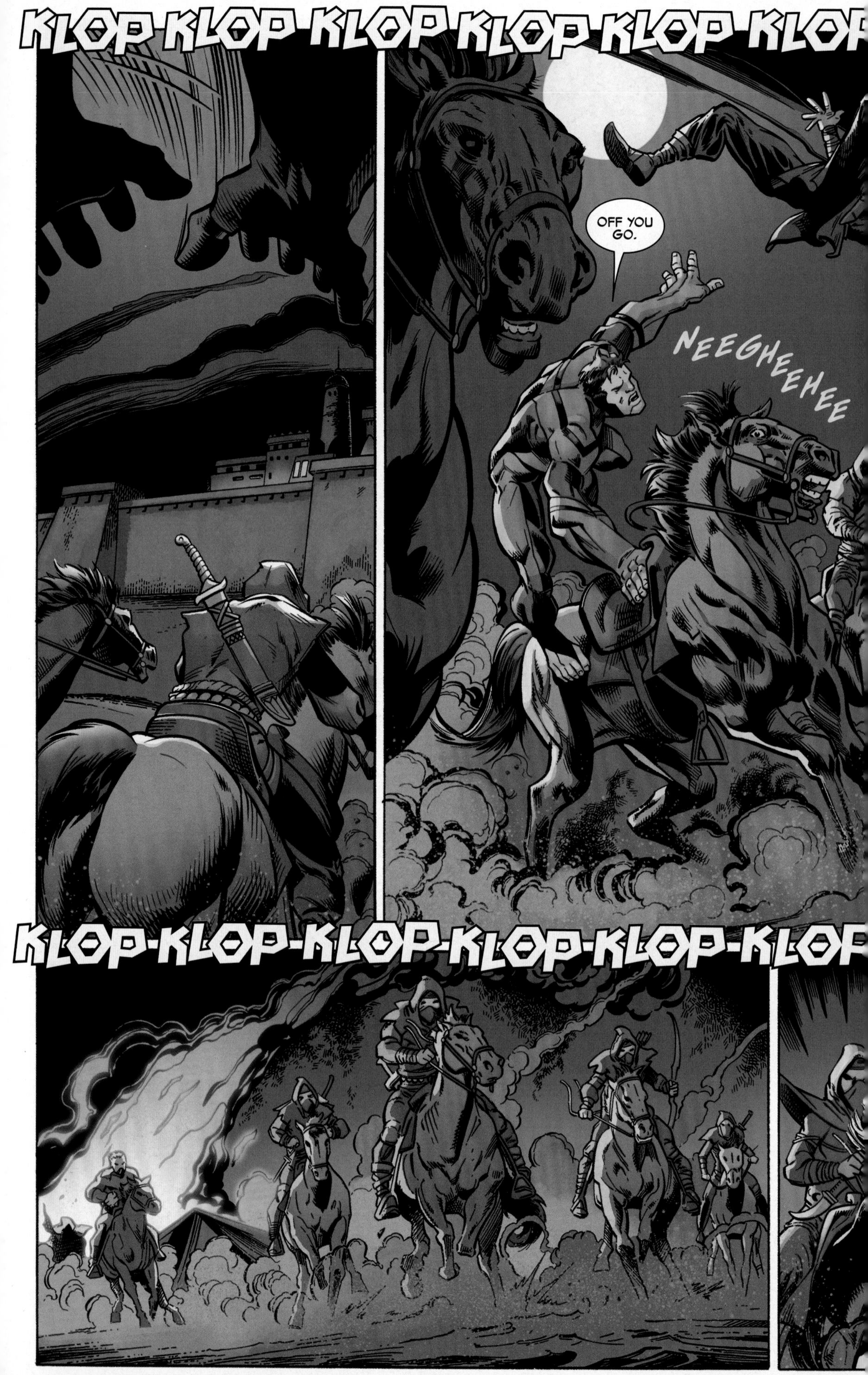

KLOP KLOP KLOP KLOP KLOP KLOP
OFF YOU GO.
NEEGHEEHEE
KLOP-KLOP-KLOP-KLOP-KLOP-KLOP

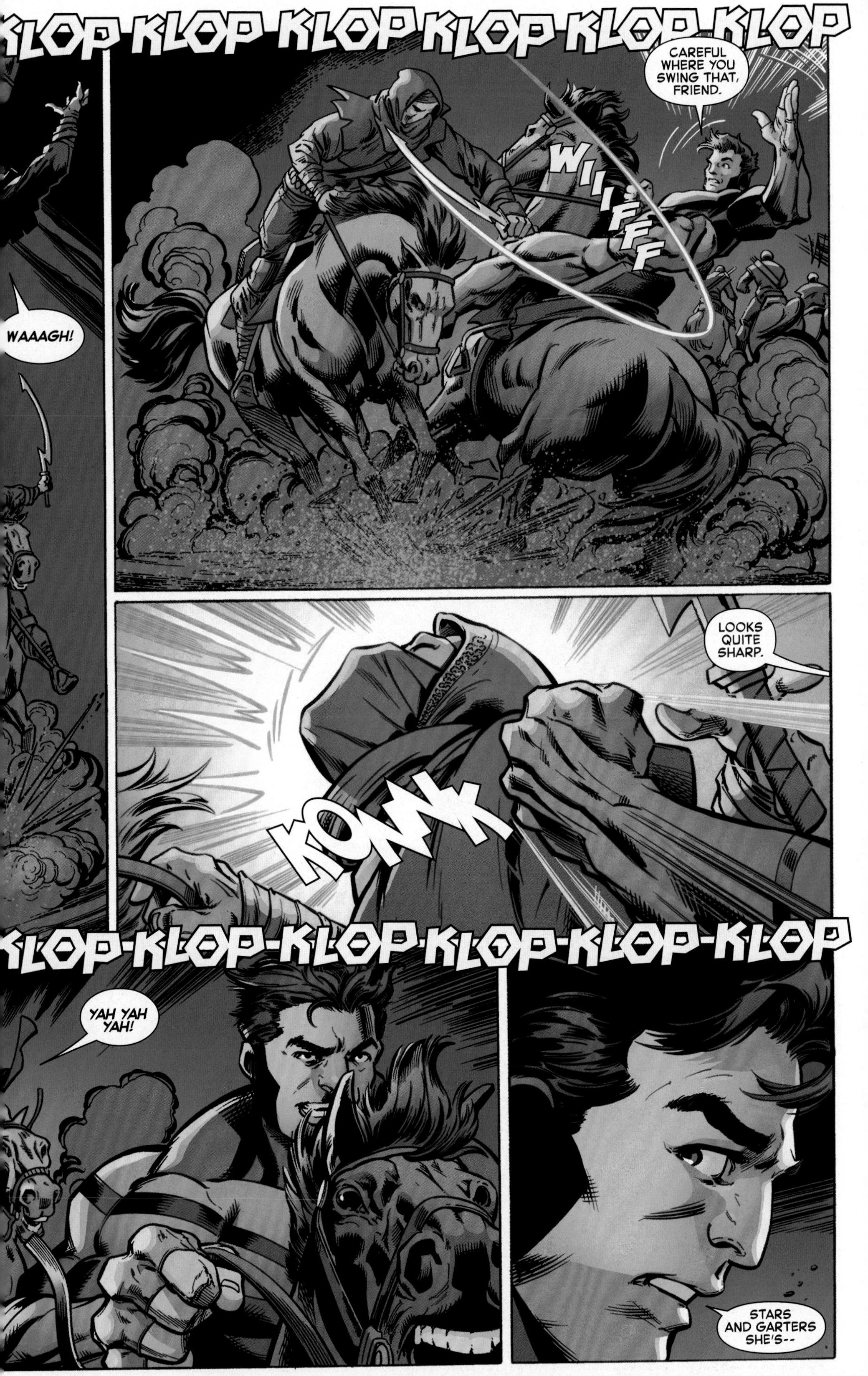
KLOP KLOP KLOP KLOP KLOP KLOP
CAREFUL WHERE YOU SWING THAT, FRIEND.
WIIIFFF
WAAAGH!
LOOKS QUITE SHARP.
KONK
KLOP-KLOP-KLOP-KLOP-KLOP-KLOP
YAH YAH YAH!
STARS AND GARTERS SHE'S--

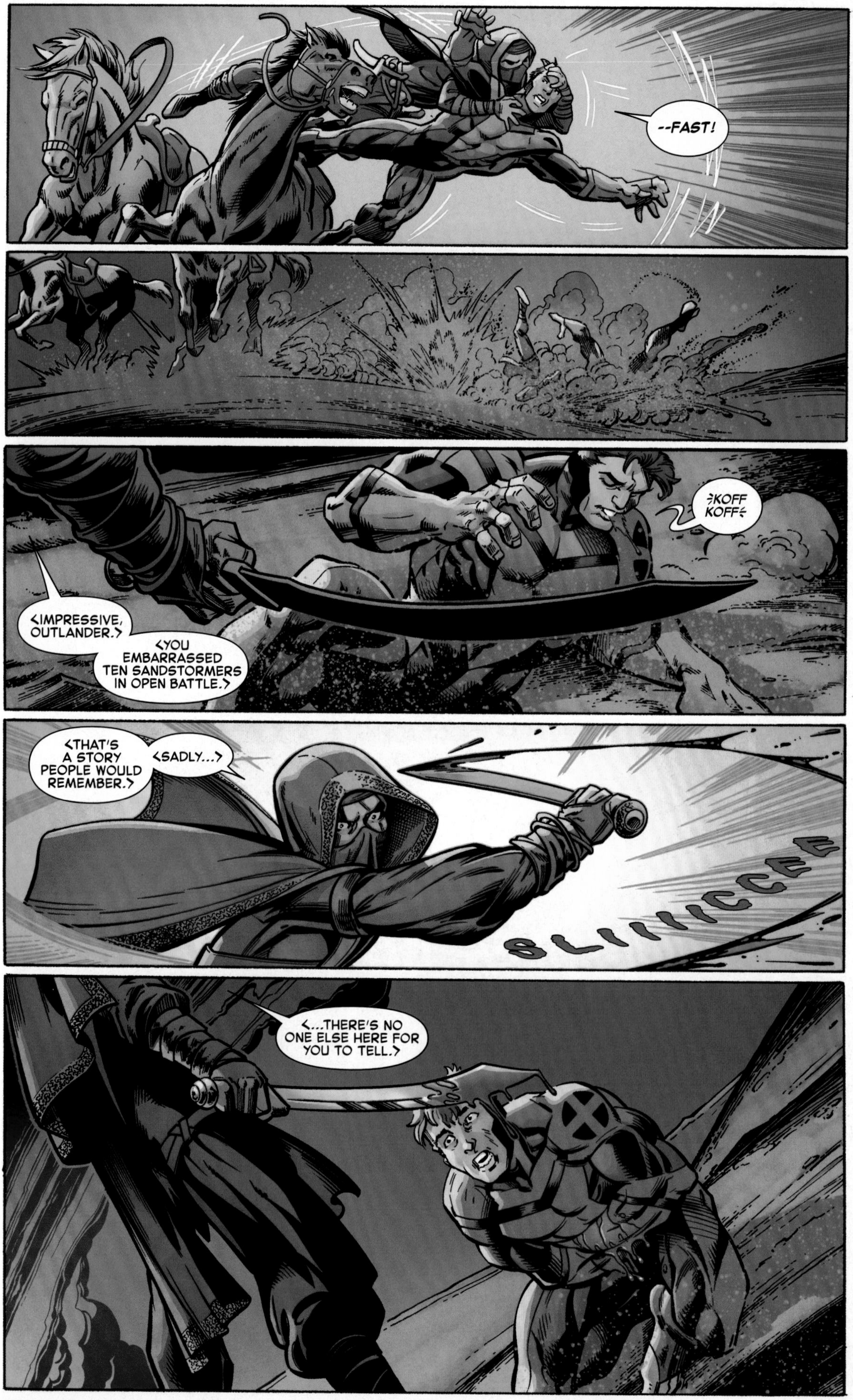
--FAST!
≠KOFF KOFF≠
<IMPRESSIVE, OUTLANDER.>
<YOU EMBARRASSED TEN SANDSTORMERS IN OPEN BATTLE.>
<THAT'S A STORY PEOPLE WOULD REMEMBER.>
<SADLY...>
SLIIIICCEE
<...THERE'S NO ONE ELSE HERE FOR YOU TO TELL.>

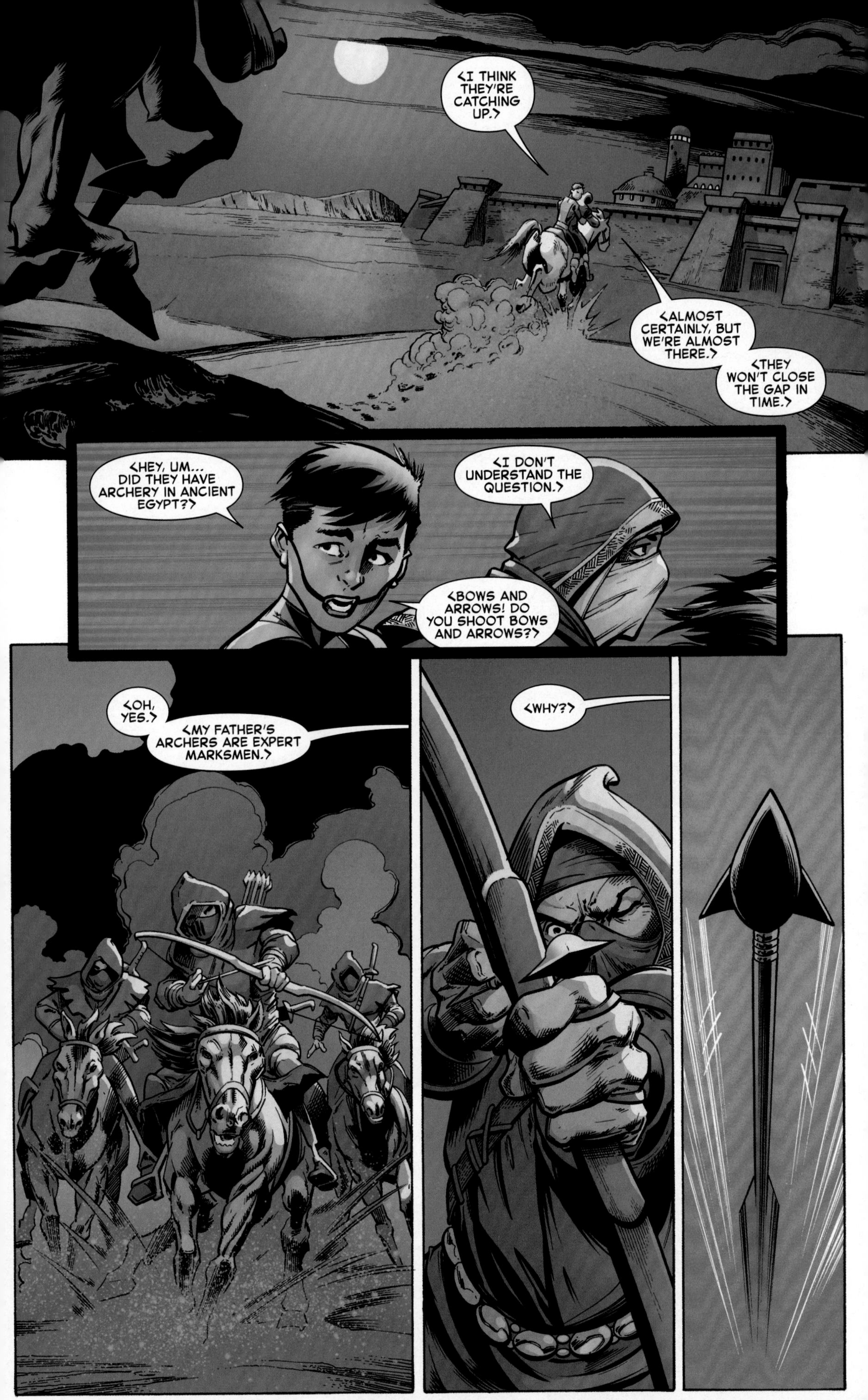

<I THINK THEY'RE CATCHING UP.>
<ALMOST CERTAINLY, BUT WE'RE ALMOST THERE.>
<THEY WON'T CLOSE THE GAP IN TIME.>
<HEY, UM... DID THEY HAVE ARCHERY IN ANCIENT EGYPT?>
<I DON'T UNDERSTAND THE QUESTION.>
<BOWS AND ARROWS! DO YOU SHOOT BOWS AND ARROWS?>
<OH, YES.>
<MY FATHER'S ARCHERS ARE EXPERT MARKSMEN.>
<WHY?>

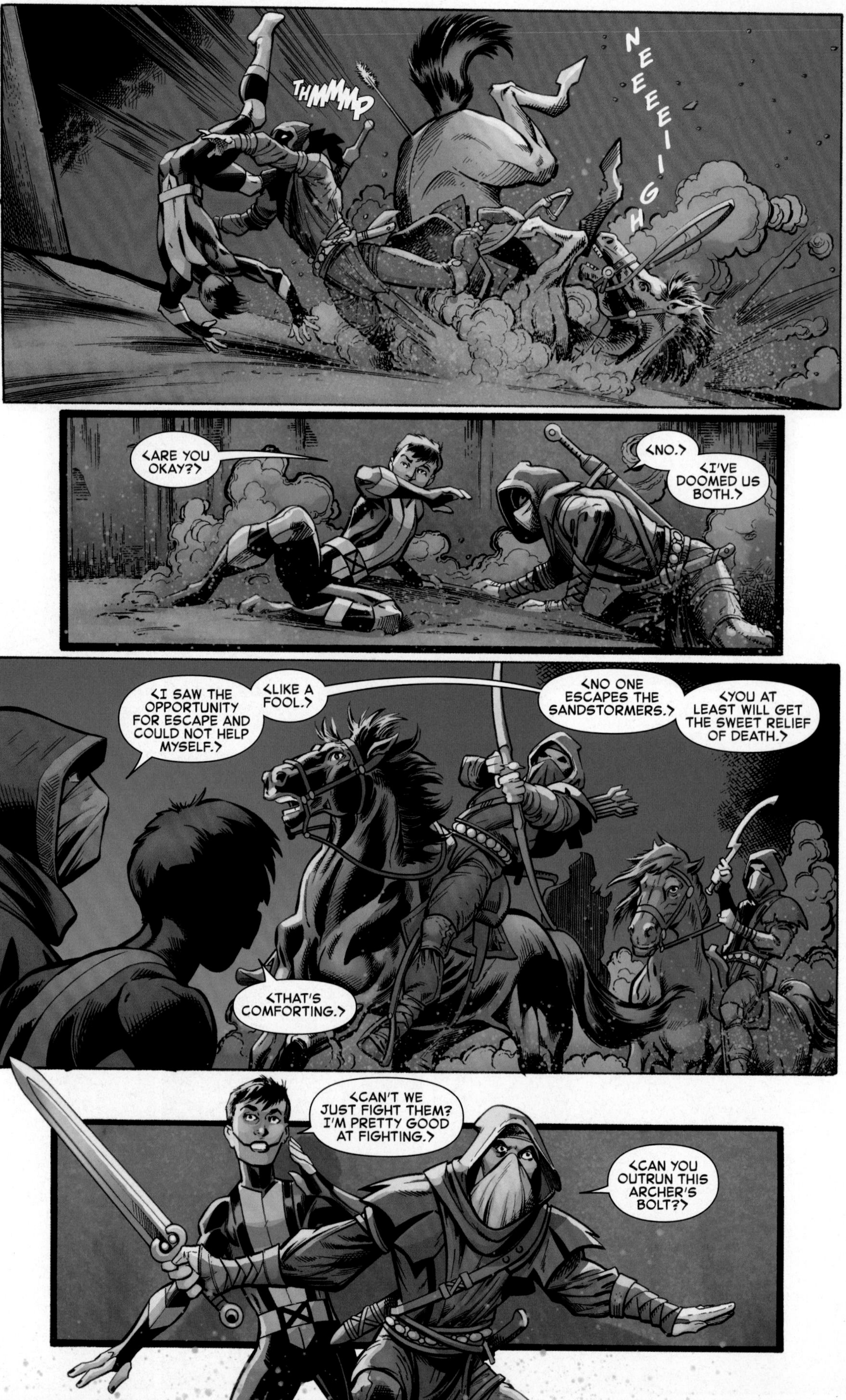
THMMMP
NEEEEIIGH
<ARE YOU OKAY?>
<NO.>
<I'VE DOOMED US BOTH.>
<I SAW THE OPPORTUNITY FOR ESCAPE AND COULD NOT HELP MYSELF.>
<LIKE A FOOL.>
<NO ONE ESCAPES THE SANDSTORMERS.>
<YOU AT LEAST WILL GET THE SWEET RELIEF OF DEATH.>
<THAT'S COMFORTING.>
<CAN'T WE JUST FIGHT THEM? I'M PRETTY GOOD AT FIGHTING.>
<CAN YOU OUTRUN THIS ARCHER'S BOLT?>

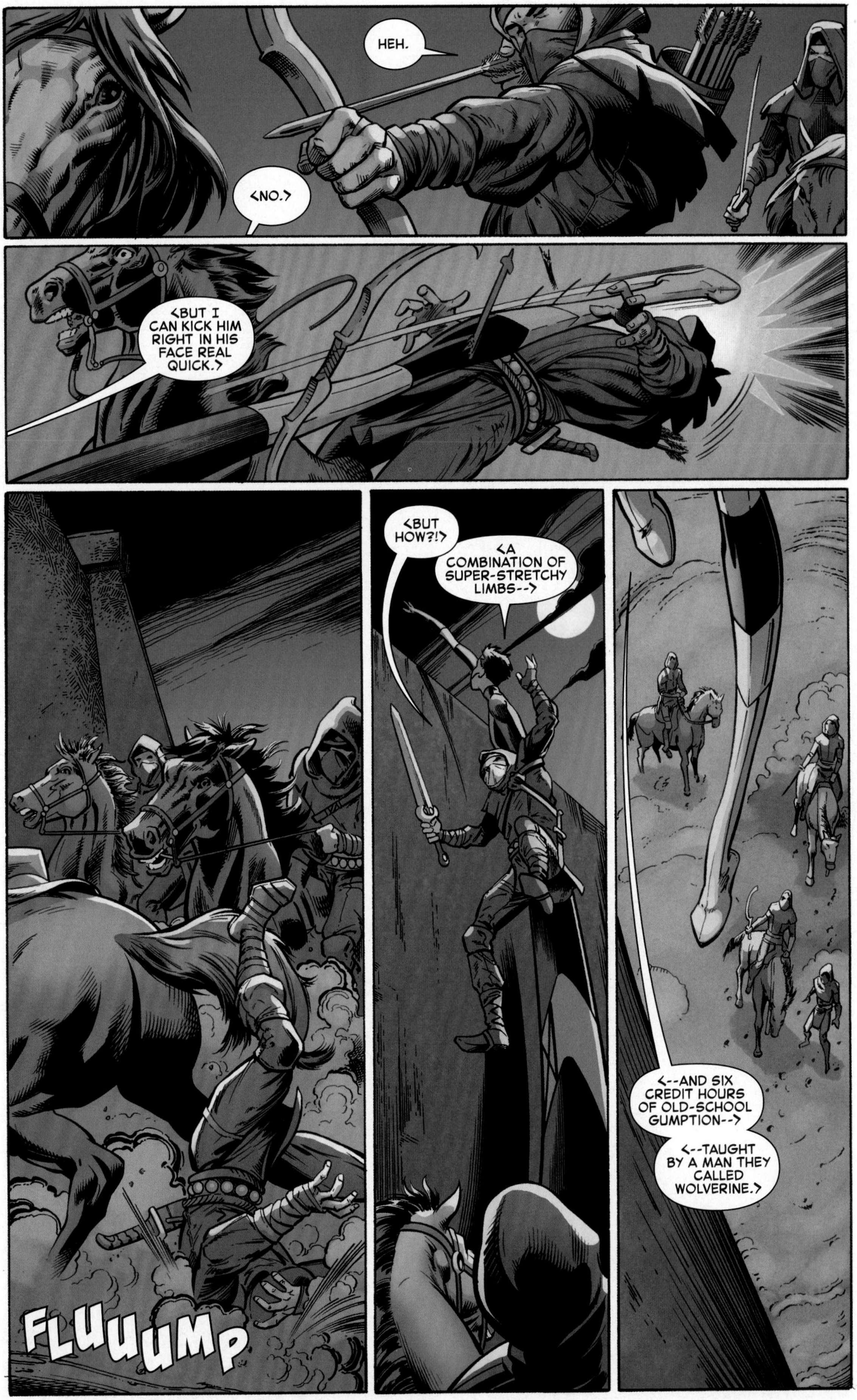
HEH.
<NO.>
<BUT I CAN KICK HIM RIGHT IN HIS FACE REAL QUICK.>
FLUUUMP
<BUT HOW?!>
<A COMBINATION OF SUPER-STRETCHY LIMBS-->
<--AND SIX CREDIT HOURS OF OLD-SCHOOL GUMPTION-->
<--TAUGHT BY A MAN THEY CALLED WOLVERINE.>

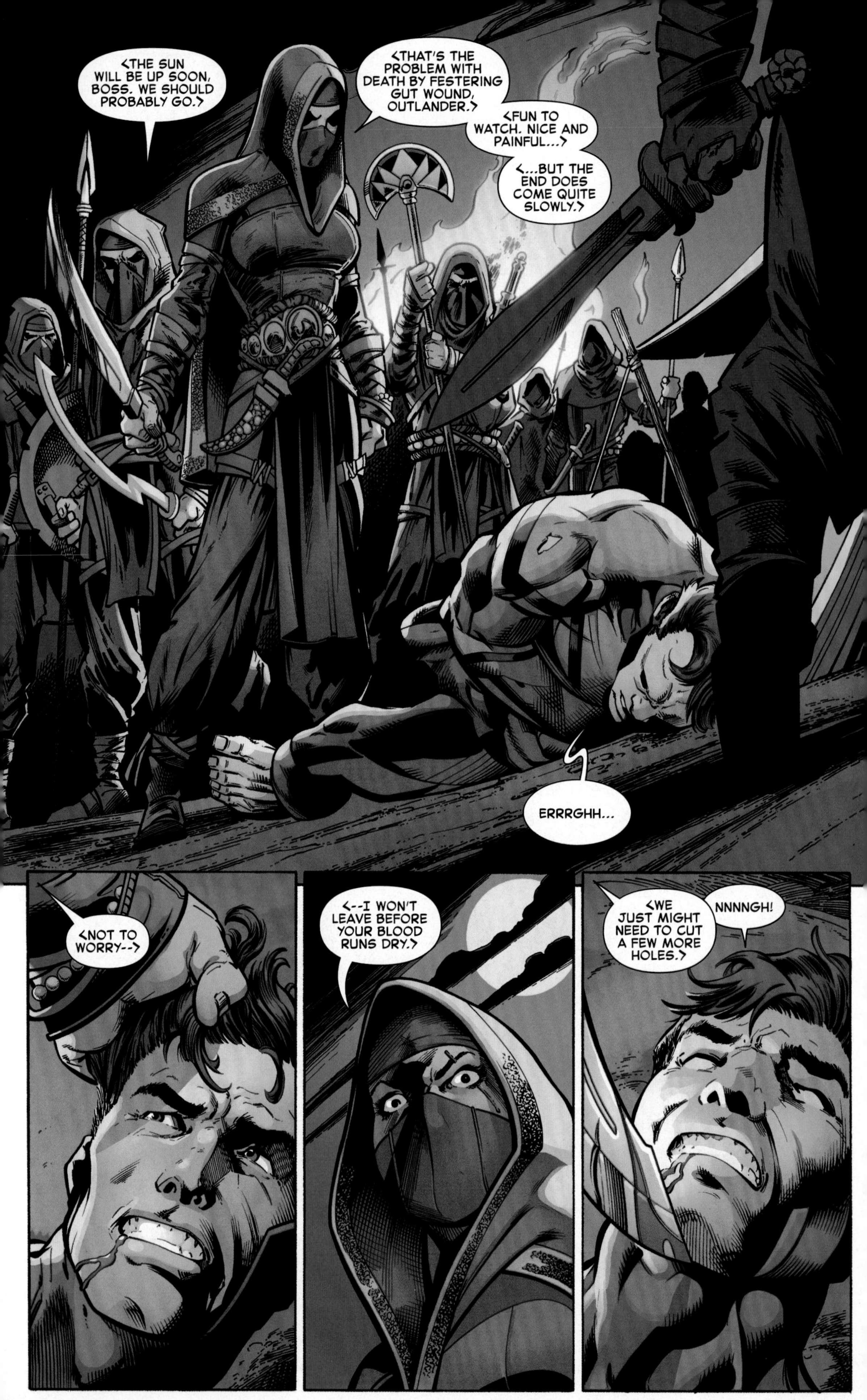
<THE SUN WILL BE UP SOON, BOSS. WE SHOULD PROBABLY GO.>
<THAT'S THE PROBLEM WITH DEATH BY FESTERING GUT WOUND, OUTLANDER.>
<FUN TO WATCH. NICE AND PAINFUL...>
<...BUT THE END DOES COME QUITE SLOWLY.>
ERRRGHH...
<NOT TO WORRY-->
<--I WON'T LEAVE BEFORE YOUR BLOOD RUNS DRY.>
<WE JUST MIGHT NEED TO CUT A FEW MORE HOLES.>
NNNNGH!

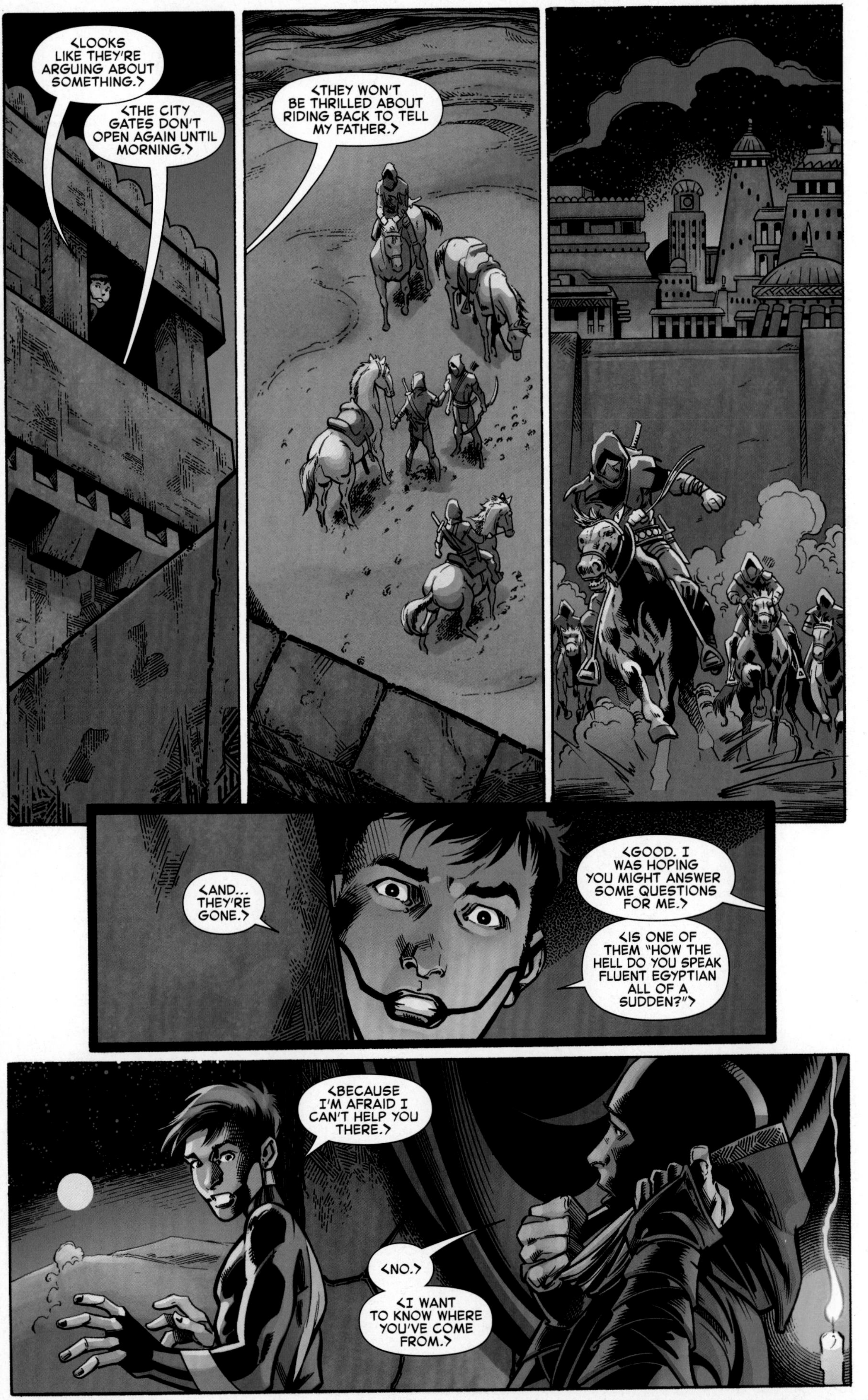
<LOOKS LIKE THEY'RE ARGUING ABOUT SOMETHING.>
<THE CITY GATES DON'T OPEN AGAIN UNTIL MORNING.>
<THEY WON'T BE THRILLED ABOUT RIDING BACK TO TELL MY FATHER.>
<AND... THEY'RE GONE.>
<GOOD. I WAS HOPING YOU MIGHT ANSWER SOME QUESTIONS FOR ME.>
<IS ONE OF THEM "HOW THE HELL DO YOU SPEAK FLUENT EGYPTIAN ALL OF A SUDDEN?">
<BECAUSE I'M AFRAID I CAN'T HELP YOU THERE.>
<NO.>
<I WANT TO KNOW WHERE YOU'VE COME FROM.>

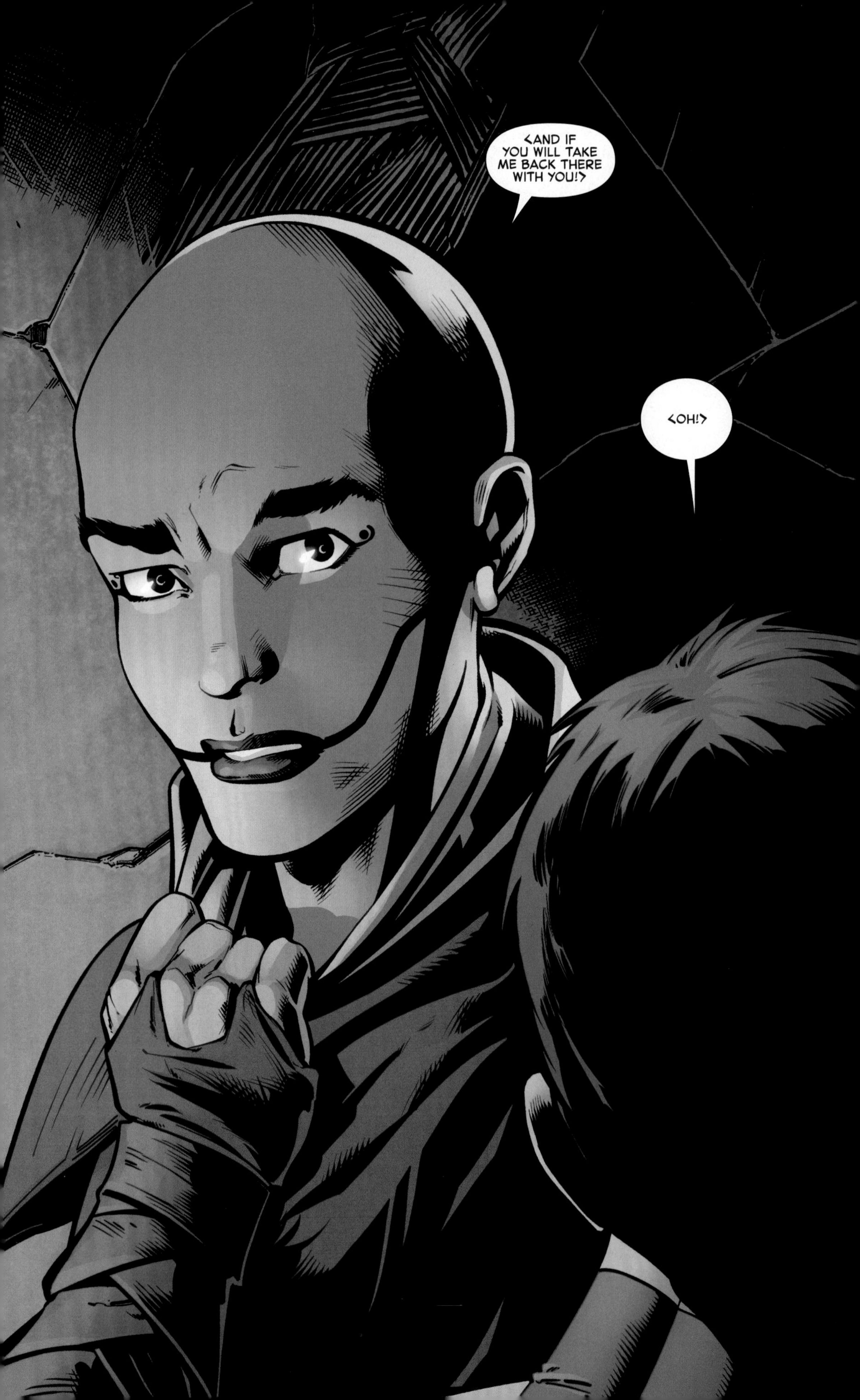
<AND IF YOU WILL TAKE ME BACK THERE WITH YOU!>
<OH!>

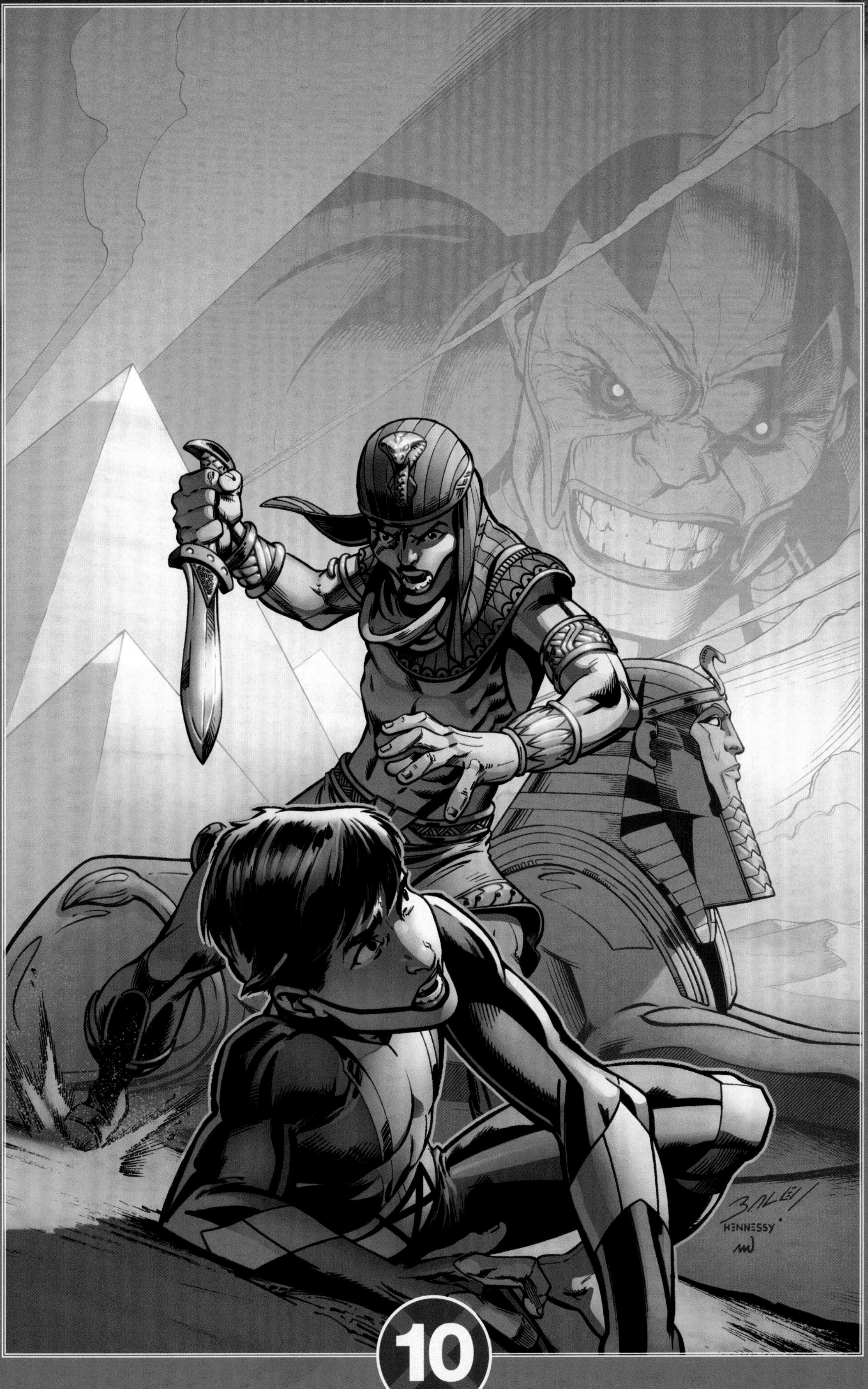
HENNESSY
10

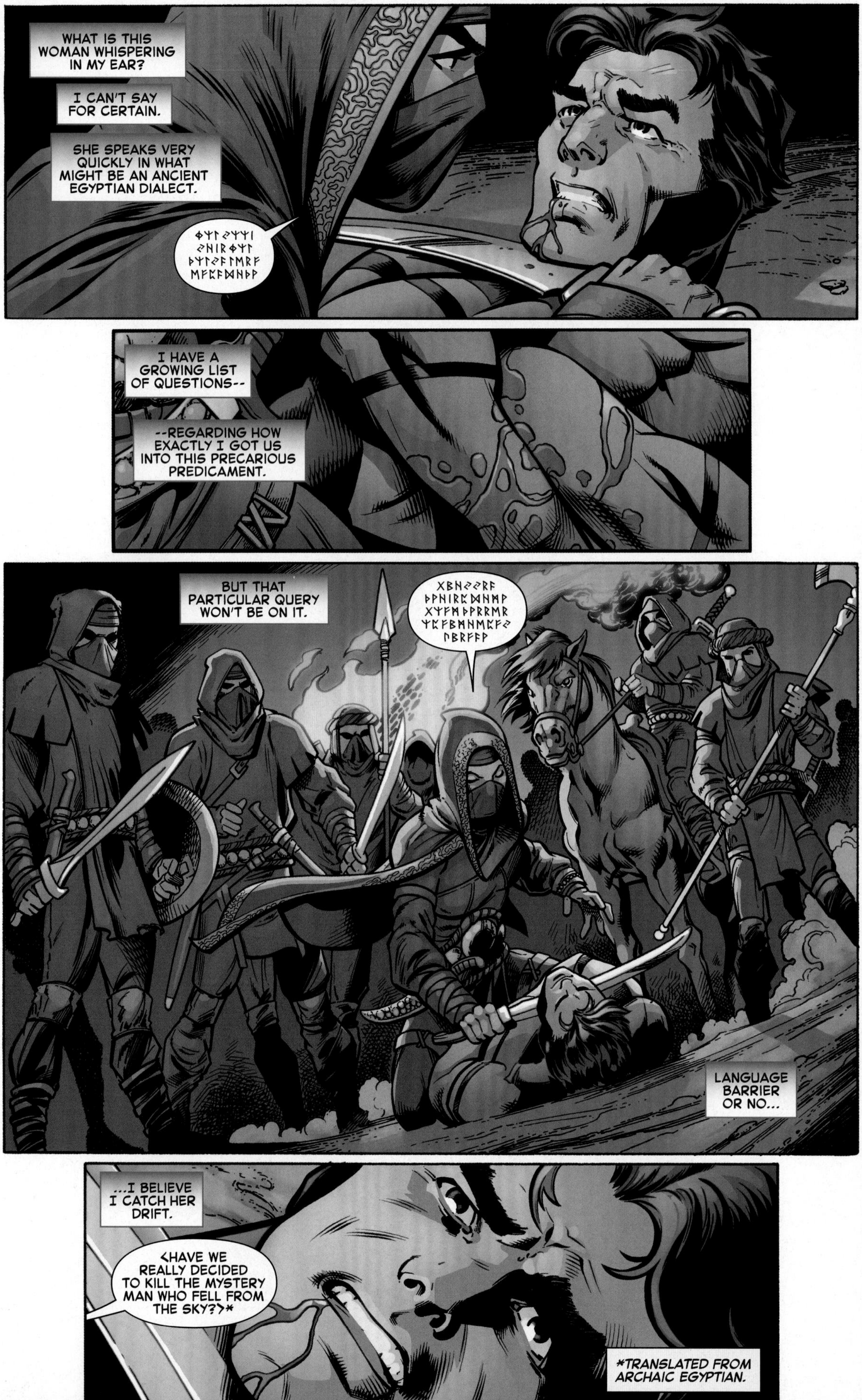
WHAT IS THIS WOMAN WHISPERING IN MY EAR?
I CAN'T SAY FOR CERTAIN.
SHE SPEAKS VERY QUICKLY IN WHAT MIGHT BE AN ANCIENT EGYPTIAN DIALECT.
I HAVE A GROWING LIST OF QUESTIONS--
--REGARDING HOW EXACTLY I GOT US INTO THIS PRECARIOUS PREDICAMENT.
BUT THAT PARTICULAR QUERY WON'T BE ON IT.
LANGUAGE BARRIER OR NO...
...I BELIEVE I CATCH HER DRIFT.
<HAVE WE REALLY DECIDED TO KILL THE MYSTERY MAN WHO FELL FROM THE SKY?>*
*TRANSLATED FROM ARCHAIC EGYPTIAN.

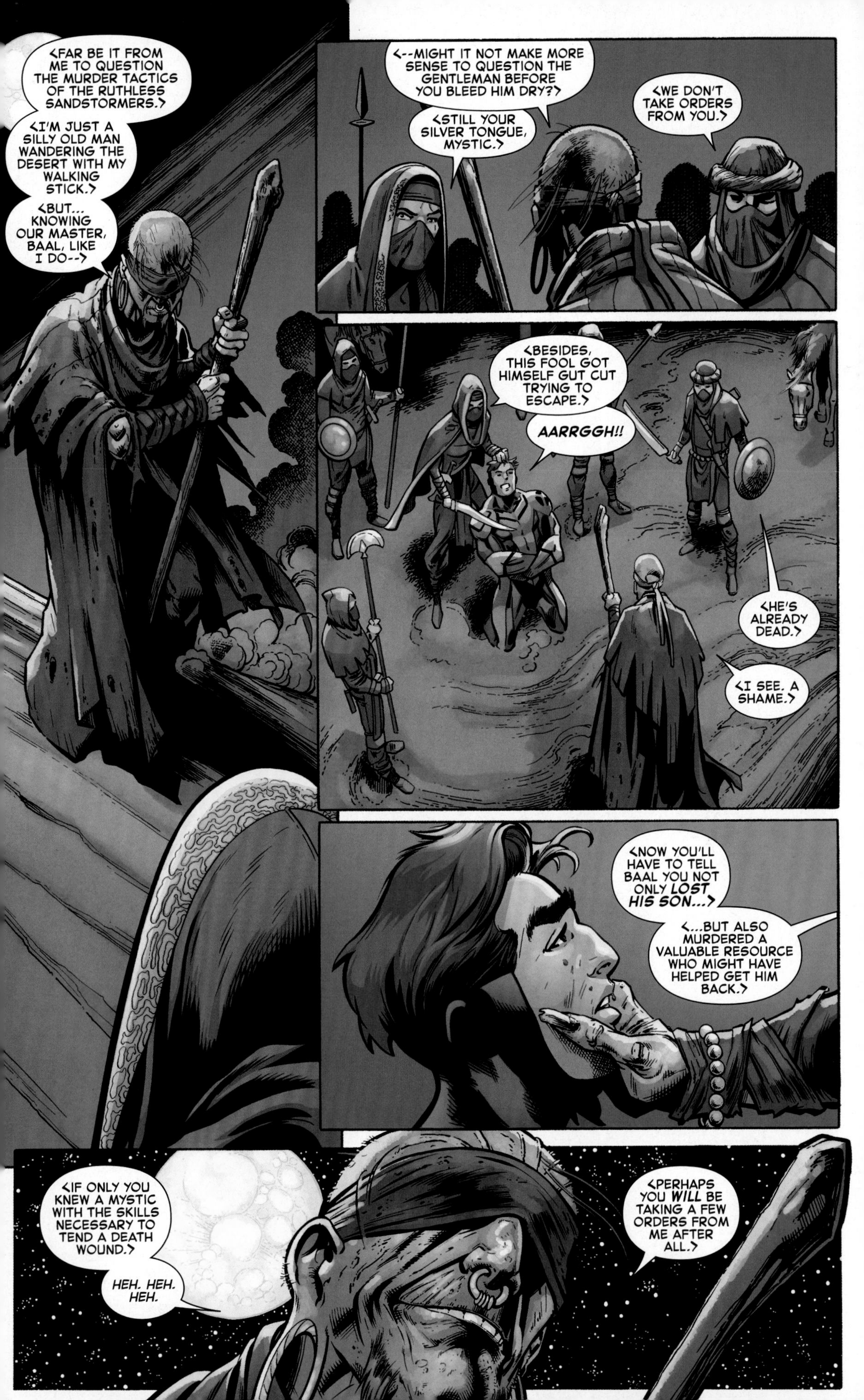
<FAR BE IT FROM ME TO QUESTION THE MURDER TACTICS OF THE RUTHLESS SANDSTORMERS.>
<I'M JUST A SILLY OLD MAN WANDERING THE DESERT WITH MY WALKING STICK.>
<BUT... KNOWING OUR MASTER, BAAL, LIKE I DO-->
<--MIGHT IT NOT MAKE MORE SENSE TO QUESTION THE GENTLEMAN BEFORE YOU BLEED HIM DRY?>
<STILL YOUR SILVER TONGUE, MYSTIC.>
<WE DON'T TAKE ORDERS FROM YOU.>
<BESIDES, THIS FOOL GOT HIMSELF GUT CUT TRYING TO ESCAPE.>
AARRGGH!!
<HE'S ALREADY DEAD.>
<I SEE. A SHAME.>
<NOW YOU'LL HAVE TO TELL BAAL YOU NOT ONLY LOST HIS SON...>
<...BUT ALSO MURDERED A VALUABLE RESOURCE WHO MIGHT HAVE HELPED GET HIM BACK.>
<IF ONLY YOU KNEW A MYSTIC WITH THE SKILLS NECESSARY TO TEND A DEATH WOUND.>
HEH. HEH. HEH.
<PERHAPS YOU WILL BE TAKING A FEW ORDERS FROM ME AFTER ALL.>

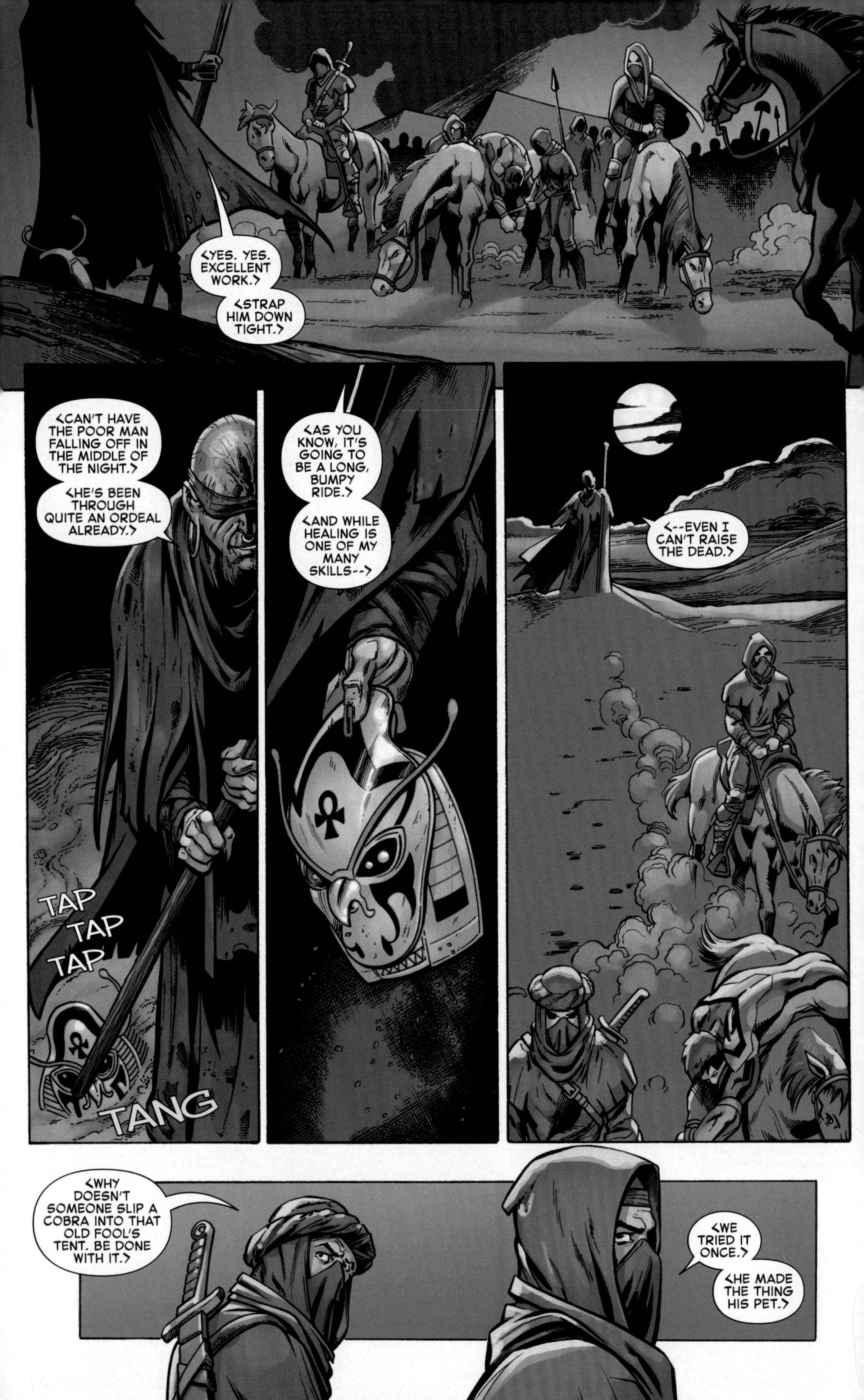
<YES. YES. EXCELLENT WORK.>
<STRAP HIM DOWN TIGHT.>
<CAN'T HAVE THE POOR MAN FALLING OFF IN THE MIDDLE OF THE NIGHT.>
<HE'S BEEN THROUGH QUITE AN ORDEAL ALREADY.>
TAP
TAP
TAP
TANG
<AS YOU KNOW, IT'S GOING TO BE A LONG, BUMPY RIDE.>
<AND WHILE HEALING IS ONE OF MY MANY SKILLS-->
<--EVEN I CAN'T RAISE THE DEAD.>
<WHY DOESN'T SOMEONE SLIP A COBRA INTO THAT OLD FOOL'S TENT. BE DONE WITH IT.>
<WE TRIED IT ONCE.>
<HE MADE THE THING HIS PET.>

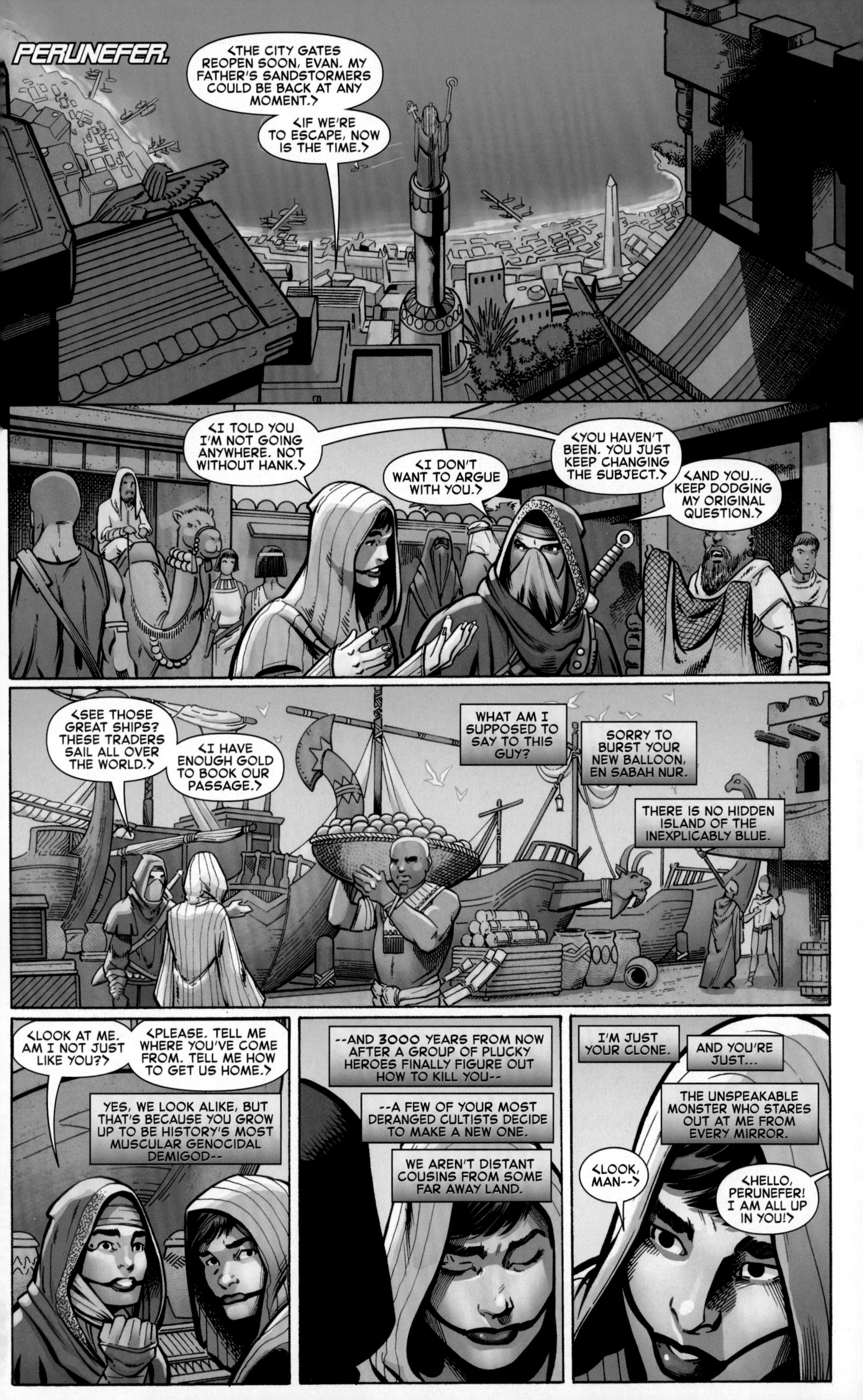
PERUNEFER.
<THE CITY GATES REOPEN SOON, EVAN. MY FATHER'S SANDSTORMERS COULD BE BACK AT ANY MOMENT.>
<IF WE'RE TO ESCAPE, NOW IS THE TIME.>
<I TOLD YOU I'M NOT GOING ANYWHERE. NOT WITHOUT HANK.>
<I DON'T WANT TO ARGUE WITH YOU.>
<YOU HAVEN'T BEEN. YOU JUST KEEP CHANGING THE SUBJECT.>
<AND YOU... KEEP DODGING MY ORIGINAL QUESTION.>
<SEE THOSE GREAT SHIPS? THESE TRADERS SAIL ALL OVER THE WORLD.>
<I HAVE ENOUGH GOLD TO BOOK OUR PASSAGE.>
WHAT AM I SUPPOSED TO SAY TO THIS GUY?
SORRY TO BURST YOUR NEW BALLOON, EN SABAH NUR.
THERE IS NO HIDDEN ISLAND OF THE INEXPLICABLY BLUE.
<LOOK AT ME. AM I NOT JUST LIKE YOU?>
<PLEASE. TELL ME WHERE YOU'VE COME FROM. TELL ME HOW TO GET US HOME.>
YES, WE LOOK ALIKE, BUT THAT'S BECAUSE YOU GROW UP TO BE HISTORY'S MOST MUSCULAR GENOCIDAL DEMIGOD--
--AND 3000 YEARS FROM NOW AFTER A GROUP OF PLUCKY HEROES FINALLY FIGURE OUT HOW TO KILL YOU--
--A FEW OF YOUR MOST DERANGED CULTISTS DECIDE TO MAKE A NEW ONE.
WE AREN'T DISTANT COUSINS FROM SOME FAR AWAY LAND.
I'M JUST YOUR CLONE.
AND YOU'RE JUST...
THE UNSPEAKABLE MONSTER WHO STARES OUT AT ME FROM EVERY MIRROR.
<LOOK, MAN-->
<HELLO, PERUNEFER! I AM ALL UP IN YOU!>

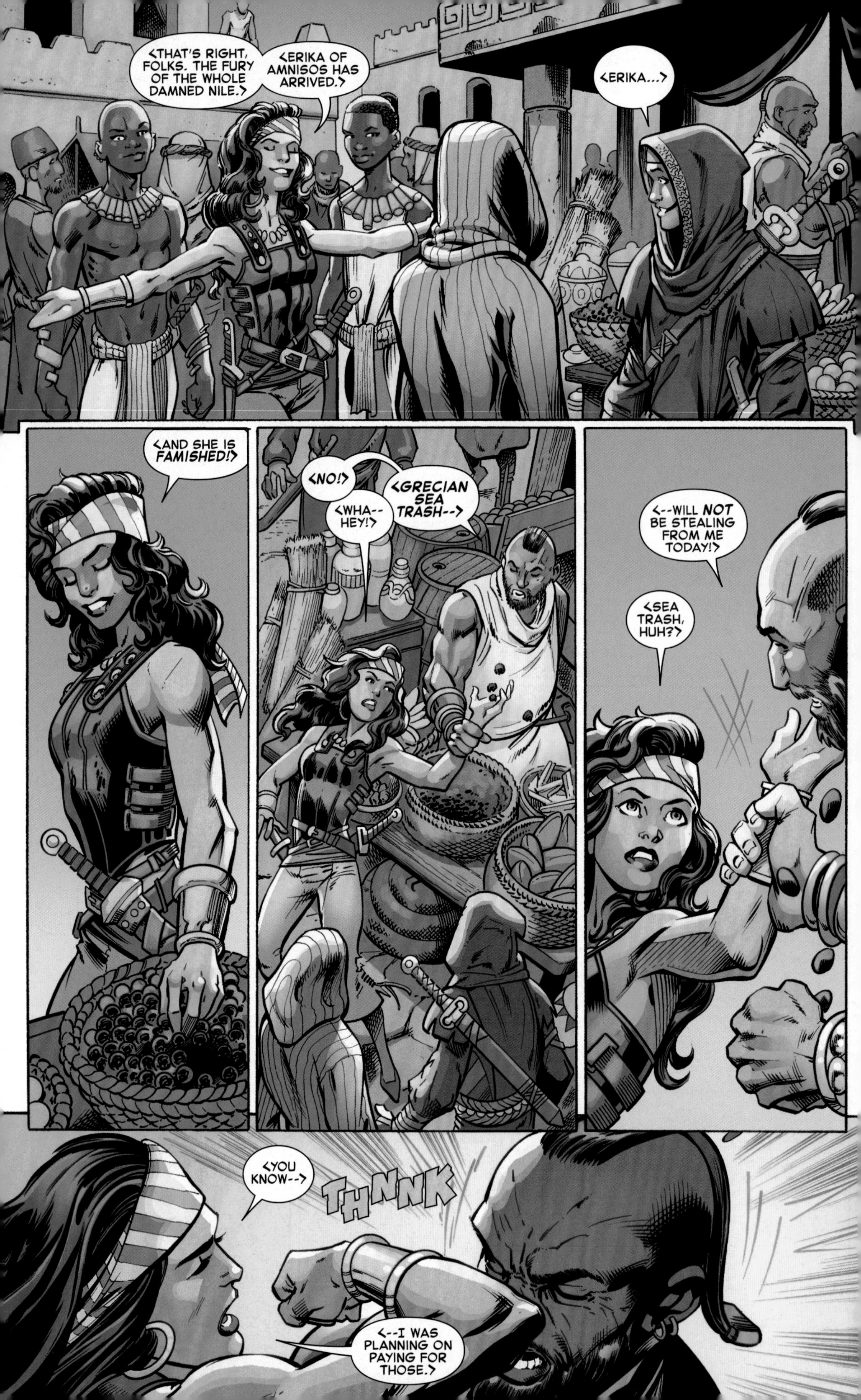
<THAT'S RIGHT, FOLKS. THE FURY OF THE WHOLE DAMNED NILE.>
<ERIKA OF AMNISOS HAS ARRIVED.>
<ERIKA...>
<AND SHE IS FAMISHED!>
<NO!>
<GRECIAN SEA TRASH-->
<WHA--HEY!>
<--WILL NOT BE STEALING FROM ME TODAY!>
<SEA TRASH, HUH?>
<YOU KNOW-->
THNNK
<--I WAS PLANNING ON PAYING FOR THOSE.>

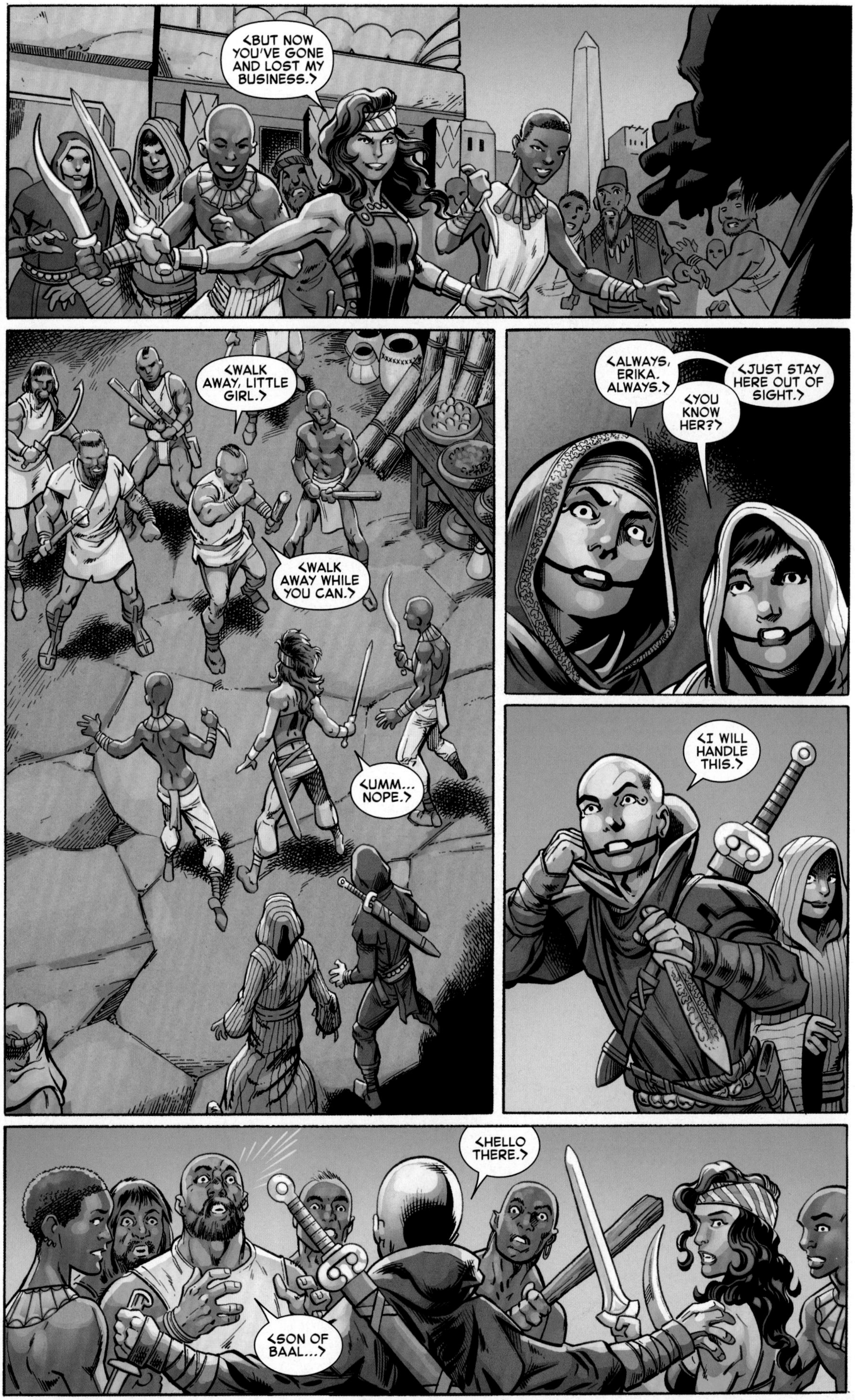
<BUT NOW YOU'VE GONE AND LOST MY BUSINESS.>
<WALK AWAY, LITTLE GIRL.>
<WALK AWAY WHILE YOU CAN.>
<UMM... NOPE.>
<ALWAYS, ERIKA. ALWAYS.>
<JUST STAY HERE OUT OF SIGHT.>
<YOU KNOW HER?>
<I WILL HANDLE THIS.>
<HELLO THERE.>
<SON OF BAAL...>

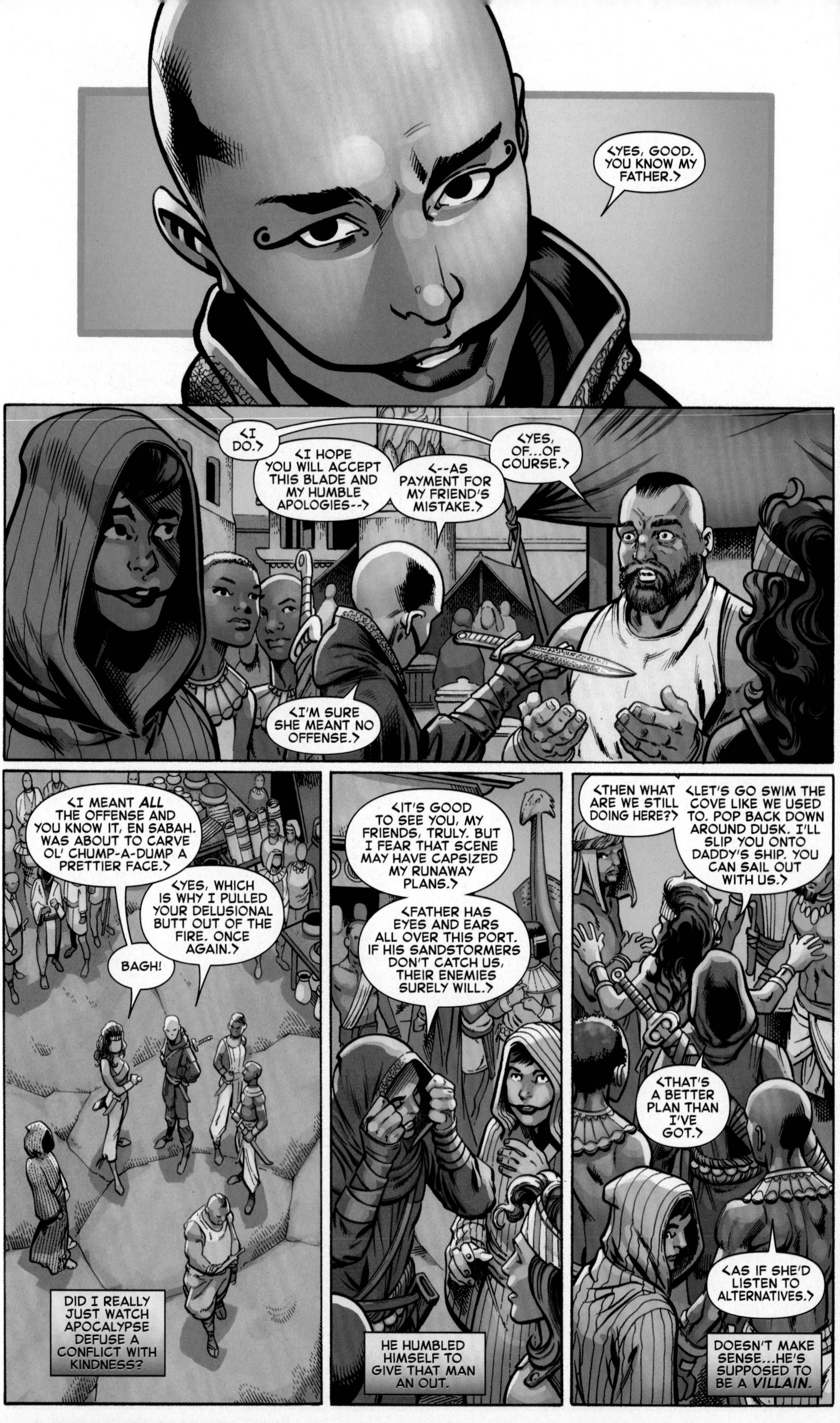
<YES, GOOD. YOU KNOW MY FATHER.>
<I DO.>
<YES, OF...OF COURSE.>
<I HOPE YOU WILL ACCEPT THIS BLADE AND MY HUMBLE APOLOGIES-->
<--AS PAYMENT FOR MY FRIEND'S MISTAKE.>
<I'M SURE SHE MEANT NO OFFENSE.>
<I MEANT *ALL* THE OFFENSE AND YOU KNOW IT, EN SABAH. WAS ABOUT TO CARVE OL' CHUMP-A-DUMP A PRETTIER FACE.>
<YES, WHICH IS WHY I PULLED YOUR DELUSIONAL BUTT OUT OF THE FIRE. ONCE AGAIN.>
BAGH!
DID I REALLY JUST WATCH APOCALYPSE DEFUSE A CONFLICT WITH KINDNESS?
<IT'S GOOD TO SEE YOU, MY FRIENDS, TRULY. BUT I FEAR THAT SCENE MAY HAVE CAPSIZED MY RUNAWAY PLANS.>
<FATHER HAS EYES AND EARS ALL OVER THIS PORT. IF HIS SANDSTORMERS DON'T CATCH US, THEIR ENEMIES SURELY WILL.>
HE HUMBLED HIMSELF TO GIVE THAT MAN AN OUT.
<THEN WHAT ARE WE STILL DOING HERE?>
<LET'S GO SWIM THE COVE LIKE WE USED TO. POP BACK DOWN AROUND DUSK. I'LL SLIP YOU ONTO DADDY'S SHIP. YOU CAN SAIL OUT WITH US.>
<THAT'S A BETTER PLAN THAN I'VE GOT.>
<AS IF SHE'D LISTEN TO ALTERNATIVES.>
DOESN'T MAKE SENSE...HE'S SUPPOSED TO BE A *VILLAIN*.

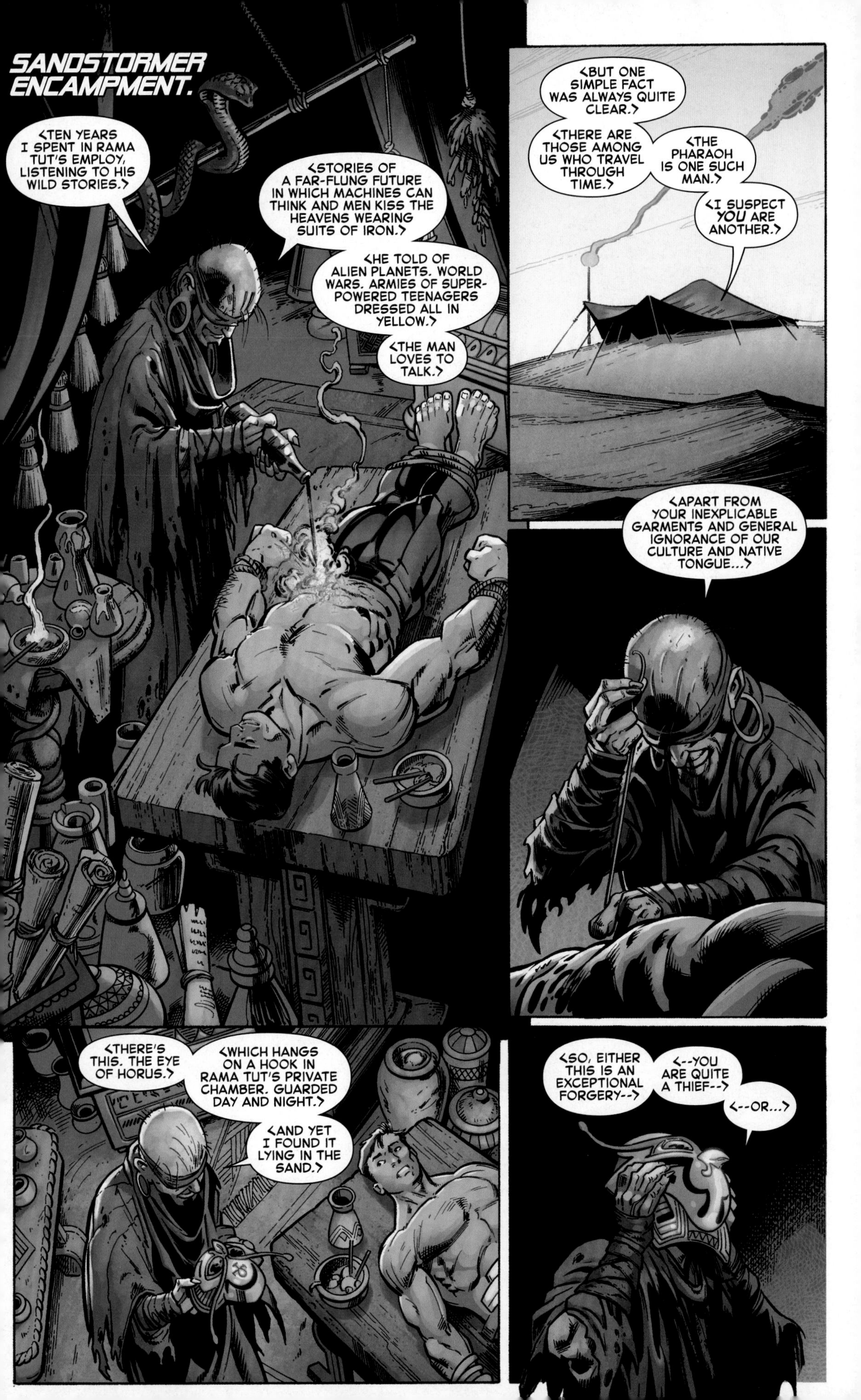
SANDSTORMER ENCAMPMENT.
<TEN YEARS I SPENT IN RAMA TUT'S EMPLOY, LISTENING TO HIS WILD STORIES.>
<STORIES OF A FAR-FLUNG FUTURE IN WHICH MACHINES CAN THINK AND MEN KISS THE HEAVENS WEARING SUITS OF IRON.>
<HE TOLD OF ALIEN PLANETS. WORLD WARS. ARMIES OF SUPER-POWERED TEENAGERS DRESSED ALL IN YELLOW.>
<THE MAN LOVES TO TALK.>
<BUT ONE SIMPLE FACT WAS ALWAYS QUITE CLEAR.>
<THERE ARE THOSE AMONG US WHO TRAVEL THROUGH TIME.>
<THE PHARAOH IS ONE SUCH MAN.>
<I SUSPECT *YOU* ARE ANOTHER.>
<APART FROM YOUR INEXPLICABLE GARMENTS AND GENERAL IGNORANCE OF OUR CULTURE AND NATIVE TONGUE...>
<THERE'S THIS. THE EYE OF HORUS.>
<WHICH HANGS ON A HOOK IN RAMA TUT'S PRIVATE CHAMBER. GUARDED DAY AND NIGHT.>
<AND YET I FOUND IT LYING IN THE SAND.>
<SO, EITHER THIS IS AN EXCEPTIONAL FORGERY-->
<--YOU ARE QUITE A THIEF-->
<--OR...>

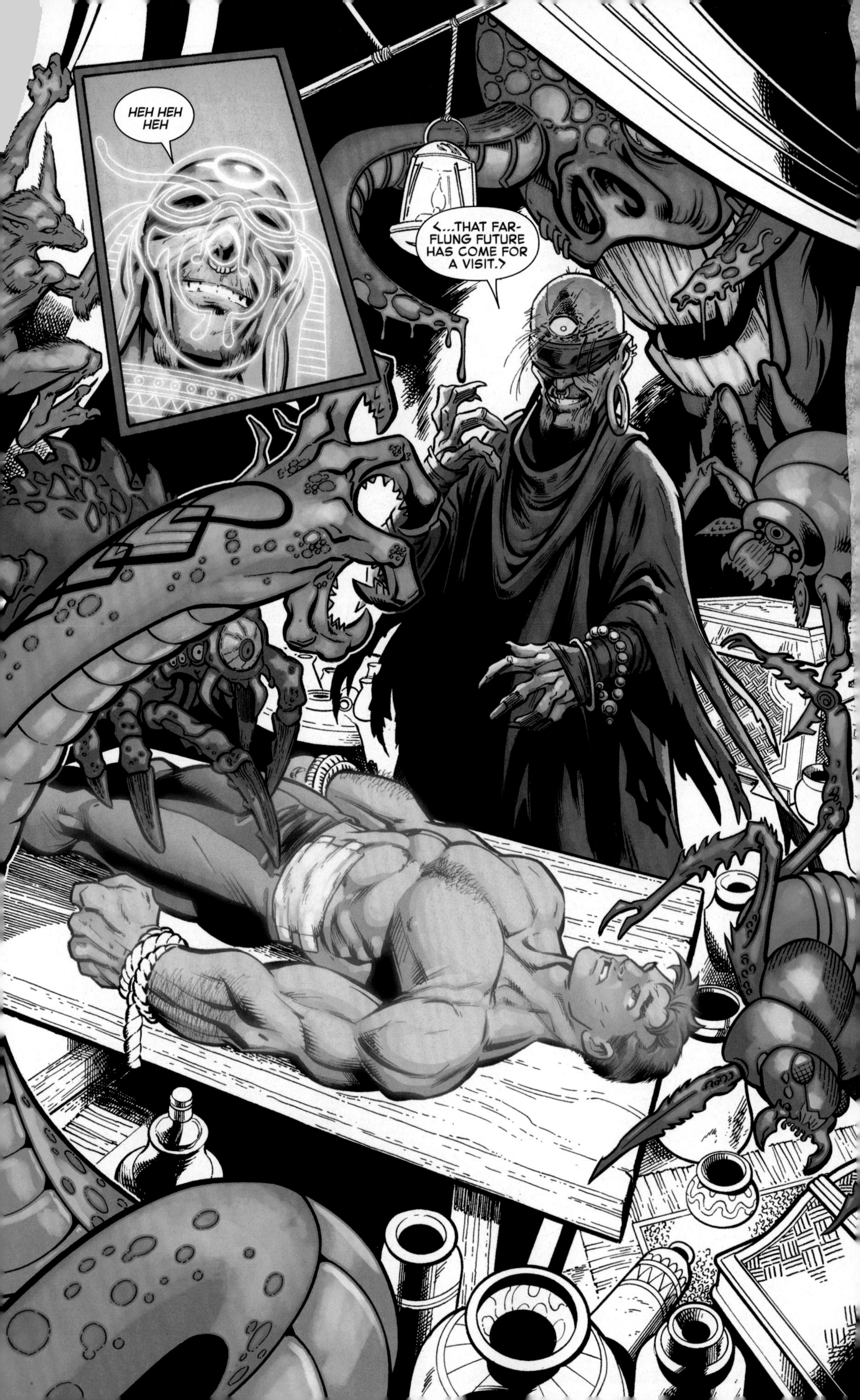
HEH HEH HEH
<...THAT FAR-FLUNG FUTURE HAS COME FOR A VISIT.>

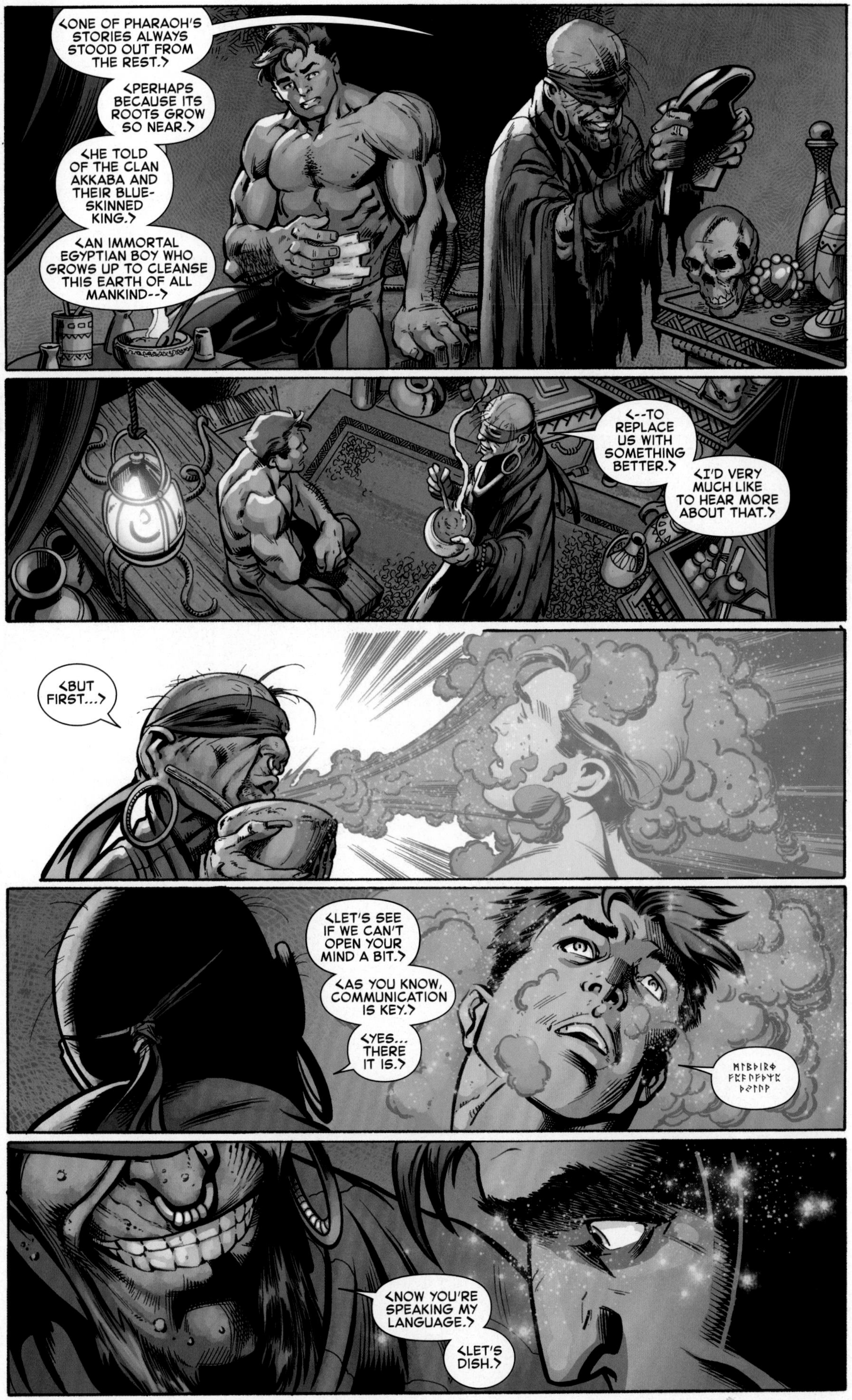
<ONE OF PHARAOH'S STORIES ALWAYS STOOD OUT FROM THE REST.>
<PERHAPS BECAUSE ITS ROOTS GROW SO NEAR.>
<HE TOLD OF THE CLAN AKKABA AND THEIR BLUE-SKINNED KING.>
<AN IMMORTAL EGYPTIAN BOY WHO GROWS UP TO CLEANSE THIS EARTH OF ALL MANKIND-->
<--TO REPLACE US WITH SOMETHING BETTER.>
<I'D VERY MUCH LIKE TO HEAR MORE ABOUT THAT.>
<BUT FIRST...>
<LET'S SEE IF WE CAN'T OPEN YOUR MIND A BIT.>
<AS YOU KNOW, COMMUNICATION IS KEY.>
<YES... THERE IT IS.>
<NOW YOU'RE SPEAKING MY LANGUAGE.>
<LET'S DISH.>

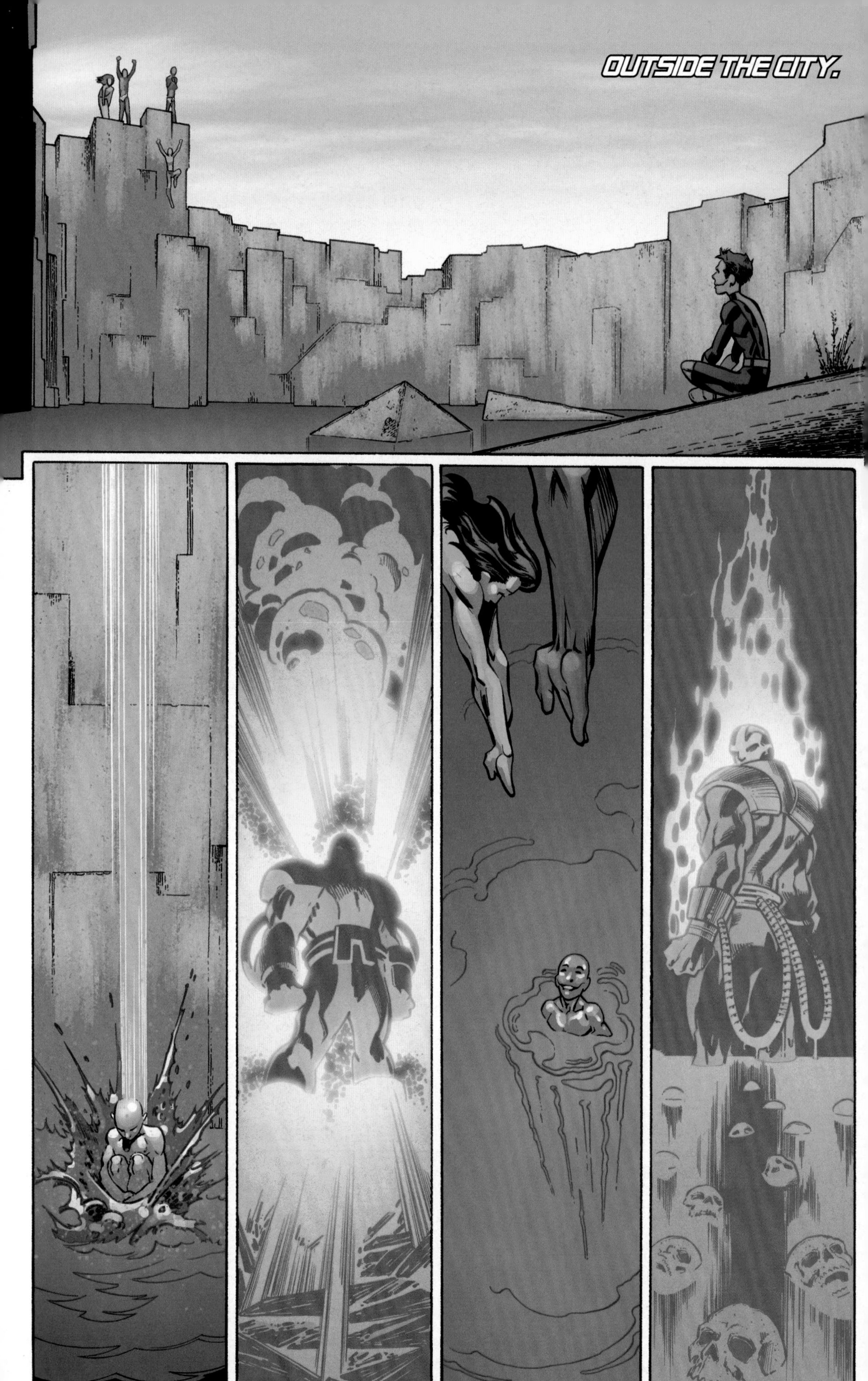
OUTSIDE THE CITY.

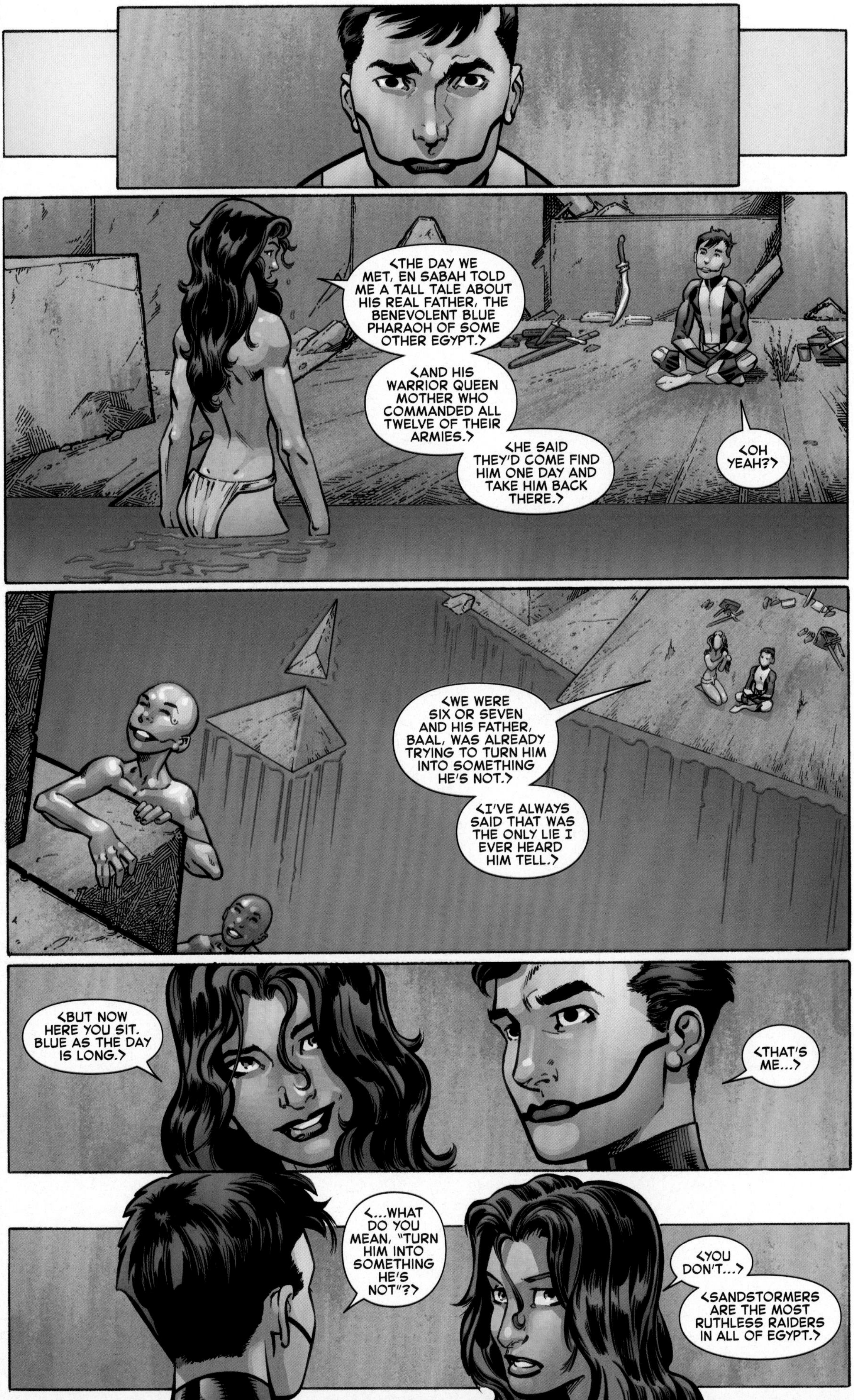

<THE DAY WE MET, EN SABAH TOLD ME A TALL TALE ABOUT HIS REAL FATHER, THE BENEVOLENT BLUE PHARAOH OF SOME OTHER EGYPT.>
<AND HIS WARRIOR QUEEN MOTHER WHO COMMANDED ALL TWELVE OF THEIR ARMIES.>
<HE SAID THEY'D COME FIND HIM ONE DAY AND TAKE HIM BACK THERE.>
<OH YEAH?>
<WE WERE SIX OR SEVEN AND HIS FATHER, BAAL, WAS ALREADY TRYING TO TURN HIM INTO SOMETHING HE'S NOT.>
<I'VE ALWAYS SAID THAT WAS THE ONLY LIE I EVER HEARD HIM TELL.>
<BUT NOW HERE YOU SIT. BLUE AS THE DAY IS LONG.>
<THAT'S ME...>
<...WHAT DO YOU MEAN, "TURN HIM INTO SOMETHING HE'S NOT"?>
<YOU DON'T...>
<SANDSTORMERS ARE THE MOST RUTHLESS RAIDERS IN ALL OF EGYPT.>

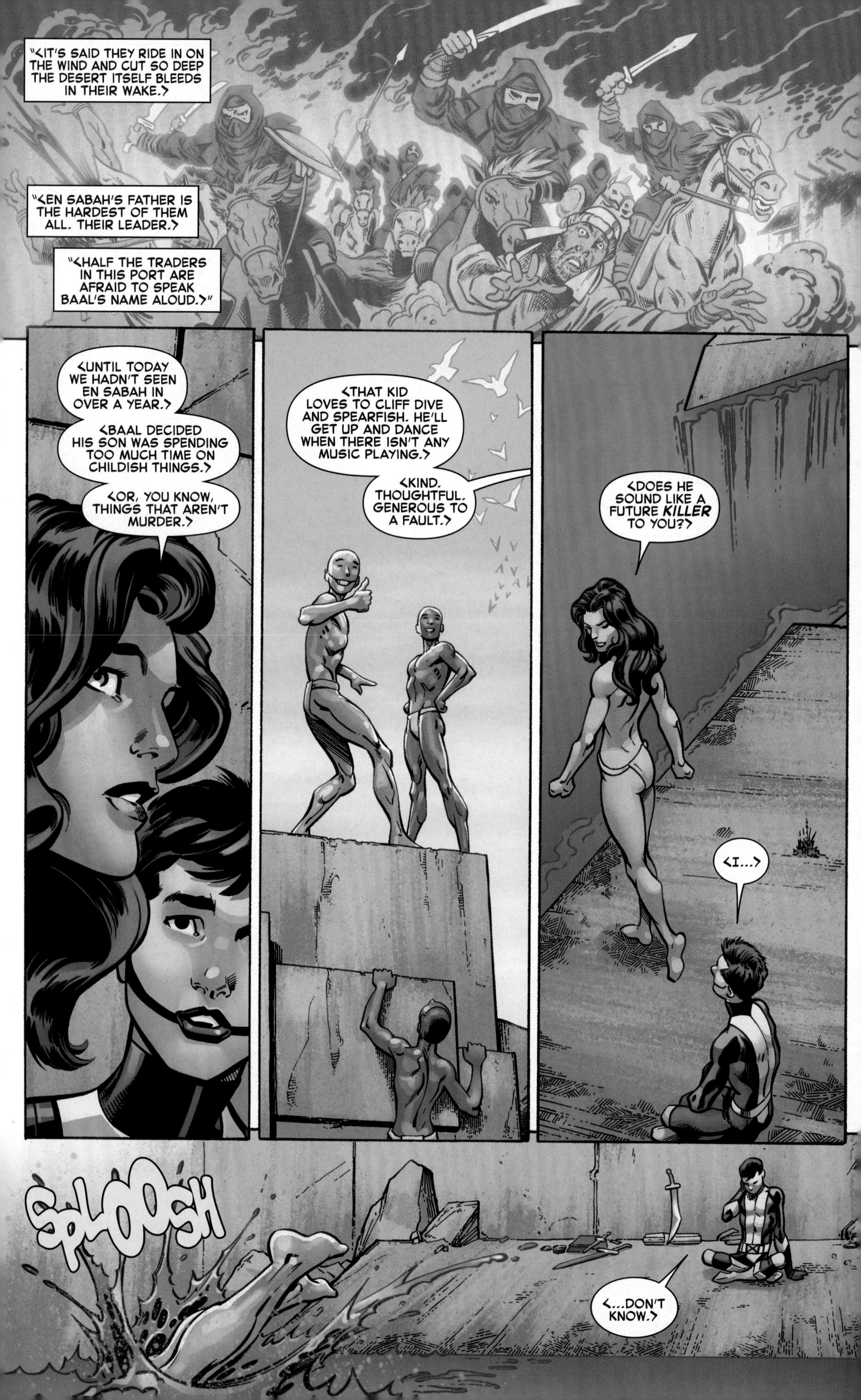
"<IT'S SAID THEY RIDE IN ON THE WIND AND CUT SO DEEP THE DESERT ITSELF BLEEDS IN THEIR WAKE.>
"<EN SABAH'S FATHER IS THE HARDEST OF THEM ALL. THEIR LEADER.>
"<HALF THE TRADERS IN THIS PORT ARE AFRAID TO SPEAK BAAL'S NAME ALOUD.>"
<UNTIL TODAY WE HADN'T SEEN EN SABAH IN OVER A YEAR.>
<BAAL DECIDED HIS SON WAS SPENDING TOO MUCH TIME ON CHILDISH THINGS.>
<OR, YOU KNOW, THINGS THAT AREN'T MURDER.>
<THAT KID LOVES TO CLIFF DIVE AND SPEARFISH. HE'LL GET UP AND DANCE WHEN THERE ISN'T ANY MUSIC PLAYING.>
<KIND. THOUGHTFUL. GENEROUS TO A FAULT.>
<DOES HE SOUND LIKE A FUTURE KILLER TO YOU?>
<I...>
SPLOOSH
<...DON'T KNOW.>

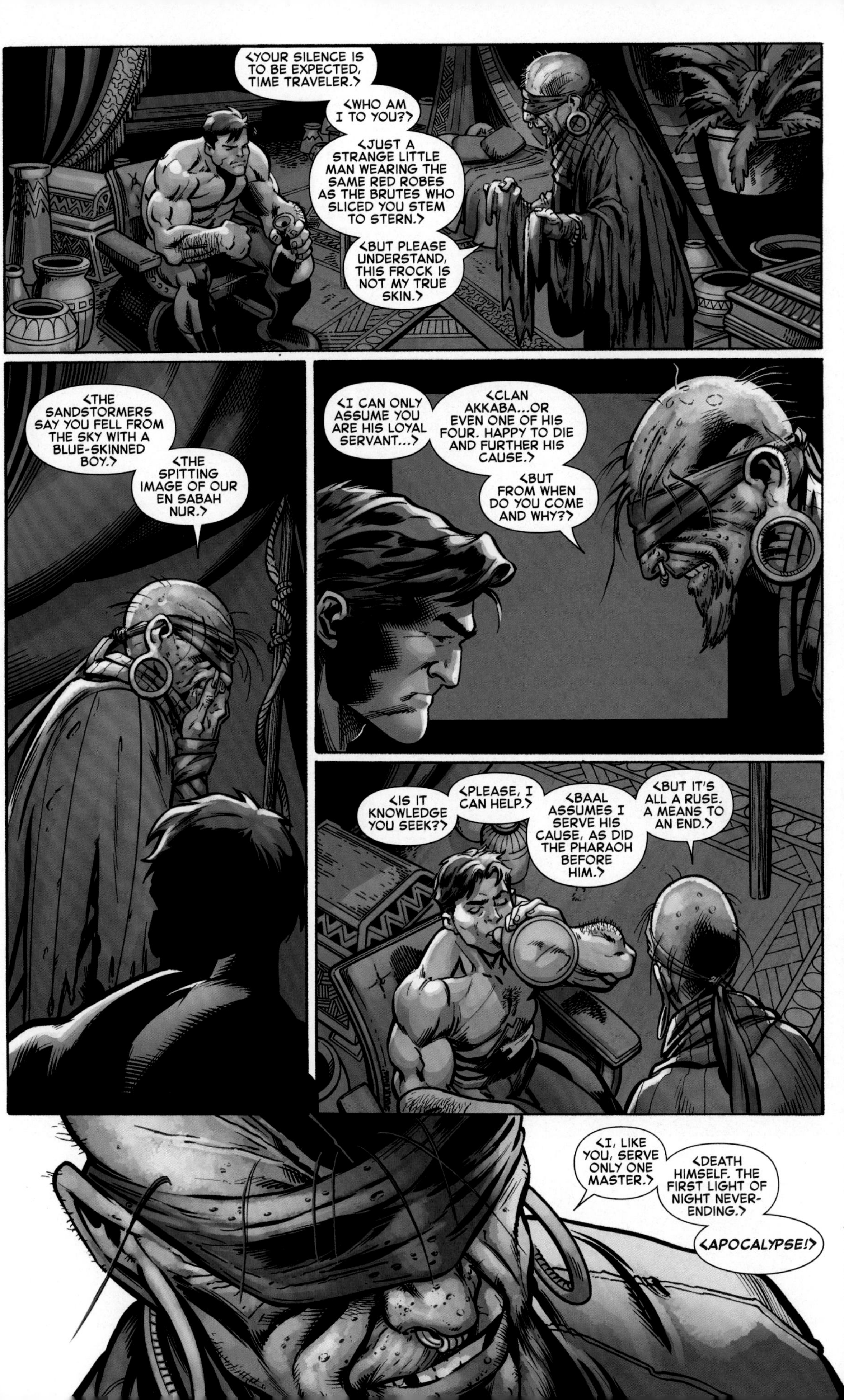
<YOUR SILENCE IS TO BE EXPECTED, TIME TRAVELER.>
<WHO AM I TO YOU?>
<JUST A STRANGE LITTLE MAN WEARING THE SAME RED ROBES AS THE BRUTES WHO SLICED YOU STEM TO STERN.>
<BUT PLEASE UNDERSTAND, THIS FROCK IS NOT MY TRUE SKIN.>
<THE SANDSTORMERS SAY YOU FELL FROM THE SKY WITH A BLUE-SKINNED BOY.>
<THE SPITTING IMAGE OF OUR EN SABAH NUR.>
<I CAN ONLY ASSUME YOU ARE HIS LOYAL SERVANT...>
<CLAN AKKABA...OR EVEN ONE OF HIS FOUR. HAPPY TO DIE AND FURTHER HIS CAUSE.>
<BUT FROM WHEN DO YOU COME AND WHY?>
<IS IT KNOWLEDGE YOU SEEK?>
<PLEASE, I CAN HELP.>
<BAAL ASSUMES I SERVE HIS CAUSE, AS DID THE PHARAOH BEFORE HIM.>
<BUT IT'S ALL A RUSE. A MEANS TO AN END.>
<I, LIKE YOU, SERVE ONLY ONE MASTER.>
<DEATH HIMSELF. THE FIRST LIGHT OF NIGHT NEVER-ENDING.>
<APOCALYPSE!>

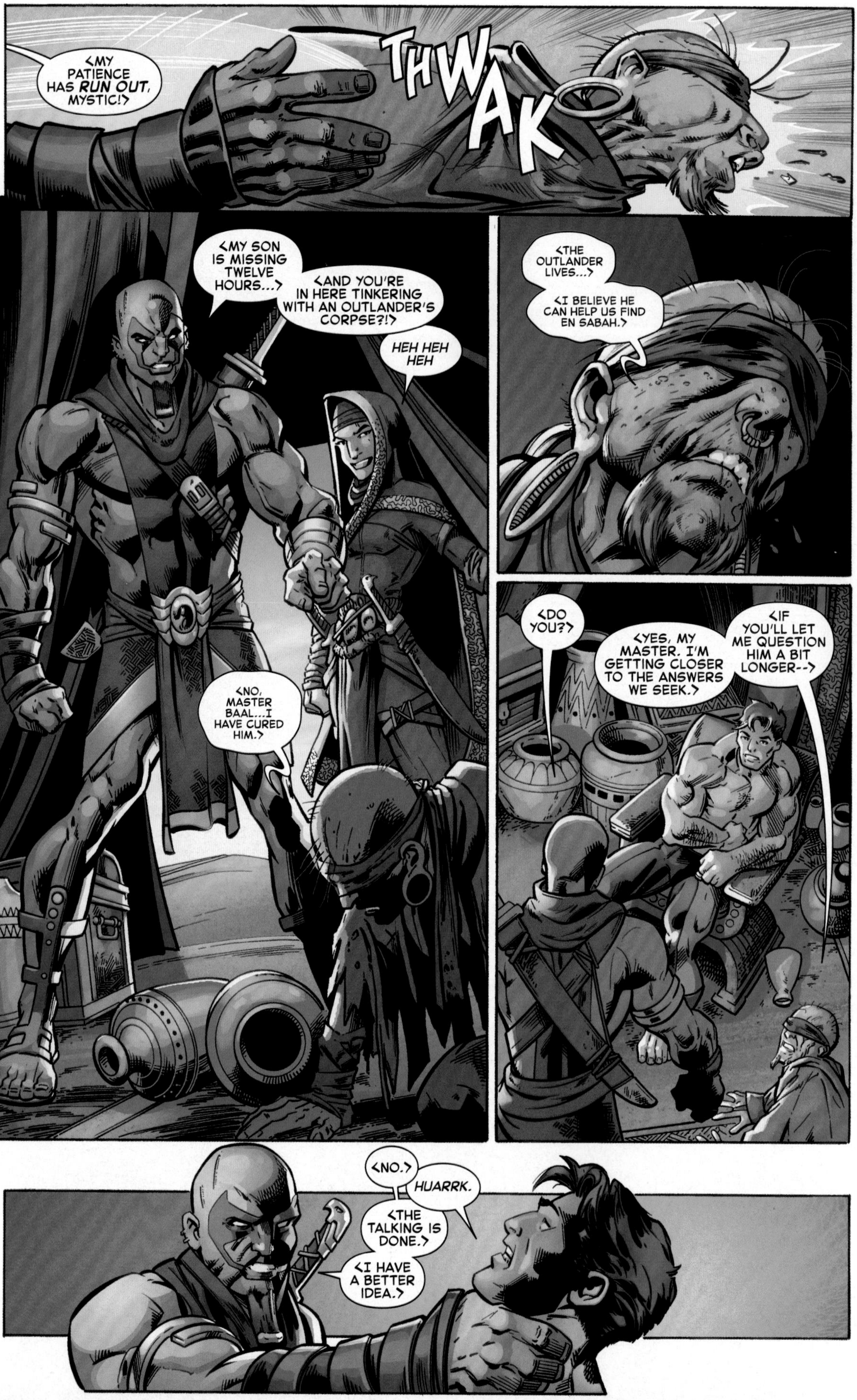
<MY PATIENCE HAS RUN OUT, MYSTIC!>
THWAK
<MY SON IS MISSING TWELVE HOURS...>
<AND YOU'RE IN HERE TINKERING WITH AN OUTLANDER'S CORPSE?!>
HEH HEH HEH
<NO, MASTER BAAL...I HAVE CURED HIM.>
<THE OUTLANDER LIVES...>
<I BELIEVE HE CAN HELP US FIND EN SABAH.>
<DO YOU?>
<YES, MY MASTER. I'M GETTING CLOSER TO THE ANSWERS WE SEEK.>
<IF YOU'LL LET ME QUESTION HIM A BIT LONGER-->
<NO.>
HUARRK.
<THE TALKING IS DONE.>
<I HAVE A BETTER IDEA.>

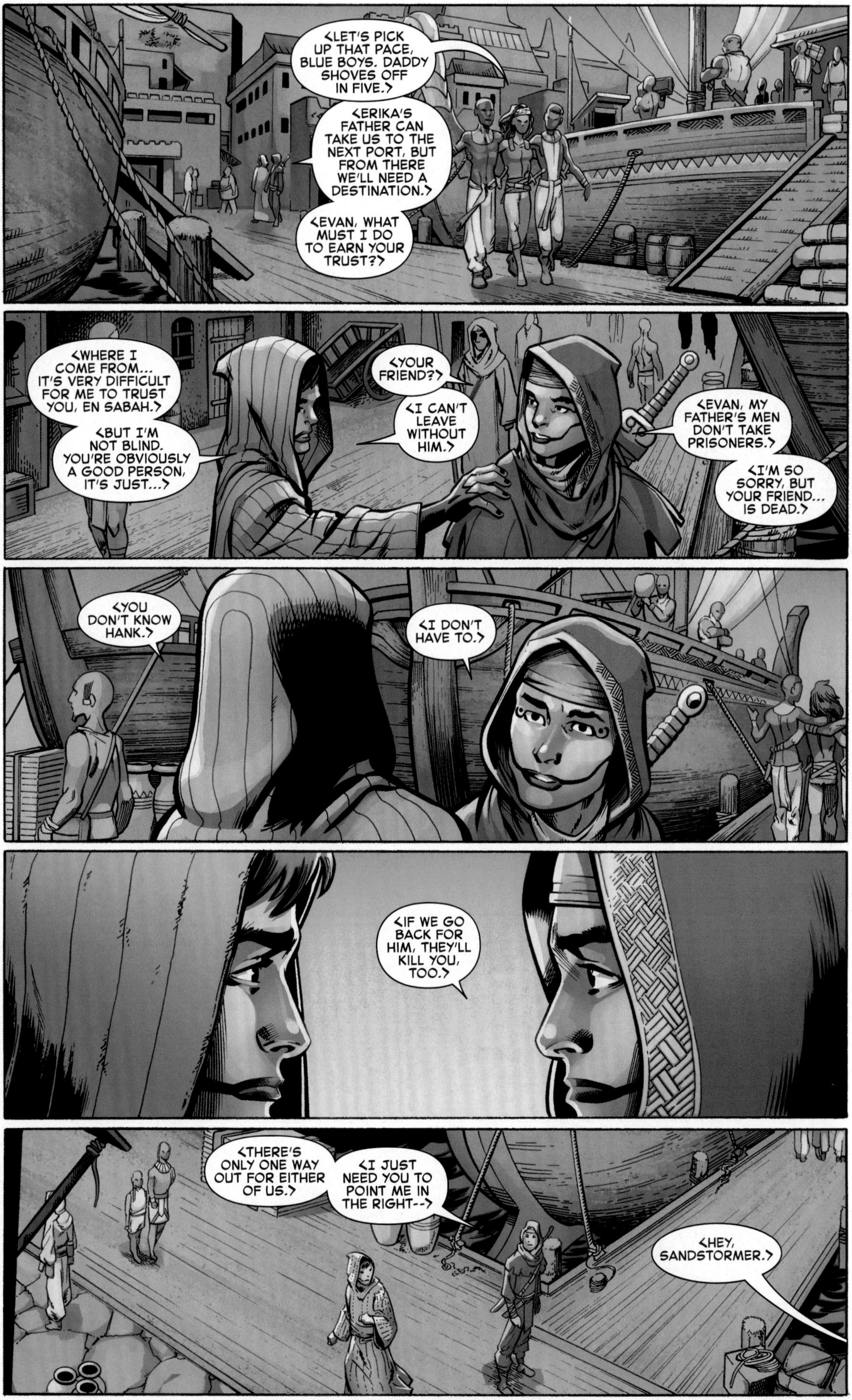

<LET'S PICK UP THAT PACE, BLUE BOYS. DADDY SHOVES OFF IN FIVE.>
<ERIKA'S FATHER CAN TAKE US TO THE NEXT PORT, BUT FROM THERE WE'LL NEED A DESTINATION.>
<EVAN, WHAT MUST I DO TO EARN YOUR TRUST?>
<WHERE I COME FROM... IT'S VERY DIFFICULT FOR ME TO TRUST YOU, EN SABAH.>
<BUT I'M NOT BLIND. YOU'RE OBVIOUSLY A GOOD PERSON, IT'S JUST...>
<YOUR FRIEND?>
<I CAN'T LEAVE WITHOUT HIM.>
<EVAN, MY FATHER'S MEN DON'T TAKE PRISONERS.>
<I'M SO SORRY, BUT YOUR FRIEND... IS DEAD.>
<YOU DON'T KNOW HANK.>
<I DON'T HAVE TO.>
<IF WE GO BACK FOR HIM, THEY'LL KILL YOU, TOO.>
<THERE'S ONLY ONE WAY OUT FOR EITHER OF US.>
<I JUST NEED YOU TO POINT ME IN THE RIGHT-->
<HEY, SANDSTORMER.>

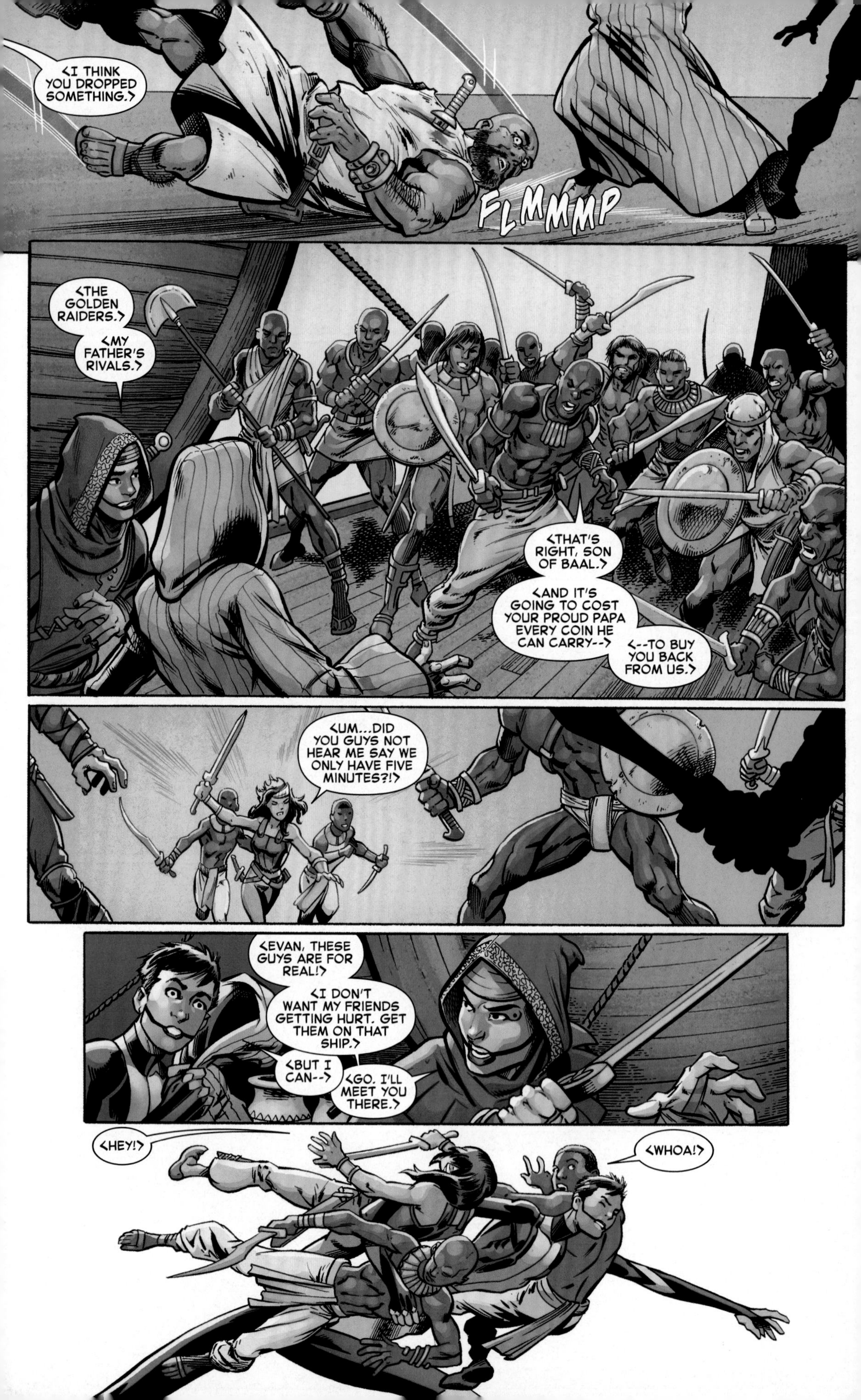

<I THINK YOU DROPPED SOMETHING.>
FLMMMMP
<THE GOLDEN RAIDERS.>
<MY FATHER'S RIVALS.>
<THAT'S RIGHT, SON OF BAAL.>
<AND IT'S GOING TO COST YOUR PROUD PAPA EVERY COIN HE CAN CARRY-->
<--TO BUY YOU BACK FROM US.>
<UM...DID YOU GUYS NOT HEAR ME SAY WE ONLY HAVE FIVE MINUTES?!>
<EVAN, THESE GUYS ARE FOR REAL!>
<I DON'T WANT MY FRIENDS GETTING HURT. GET THEM ON THAT SHIP.>
<BUT I CAN-->
<GO. I'LL MEET YOU THERE.>
<HEY!>
<WHOA!>

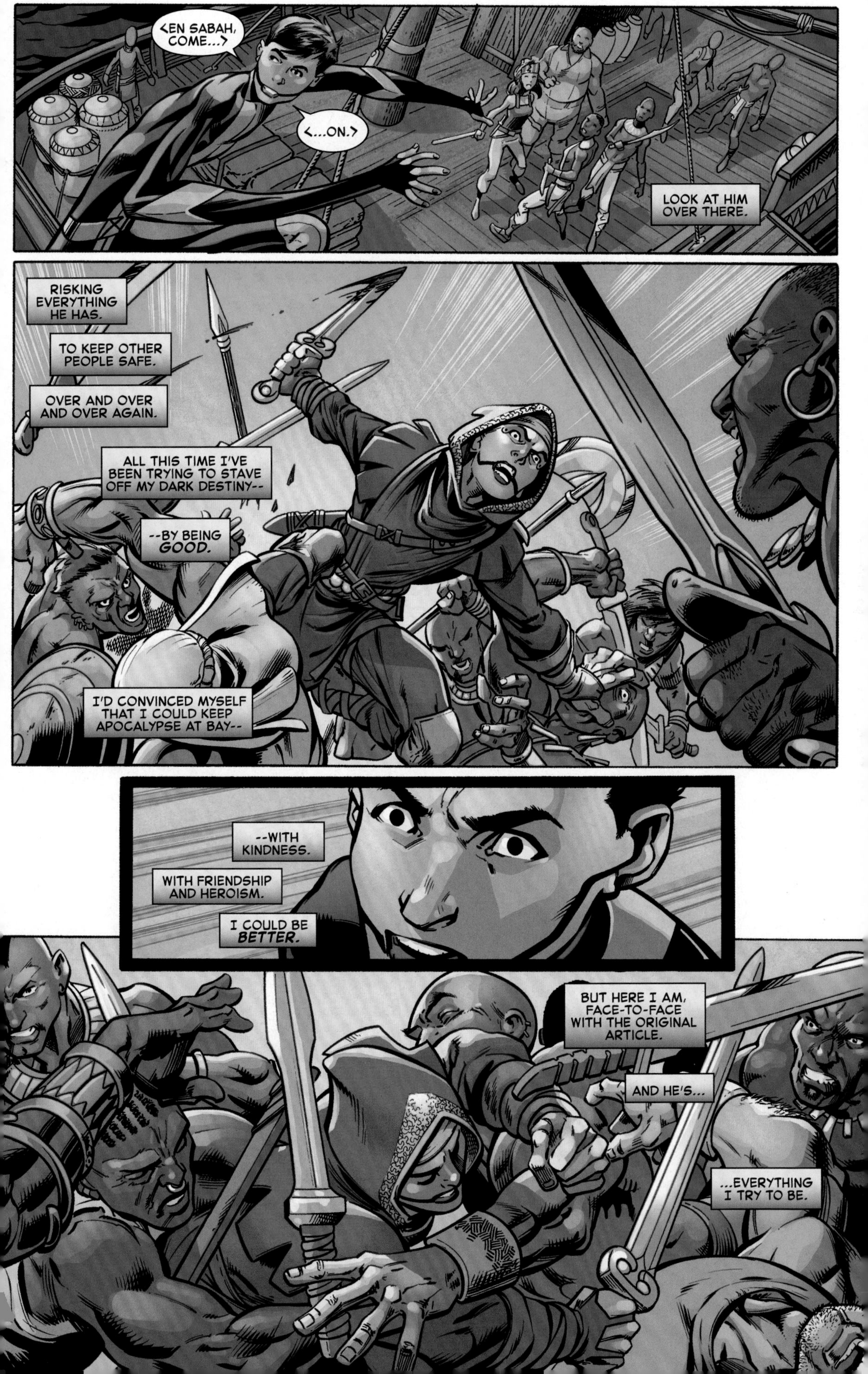

<EN SABAH, COME...>
<...ON.>
LOOK AT HIM OVER THERE.
RISKING EVERYTHING HE HAS.
TO KEEP OTHER PEOPLE SAFE.
OVER AND OVER AND OVER AGAIN.
ALL THIS TIME I'VE BEEN TRYING TO STAVE OFF MY DARK DESTINY--
--BY BEING *GOOD.*
I'D CONVINCED MYSELF THAT I COULD KEEP APOCALYPSE AT BAY--
--WITH KINDNESS.
WITH FRIENDSHIP AND HEROISM.
I COULD BE *BETTER.*
BUT HERE I AM, FACE-TO-FACE WITH THE ORIGINAL ARTICLE.
AND HE'S...
...EVERYTHING I TRY TO BE.

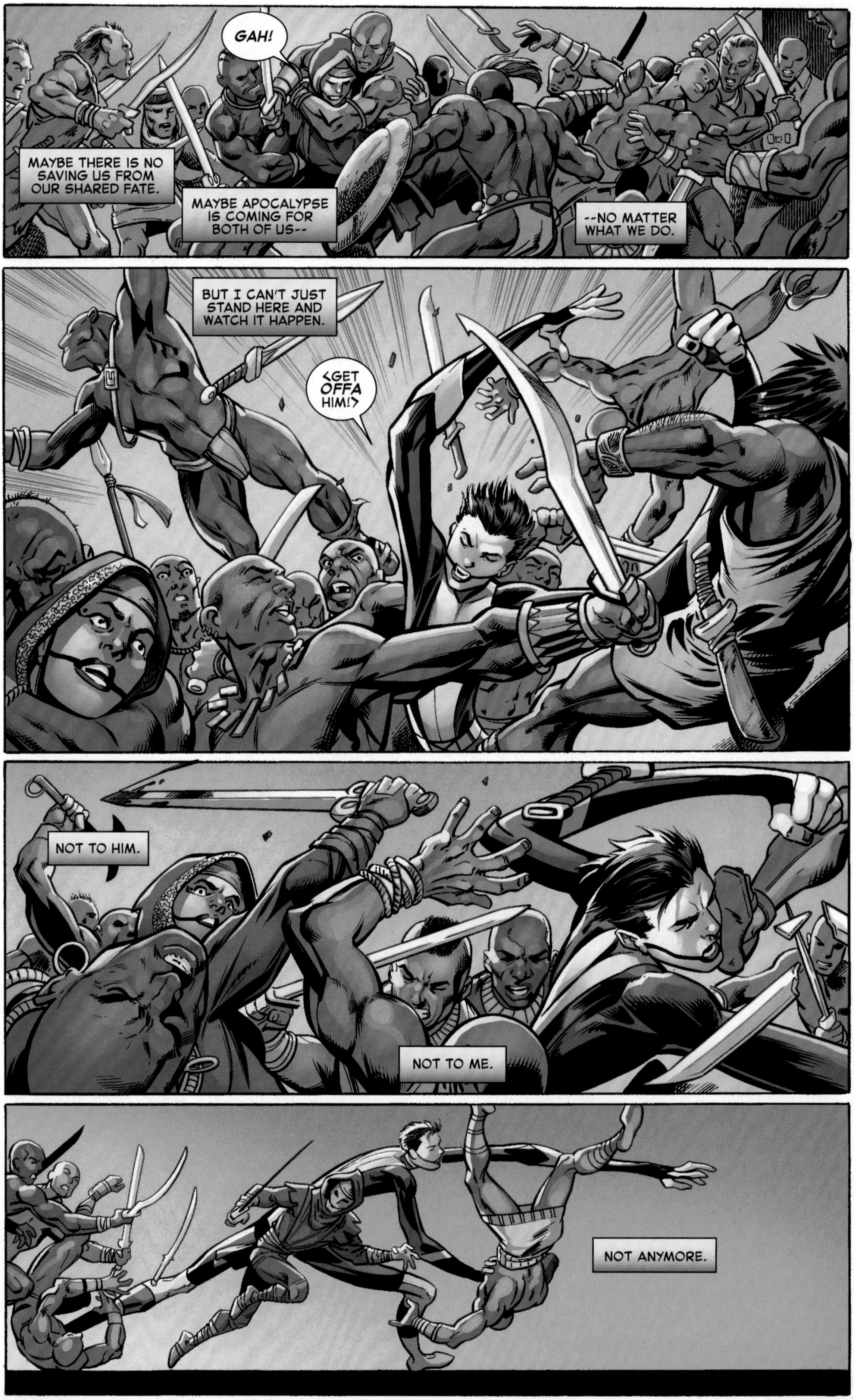

GAH!
MAYBE THERE IS NO SAVING US FROM OUR SHARED FATE.
MAYBE APOCALYPSE IS COMING FOR BOTH OF US--
--NO MATTER WHAT WE DO.
BUT I CAN'T JUST STAND HERE AND WATCH IT HAPPEN.
<GET OFFA HIM!>
NOT TO HIM.
NOT TO ME.
NOT ANYMORE.

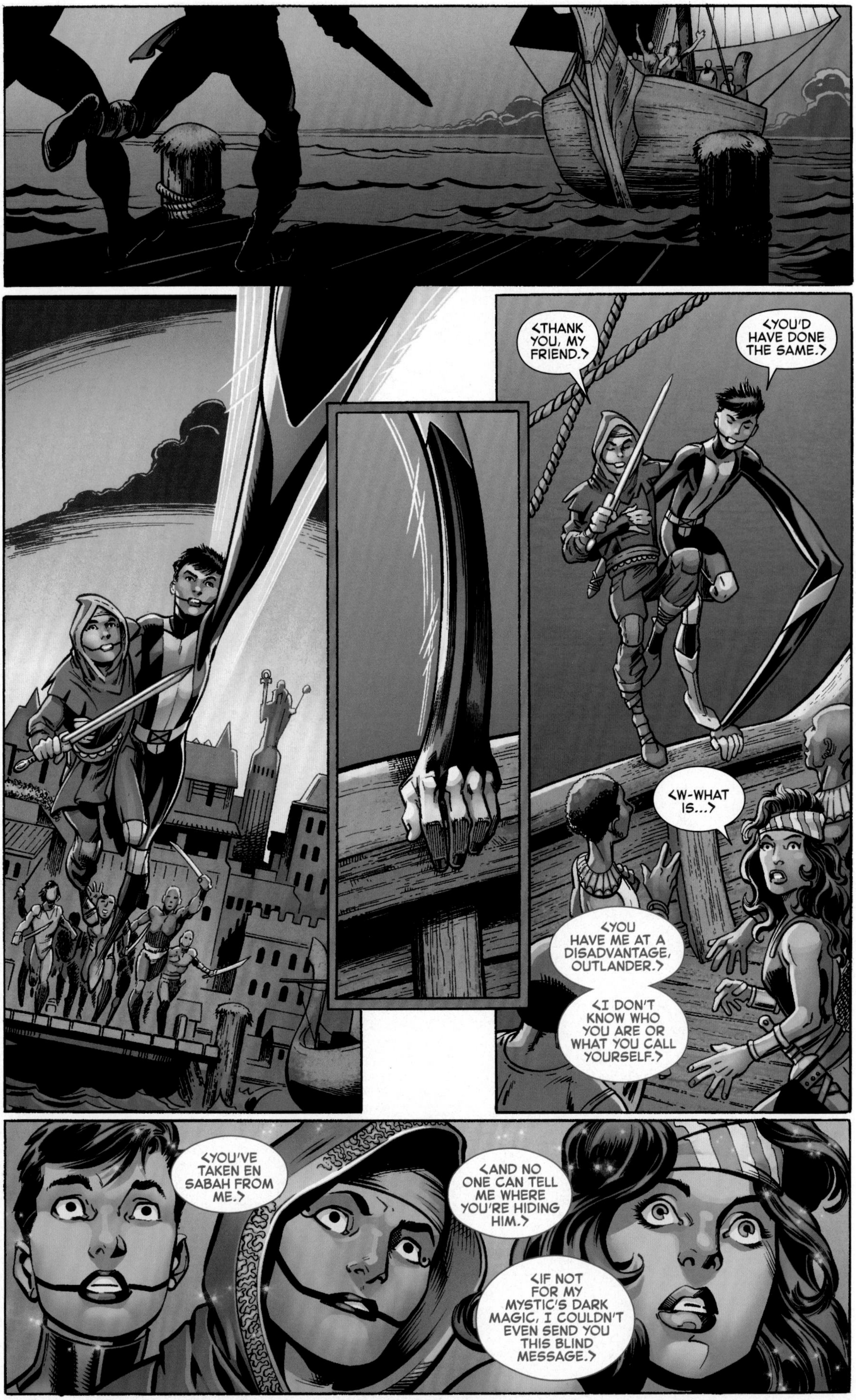

<THANK YOU, MY FRIEND.>
<YOU'D HAVE DONE THE SAME.>
<W-WHAT IS...>
<YOU HAVE ME AT A DISADVANTAGE, OUTLANDER.>
<I DON'T KNOW WHO YOU ARE OR WHAT YOU CALL YOURSELF.>
<YOU'VE TAKEN EN SABAH FROM ME.>
<AND NO ONE CAN TELL ME WHERE YOU'RE HIDING HIM.>
<IF NOT FOR MY MYSTIC'S DARK MAGIC, I COULDN'T EVEN SEND YOU THIS BLIND MESSAGE.>

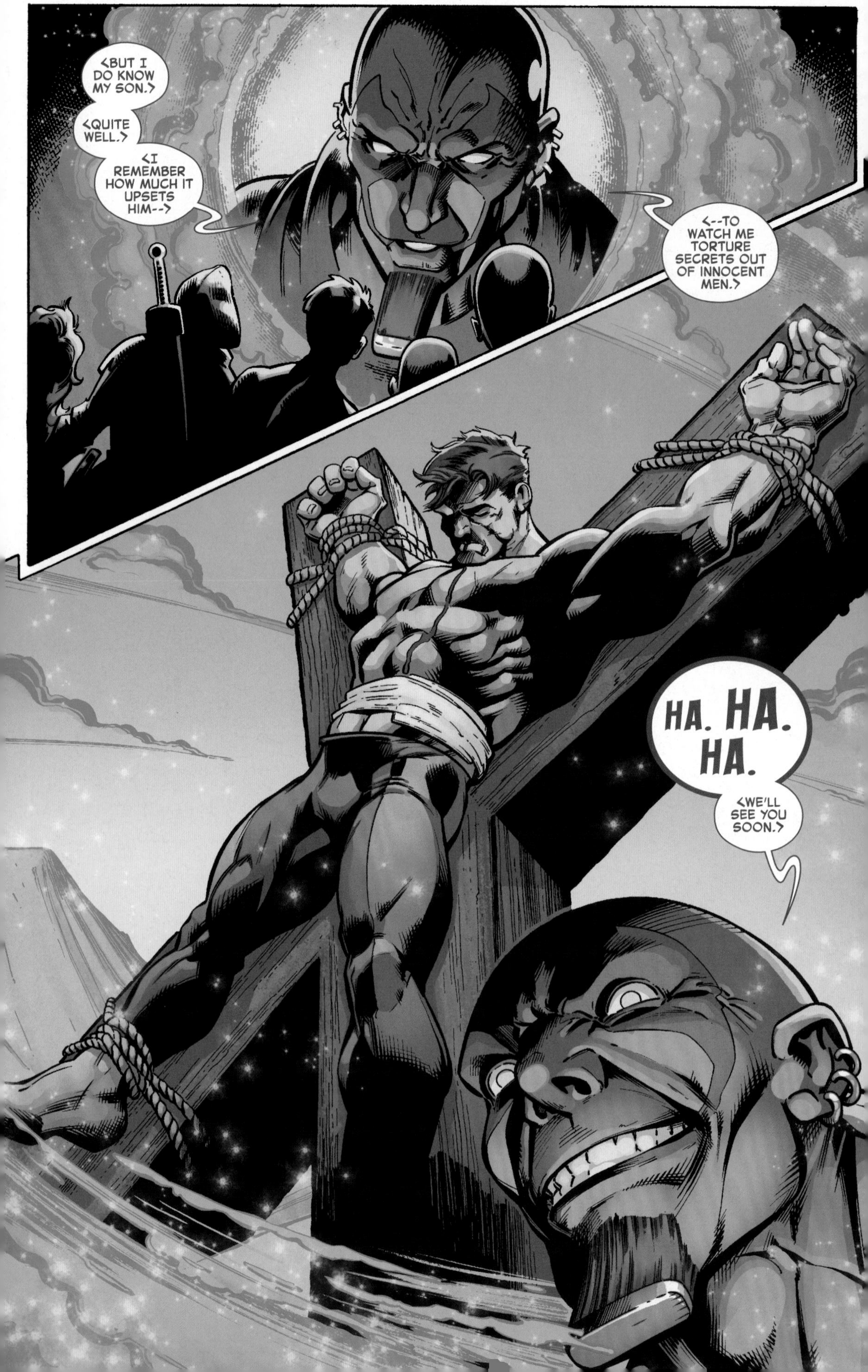
<BUT I DO KNOW MY SON.>
<QUITE WELL.>
<I REMEMBER HOW MUCH IT UPSETS HIM-->
<--TO WATCH ME TORTURE SECRETS OUT OF INNOCENT MEN.>
HA. HA. HA.
<WE'LL SEE YOU SOON.>

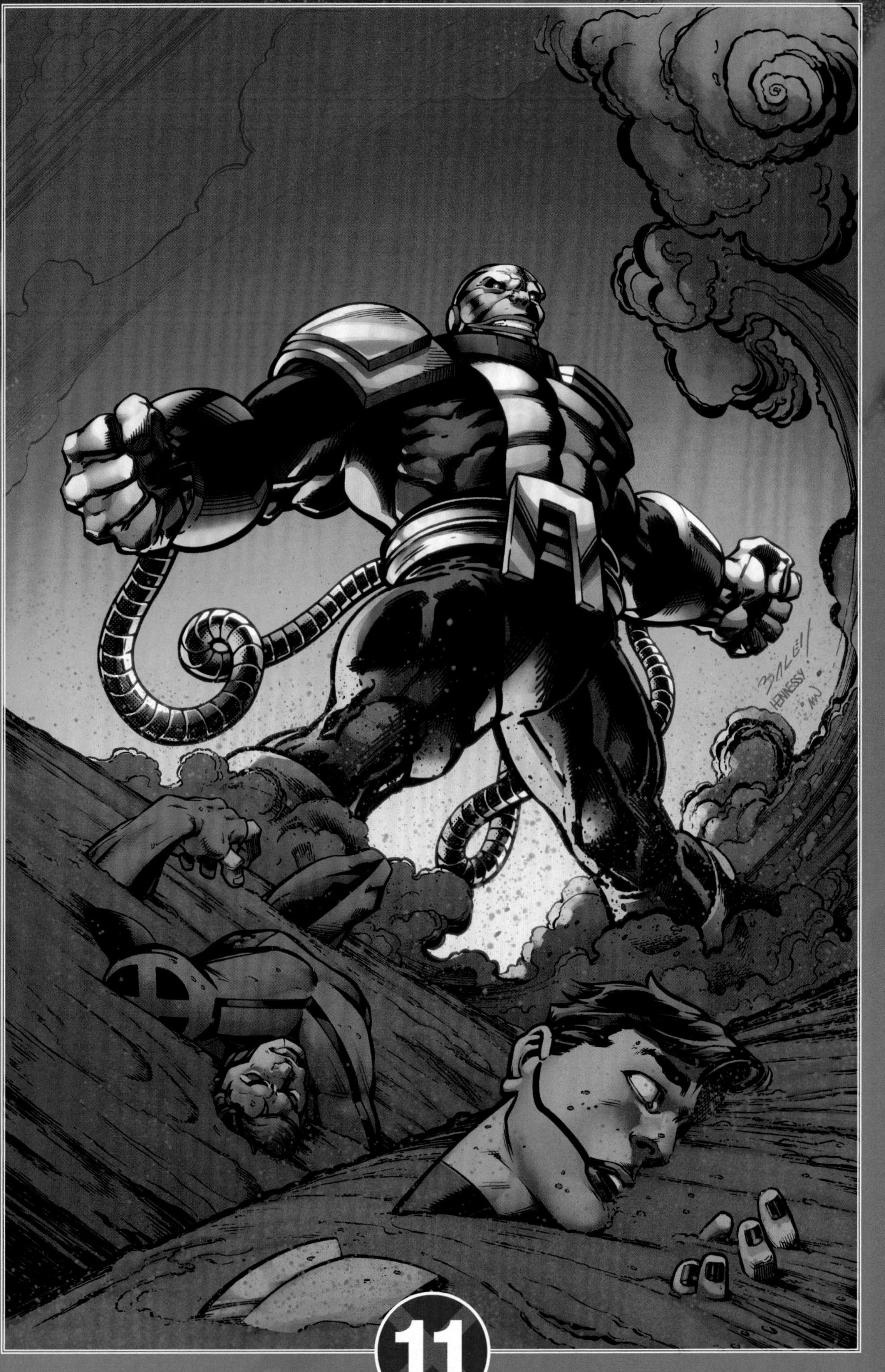

11

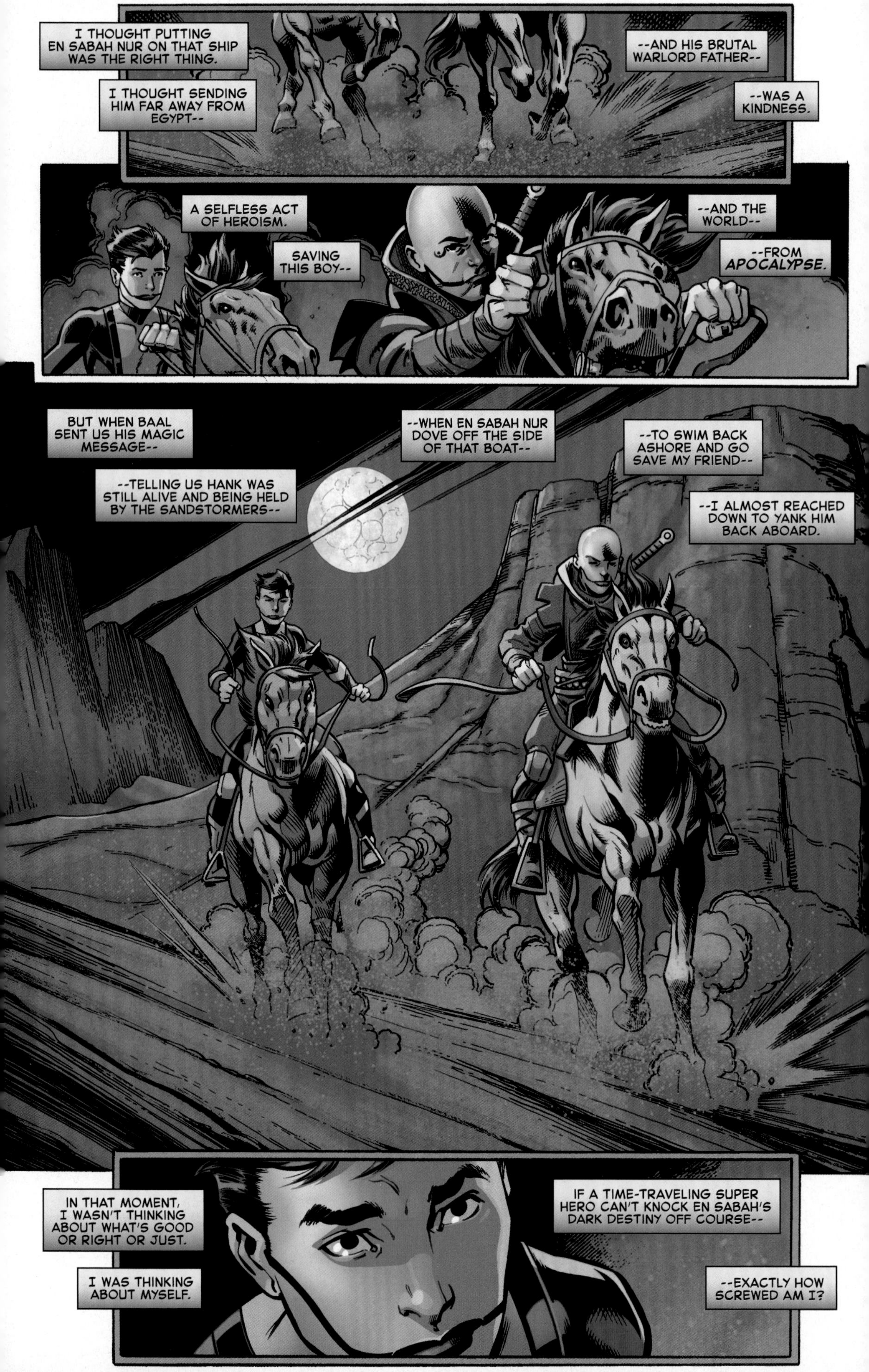
I THOUGHT PUTTING EN SABAH NUR ON THAT SHIP WAS THE RIGHT THING.
I THOUGHT SENDING HIM FAR AWAY FROM EGYPT--
--AND HIS BRUTAL WARLORD FATHER--
--WAS A KINDNESS.
A SELFLESS ACT OF HEROISM.
SAVING THIS BOY--
--AND THE WORLD--
--FROM *APOCALYPSE.*
BUT WHEN BAAL SENT US HIS MAGIC MESSAGE--
--TELLING US HANK WAS STILL ALIVE AND BEING HELD BY THE SANDSTORMERS--
--WHEN EN SABAH NUR DOVE OFF THE SIDE OF THAT BOAT--
--TO SWIM BACK ASHORE AND GO SAVE MY FRIEND--
--I ALMOST REACHED DOWN TO YANK HIM BACK ABOARD.
IN THAT MOMENT, I WASN'T THINKING ABOUT WHAT'S GOOD OR RIGHT OR JUST.
I WAS THINKING ABOUT MYSELF.
IF A TIME-TRAVELING SUPER HERO CAN'T KNOCK EN SABAH'S DARK DESTINY OFF COURSE--
--EXACTLY HOW SCREWED AM I?

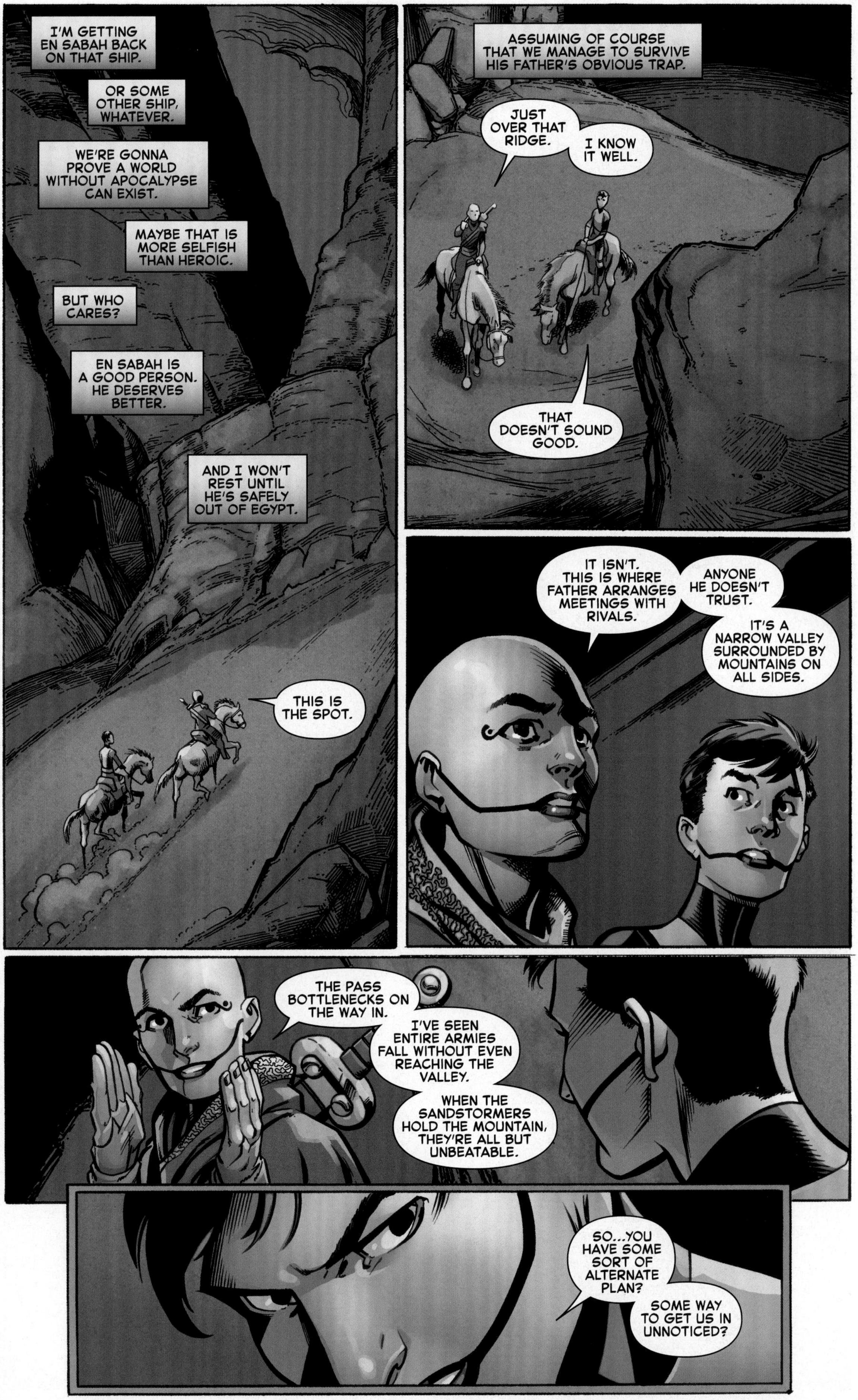
I'M GETTING EN SABAH BACK ON THAT SHIP.
OR SOME OTHER SHIP, WHATEVER.
WE'RE GONNA PROVE A WORLD WITHOUT APOCALYPSE CAN EXIST.
MAYBE THAT IS MORE SELFISH THAN HEROIC.
BUT WHO CARES?
EN SABAH IS A GOOD PERSON. HE DESERVES BETTER.
AND I WON'T REST UNTIL HE'S SAFELY OUT OF EGYPT.
THIS IS THE SPOT.
ASSUMING OF COURSE THAT WE MANAGE TO SURVIVE HIS FATHER'S OBVIOUS TRAP.
JUST OVER THAT RIDGE.
I KNOW IT WELL.
THAT DOESN'T SOUND GOOD.
IT ISN'T. THIS IS WHERE FATHER ARRANGES MEETINGS WITH RIVALS.
ANYONE HE DOESN'T TRUST.
IT'S A NARROW VALLEY SURROUNDED BY MOUNTAINS ON ALL SIDES.
THE PASS BOTTLENECKS ON THE WAY IN.
I'VE SEEN ENTIRE ARMIES FALL WITHOUT EVEN REACHING THE VALLEY.
WHEN THE SANDSTORMERS HOLD THE MOUNTAIN, THEY'RE ALL BUT UNBEATABLE.
SO...YOU HAVE SOME SORT OF ALTERNATE PLAN?
SOME WAY TO GET US IN UNNOTICED?

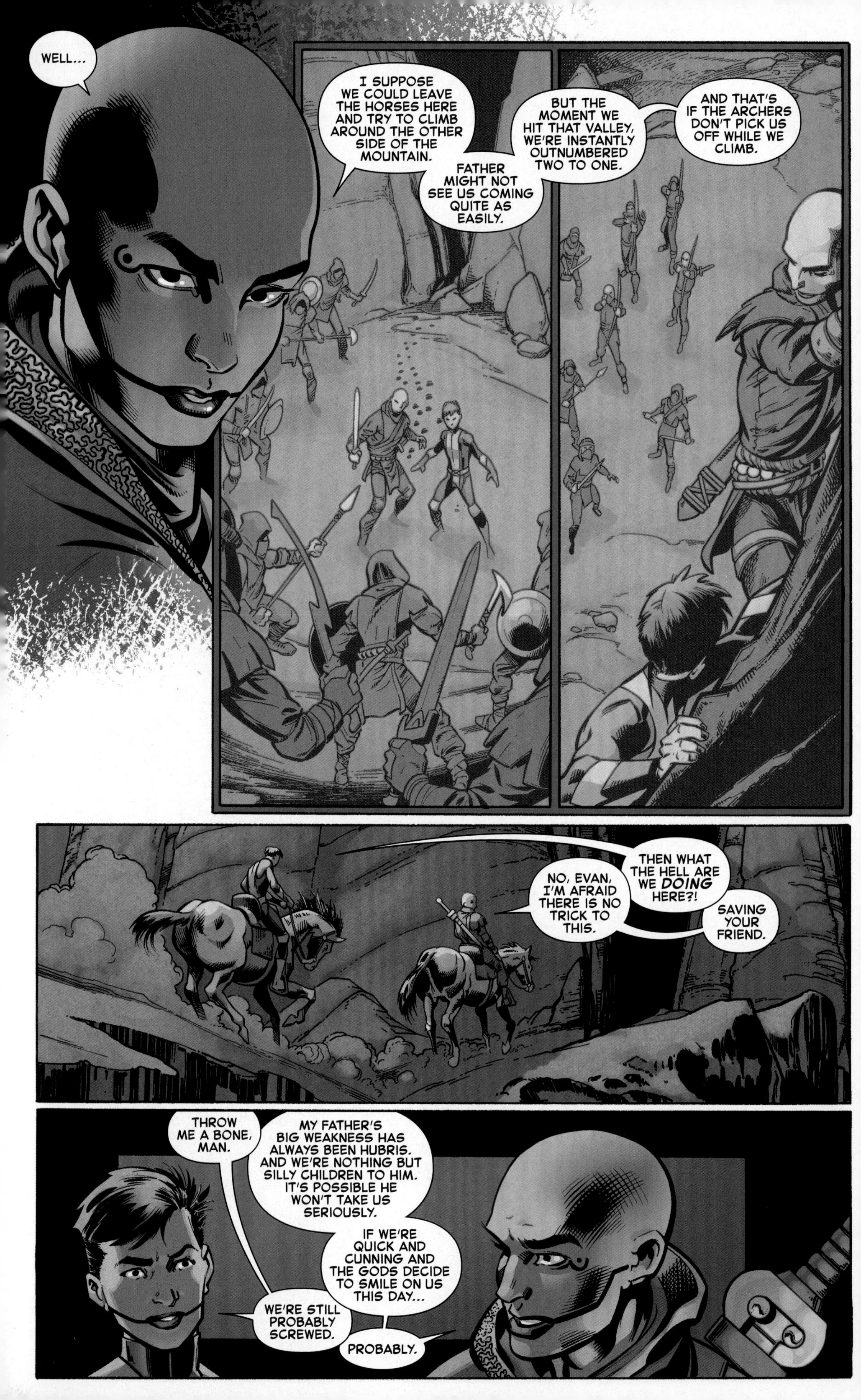

WELL...
I SUPPOSE WE COULD LEAVE THE HORSES HERE AND TRY TO CLIMB AROUND THE OTHER SIDE OF THE MOUNTAIN.
FATHER MIGHT NOT SEE US COMING QUITE AS EASILY.
BUT THE MOMENT WE HIT THAT VALLEY, WE'RE INSTANTLY OUTNUMBERED TWO TO ONE.
AND THAT'S IF THE ARCHERS DON'T PICK US OFF WHILE WE CLIMB.
NO, EVAN, I'M AFRAID THERE IS NO TRICK TO THIS.
THEN WHAT THE HELL ARE WE DOING HERE?!
SAVING YOUR FRIEND.
THROW ME A BONE, MAN.
MY FATHER'S BIG WEAKNESS HAS ALWAYS BEEN HUBRIS. AND WE'RE NOTHING BUT SILLY CHILDREN TO HIM. IT'S POSSIBLE HE WON'T TAKE US SERIOUSLY.
IF WE'RE QUICK AND CUNNING AND THE GODS DECIDE TO SMILE ON US THIS DAY...
WE'RE STILL PROBABLY SCREWED.
PROBABLY.

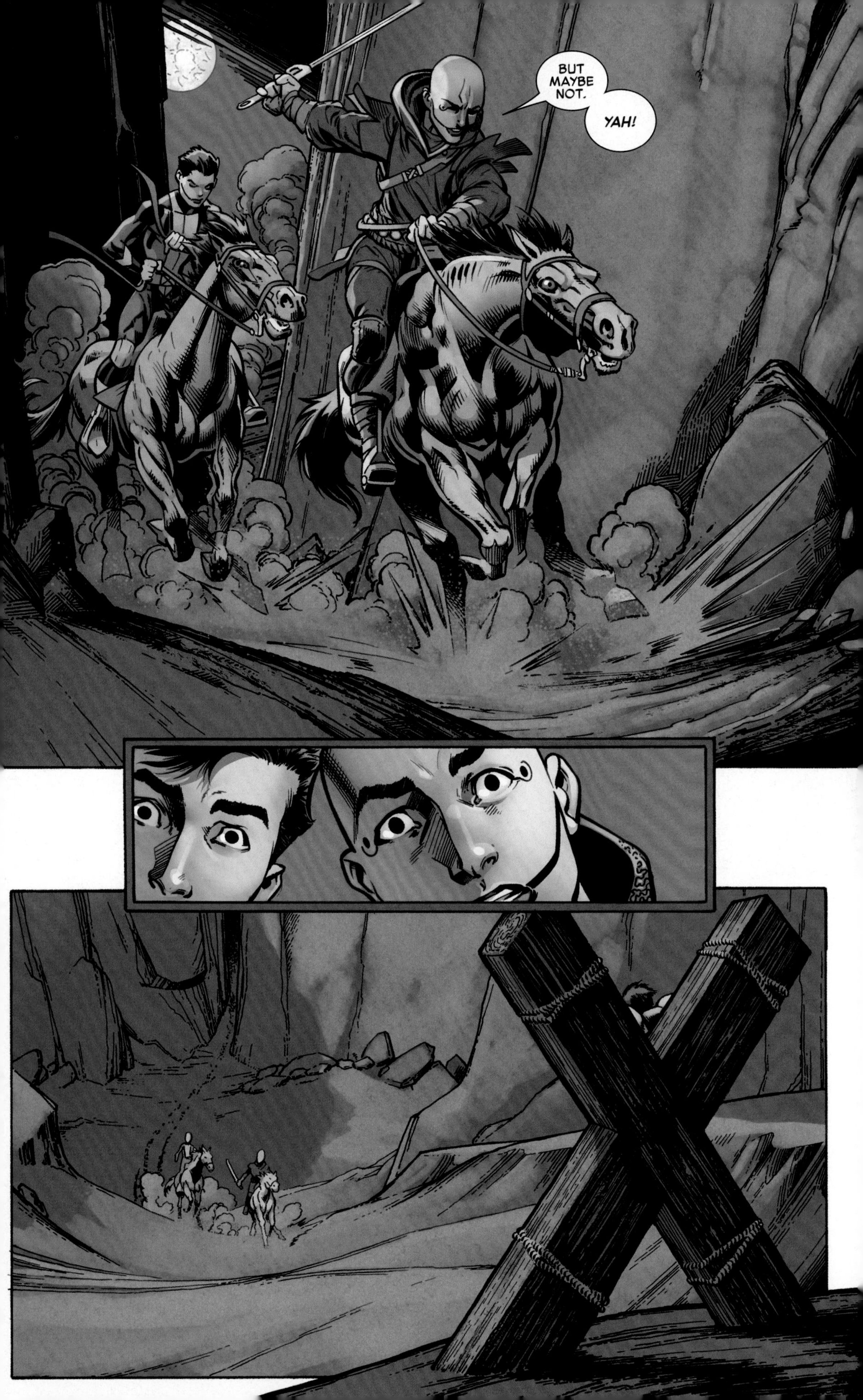
BUT MAYBE NOT.
YAH!

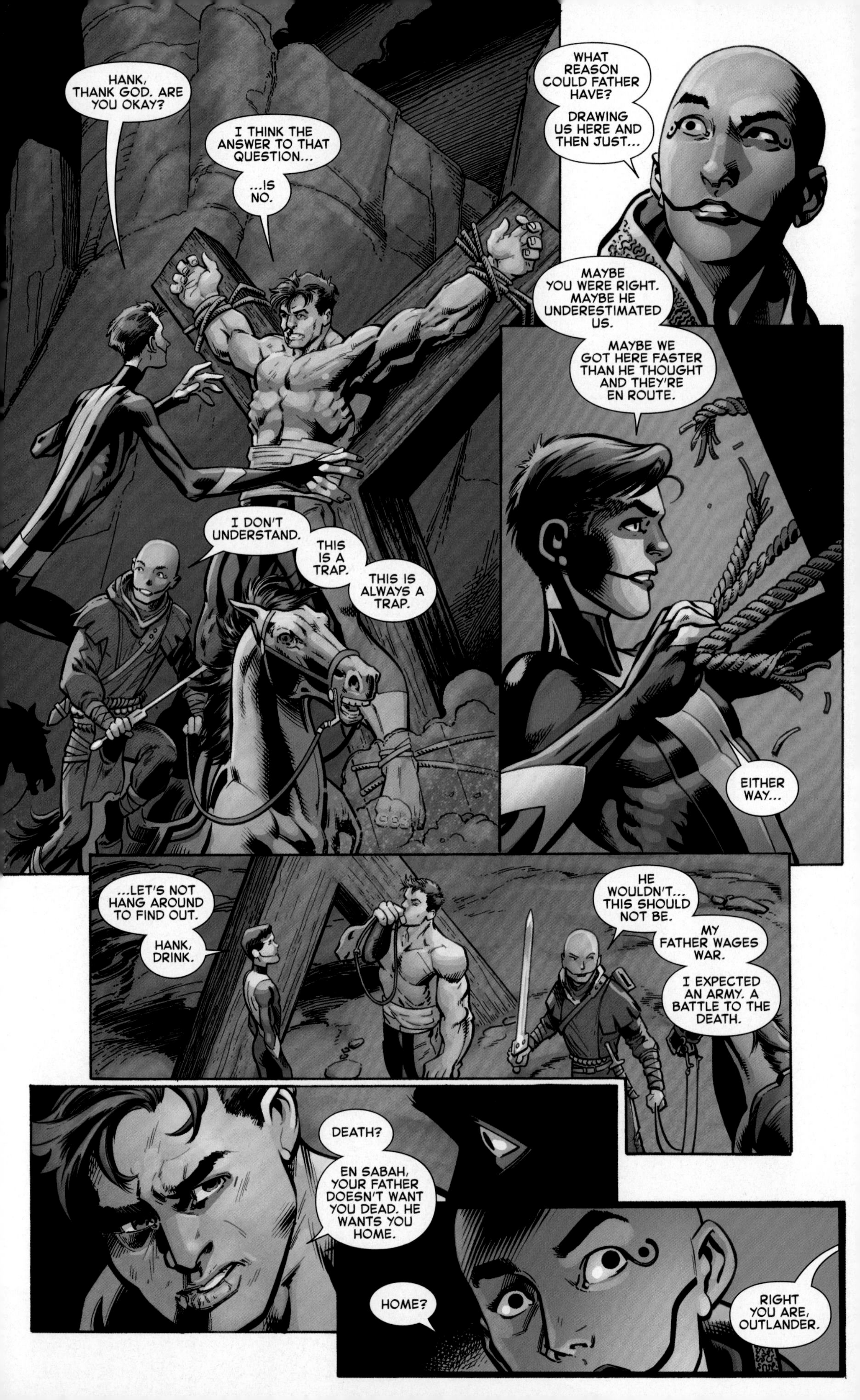
HANK, THANK GOD. ARE YOU OKAY?
I THINK THE ANSWER TO THAT QUESTION...
...IS NO.
WHAT REASON COULD FATHER HAVE?
DRAWING US HERE AND THEN JUST...
I DON'T UNDERSTAND.
THIS IS A TRAP.
THIS IS ALWAYS A TRAP.
MAYBE YOU WERE RIGHT. MAYBE HE UNDERESTIMATED US.
MAYBE WE GOT HERE FASTER THAN HE THOUGHT AND THEY'RE EN ROUTE.
EITHER WAY...
...LET'S NOT HANG AROUND TO FIND OUT.
HANK, DRINK.
HE WOULDN'T... THIS SHOULD NOT BE.
MY FATHER WAGES WAR.
I EXPECTED AN ARMY. A BATTLE TO THE DEATH.
DEATH?
EN SABAH, YOUR FATHER DOESN'T WANT YOU DEAD. HE WANTS YOU HOME.
HOME?
RIGHT YOU ARE, OUTLANDER.

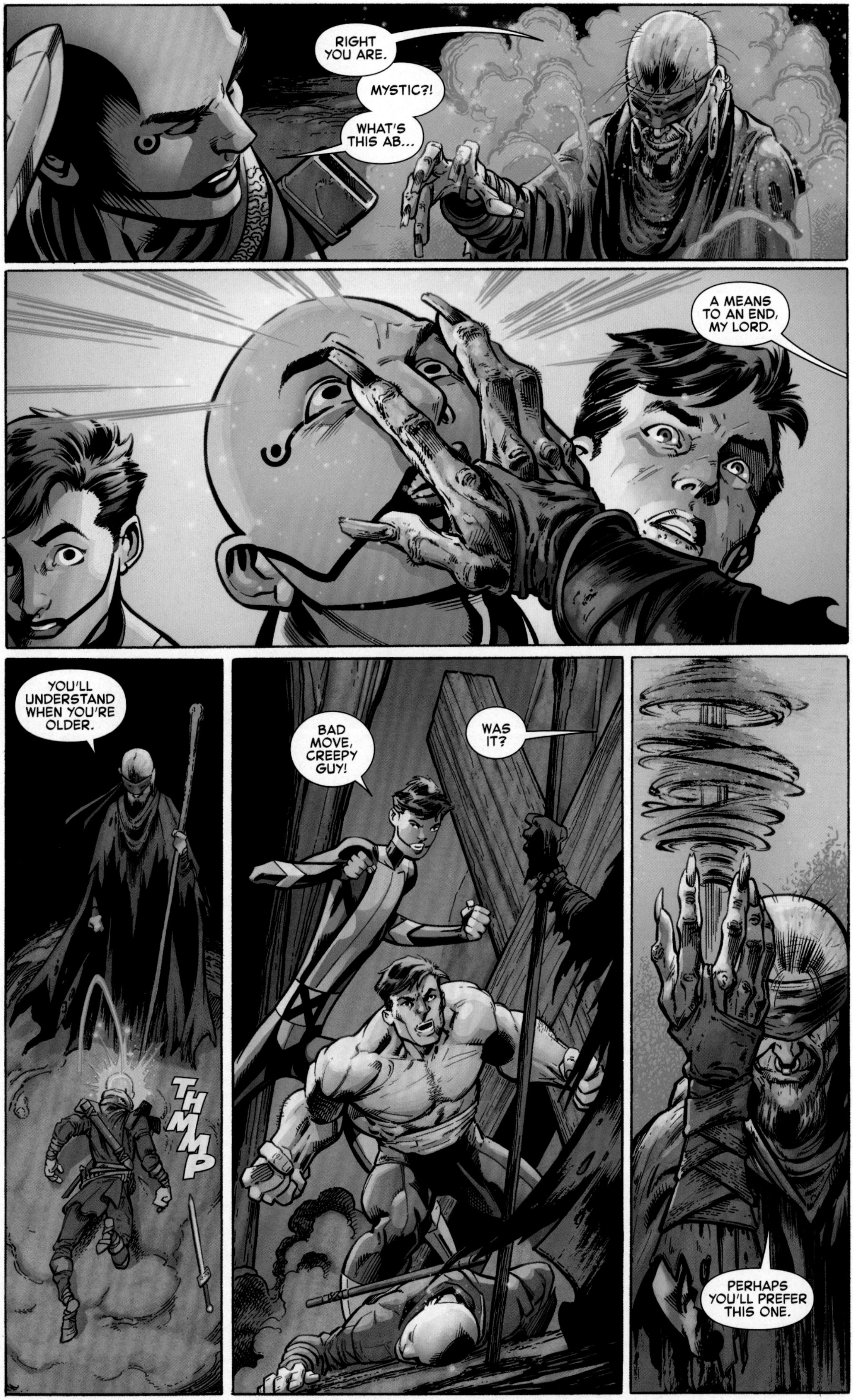
RIGHT YOU ARE.
MYSTIC?!
WHAT'S THIS AB...
A MEANS TO AN END, MY LORD.
YOU'LL UNDERSTAND WHEN YOU'RE OLDER.
THMMP
BAD MOVE, CREEPY GUY!
WAS IT?
PERHAPS YOU'LL PREFER THIS ONE.

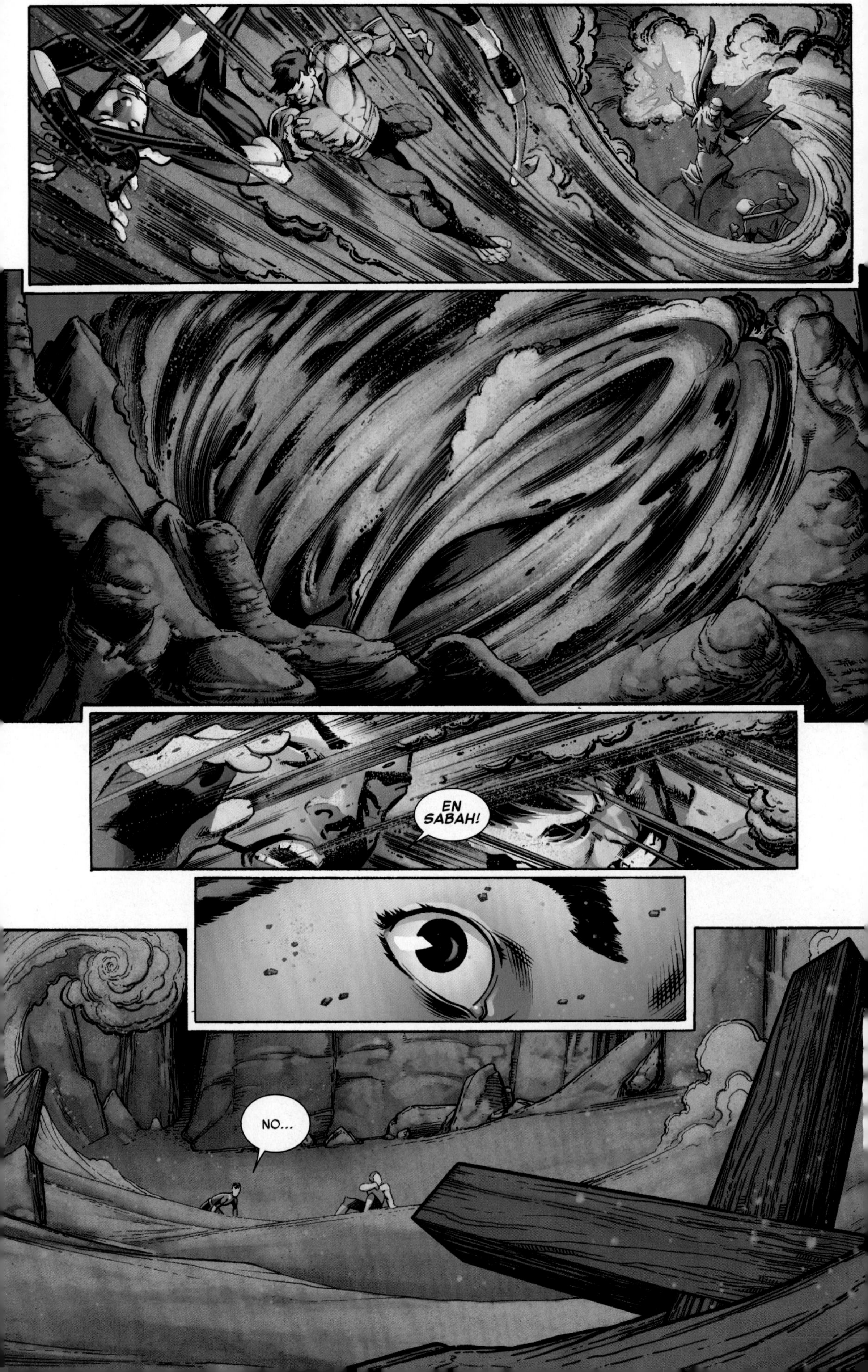
EN SABAH!
NO...

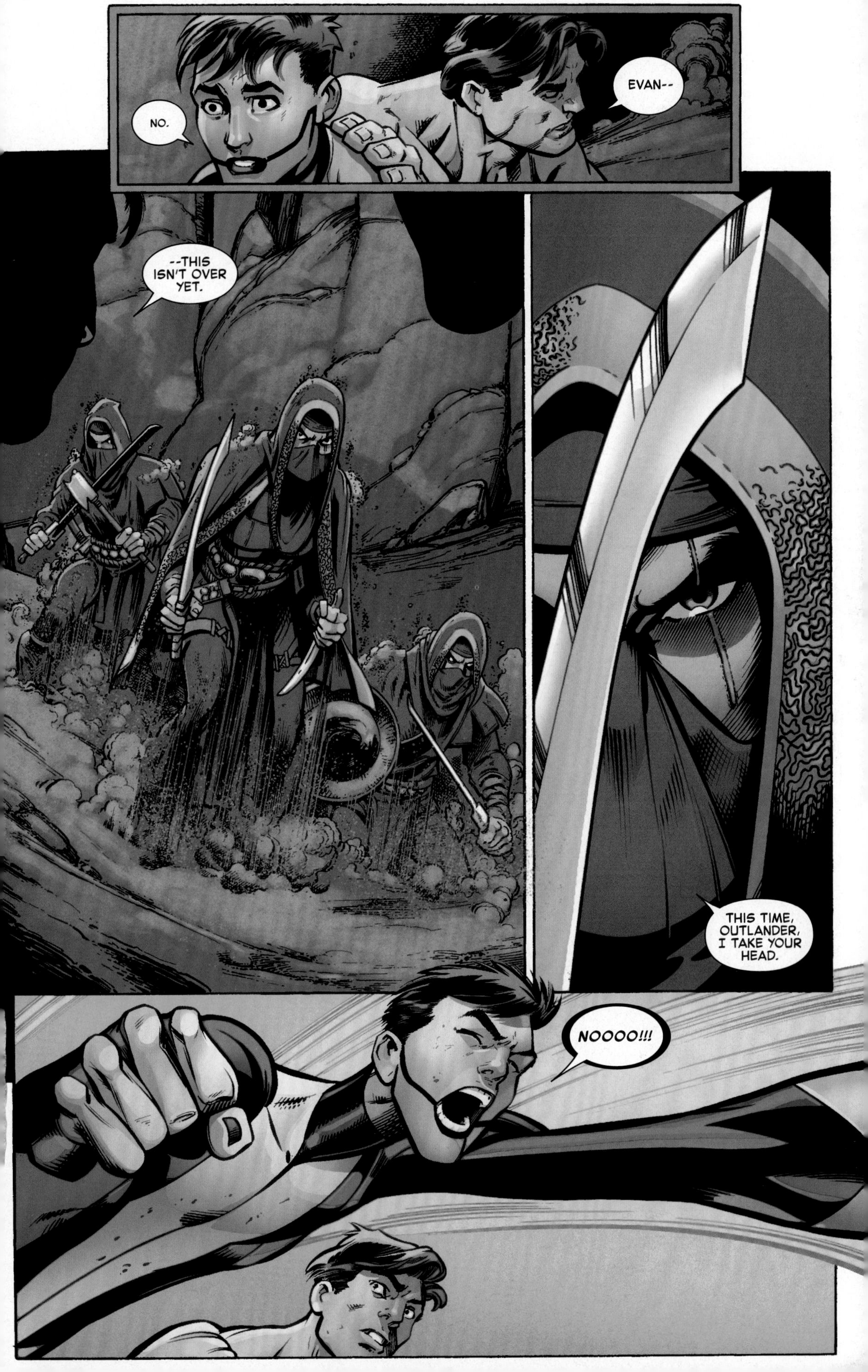
NO.
EVAN--
--THIS ISN'T OVER YET.
THIS TIME, OUTLANDER, I TAKE YOUR HEAD.
NOOOO!!!

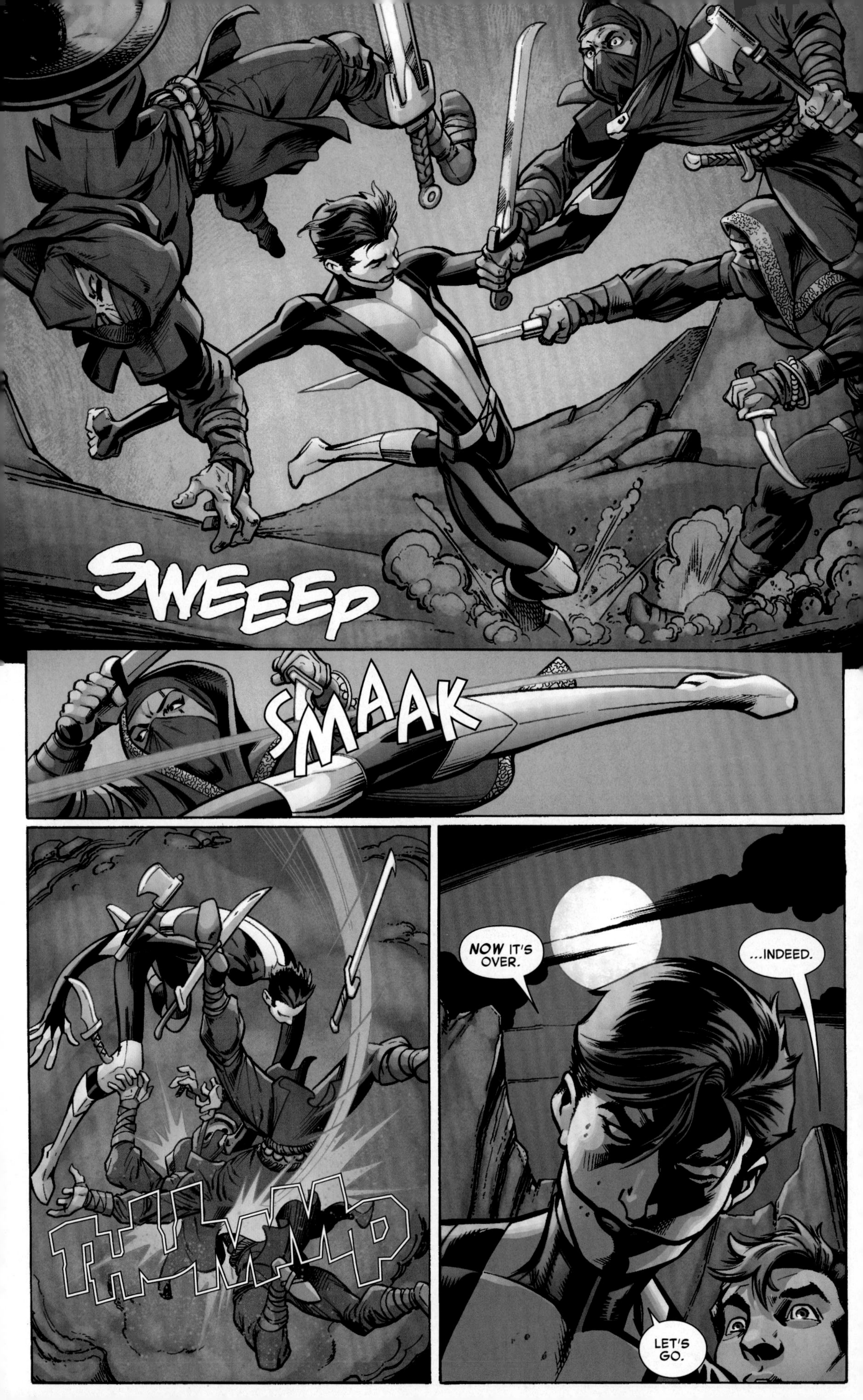
SWEEEP
SMAAK
THUMP
NOW IT'S OVER.
...INDEED.
LET'S GO.

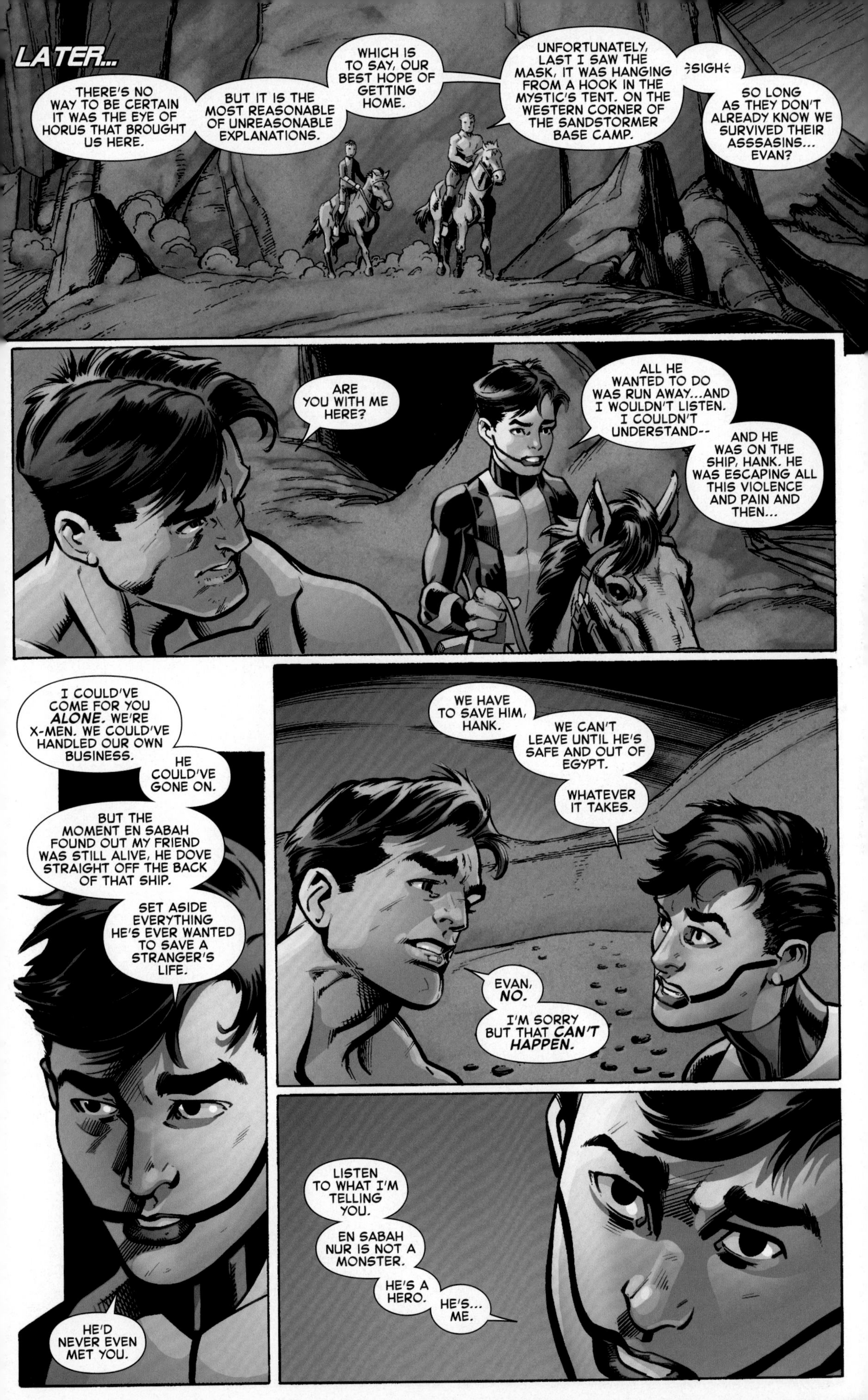
LATER...
THERE'S NO WAY TO BE CERTAIN IT WAS THE EYE OF HORUS THAT BROUGHT US HERE.
BUT IT IS THE MOST REASONABLE OF UNREASONABLE EXPLANATIONS.
WHICH IS TO SAY, OUR BEST HOPE OF GETTING HOME.
UNFORTUNATELY, LAST I SAW THE MASK, IT WAS HANGING FROM A HOOK IN THE MYSTIC'S TENT. ON THE WESTERN CORNER OF THE SANDSTORMER BASE CAMP.
SIGH
SO LONG AS THEY DON'T ALREADY KNOW WE SURVIVED THEIR ASSSASINS... EVAN?
ARE YOU WITH ME HERE?
ALL HE WANTED TO DO WAS RUN AWAY...AND I WOULDN'T LISTEN. I COULDN'T UNDERSTAND--
AND HE WAS ON THE SHIP, HANK. HE WAS ESCAPING ALL THIS VIOLENCE AND PAIN AND THEN...
I COULD'VE COME FOR YOU ALONE. WE'RE X-MEN. WE COULD'VE HANDLED OUR OWN BUSINESS.
HE COULD'VE GONE ON.
BUT THE MOMENT EN SABAH FOUND OUT MY FRIEND WAS STILL ALIVE, HE DOVE STRAIGHT OFF THE BACK OF THAT SHIP.
SET ASIDE EVERYTHING HE'S EVER WANTED TO SAVE A STRANGER'S LIFE.
HE'D NEVER EVEN MET YOU.
WE HAVE TO SAVE HIM, HANK.
WE CAN'T LEAVE UNTIL HE'S SAFE AND OUT OF EGYPT.
WHATEVER IT TAKES.
EVAN, NO.
I'M SORRY BUT THAT CAN'T HAPPEN.
LISTEN TO WHAT I'M TELLING YOU.
EN SABAH NUR IS NOT A MONSTER.
HE'S A HERO.
HE'S... ME.

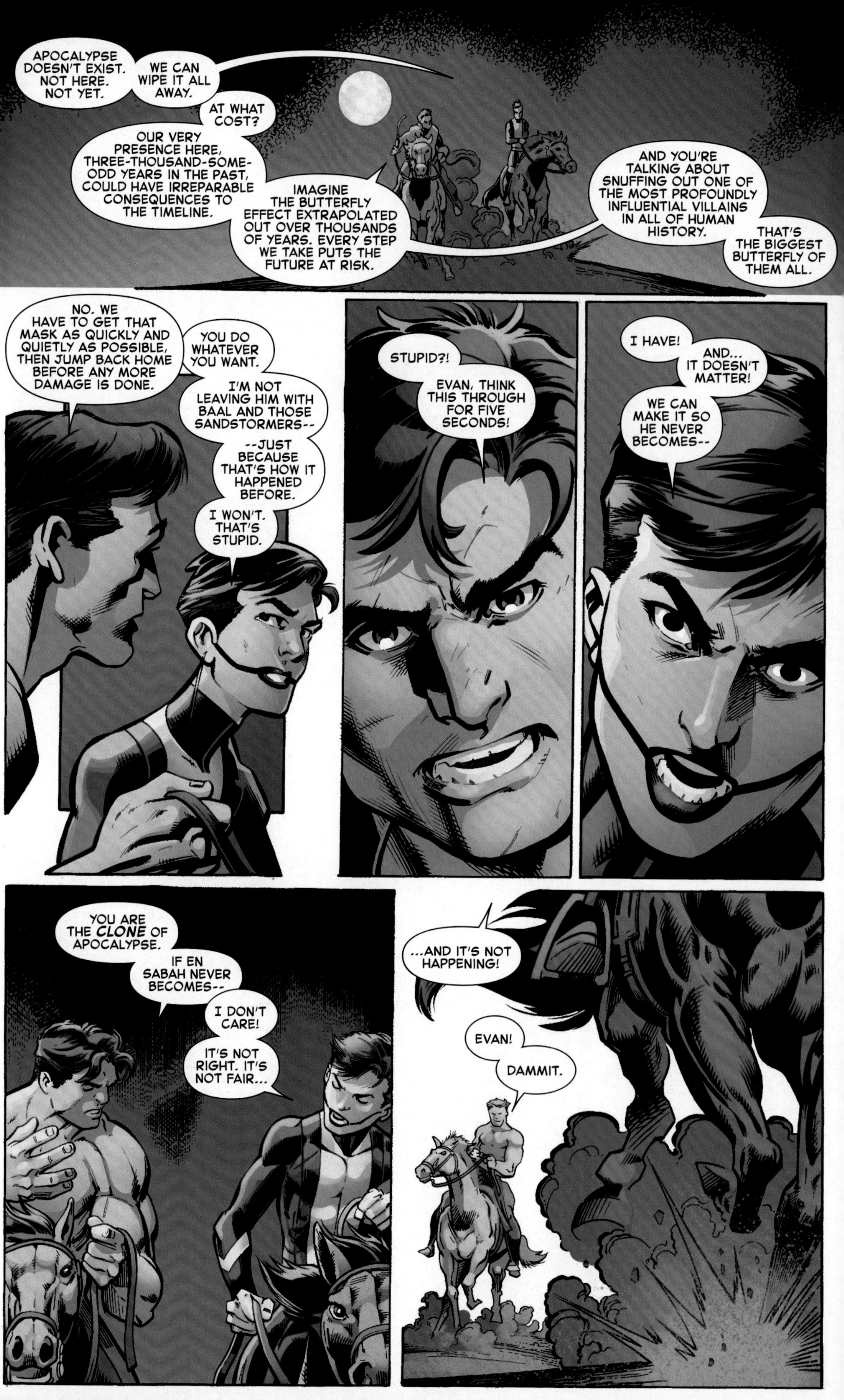
APOCALYPSE DOESN'T EXIST. NOT HERE. NOT YET.
WE CAN WIPE IT ALL AWAY.
AT WHAT COST?
OUR VERY PRESENCE HERE, THREE-THOUSAND-SOME-ODD YEARS IN THE PAST, COULD HAVE IRREPARABLE CONSEQUENCES TO THE TIMELINE.
IMAGINE THE BUTTERFLY EFFECT EXTRAPOLATED OUT OVER THOUSANDS OF YEARS. EVERY STEP WE TAKE PUTS THE FUTURE AT RISK.
AND YOU'RE TALKING ABOUT SNUFFING OUT ONE OF THE MOST PROFOUNDLY INFLUENTIAL VILLAINS IN ALL OF HUMAN HISTORY.
THAT'S THE BIGGEST BUTTERFLY OF THEM ALL.
NO. WE HAVE TO GET THAT MASK AS QUICKLY AND QUIETLY AS POSSIBLE, THEN JUMP BACK HOME BEFORE ANY MORE DAMAGE IS DONE.
YOU DO WHATEVER YOU WANT.
I'M NOT LEAVING HIM WITH BAAL AND THOSE SANDSTORMERS--
--JUST BECAUSE THAT'S HOW IT HAPPENED BEFORE.
I WON'T. THAT'S STUPID.
STUPID?!
EVAN, THINK THIS THROUGH FOR FIVE SECONDS!
I HAVE!
AND... IT DOESN'T MATTER!
WE CAN MAKE IT SO HE NEVER BECOMES--
YOU ARE THE *CLONE* OF APOCALYPSE.
IF EN SABAH NEVER BECOMES--
I DON'T CARE!
IT'S NOT RIGHT. IT'S NOT FAIR...
...AND IT'S NOT HAPPENING!
EVAN!
DAMMIT.

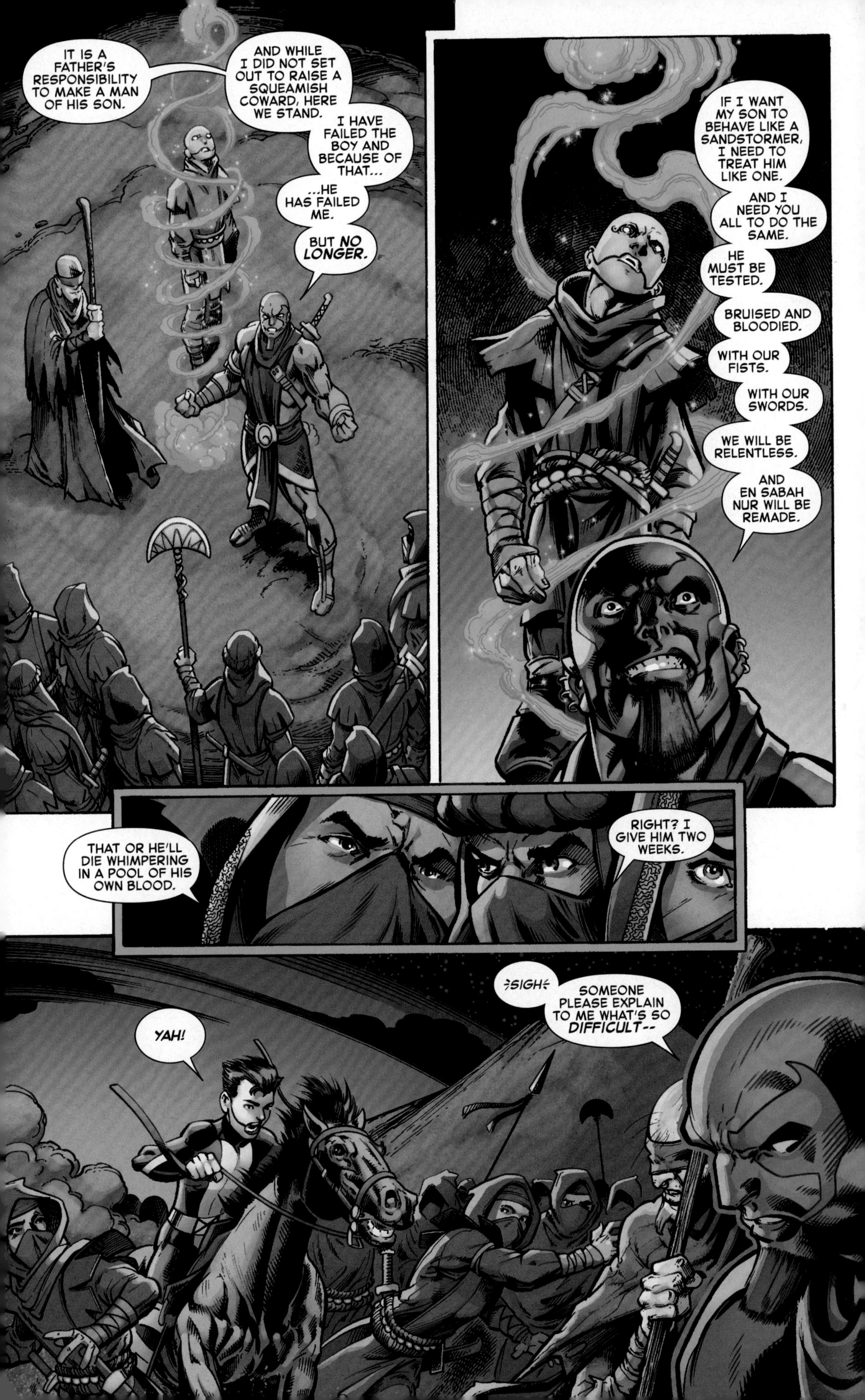
IT IS A FATHER'S RESPONSIBILITY TO MAKE A MAN OF HIS SON.
AND WHILE I DID NOT SET OUT TO RAISE A SQUEAMISH COWARD, HERE WE STAND.
I HAVE FAILED THE BOY AND BECAUSE OF THAT...
...HE HAS FAILED ME.
BUT NO LONGER.
IF I WANT MY SON TO BEHAVE LIKE A SANDSTORMER, I NEED TO TREAT HIM LIKE ONE.
AND I NEED YOU ALL TO DO THE SAME.
HE MUST BE TESTED.
BRUISED AND BLOODIED.
WITH OUR FISTS.
WITH OUR SWORDS.
WE WILL BE RELENTLESS.
AND EN SABAH NUR WILL BE REMADE.
THAT OR HE'LL DIE WHIMPERING IN A POOL OF HIS OWN BLOOD.
RIGHT? I GIVE HIM TWO WEEKS.
YAH!
SIGH
SOMEONE PLEASE EXPLAIN TO ME WHAT'S SO DIFFICULT--

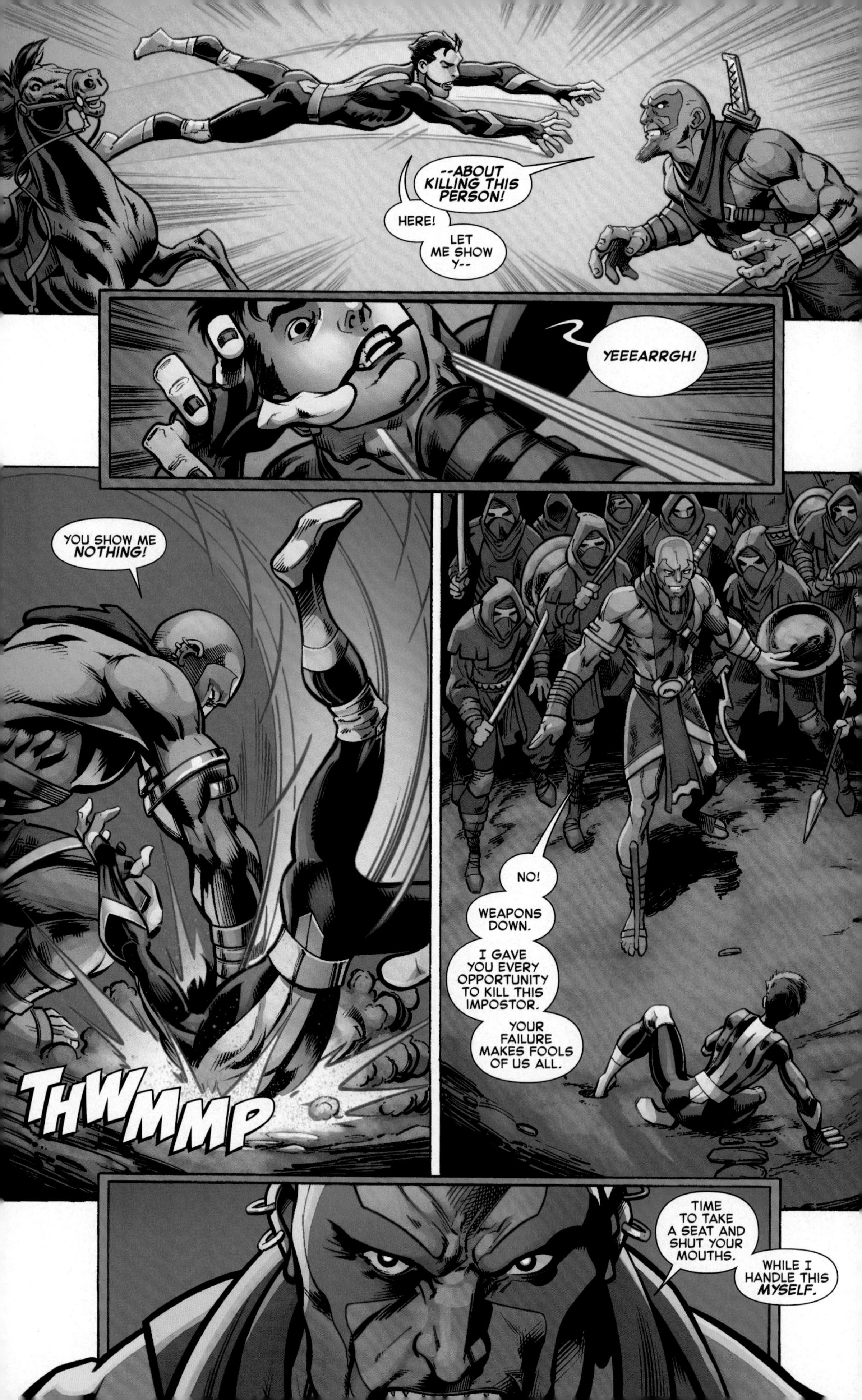
--ABOUT KILLING THIS PERSON!
HERE!
LET ME SHOW Y--
YEEEARRGH!
YOU SHOW ME NOTHING!
THWMMP
NO!
WEAPONS DOWN.
I GAVE YOU EVERY OPPORTUNITY TO KILL THIS IMPOSTOR.
YOUR FAILURE MAKES FOOLS OF US ALL.
TIME TO TAKE A SEAT AND SHUT YOUR MOUTHS.
WHILE I HANDLE THIS MYSELF.

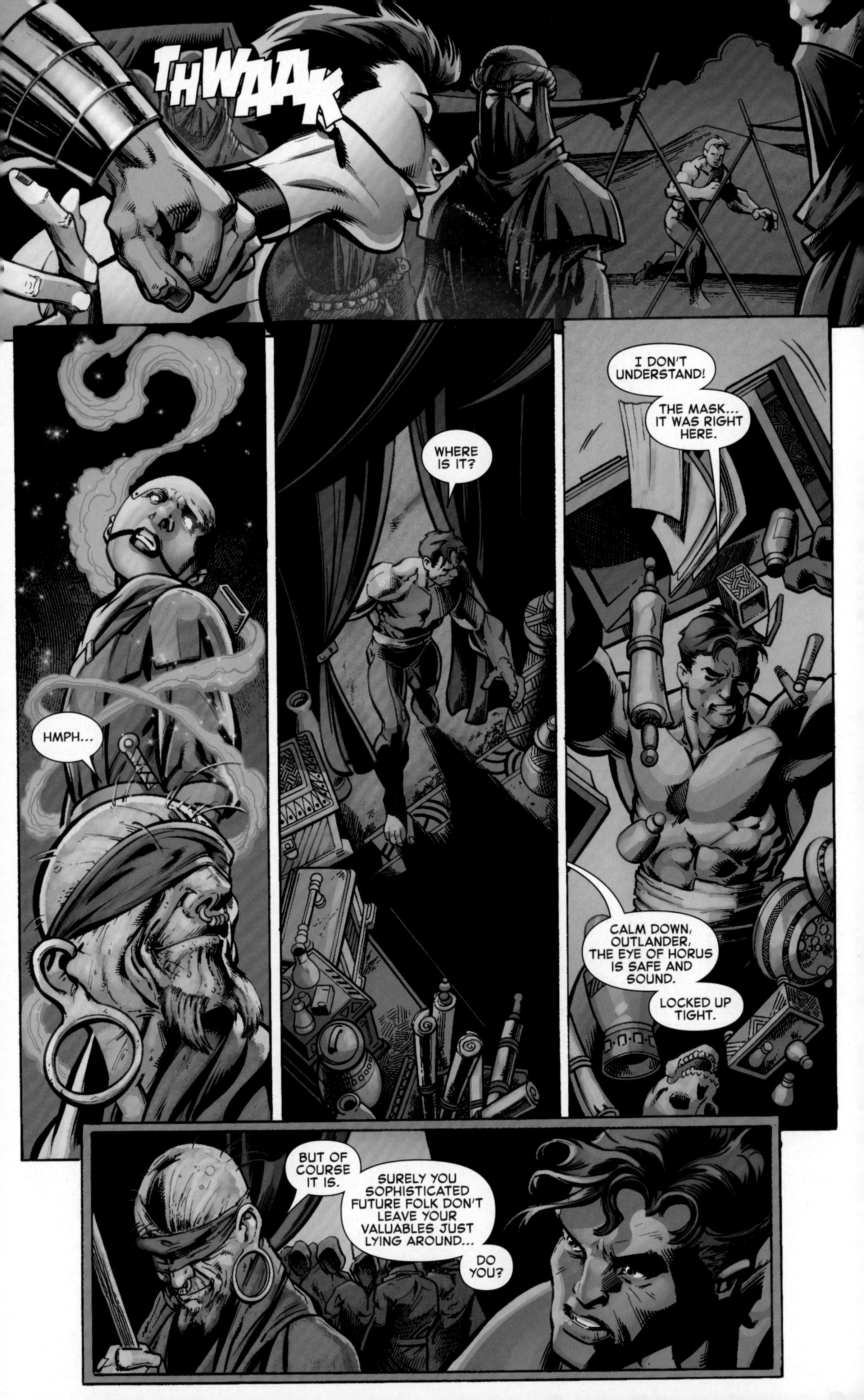
THWAAK
HMPH...
WHERE IS IT?
I DON'T UNDERSTAND!
THE MASK... IT WAS RIGHT HERE.
CALM DOWN, OUTLANDER, THE EYE OF HORUS IS SAFE AND SOUND.
LOCKED UP TIGHT.
BUT OF COURSE IT IS.
SURELY YOU SOPHISTICATED FUTURE FOLK DON'T LEAVE YOUR VALUABLES JUST LYING AROUND...
DO YOU?

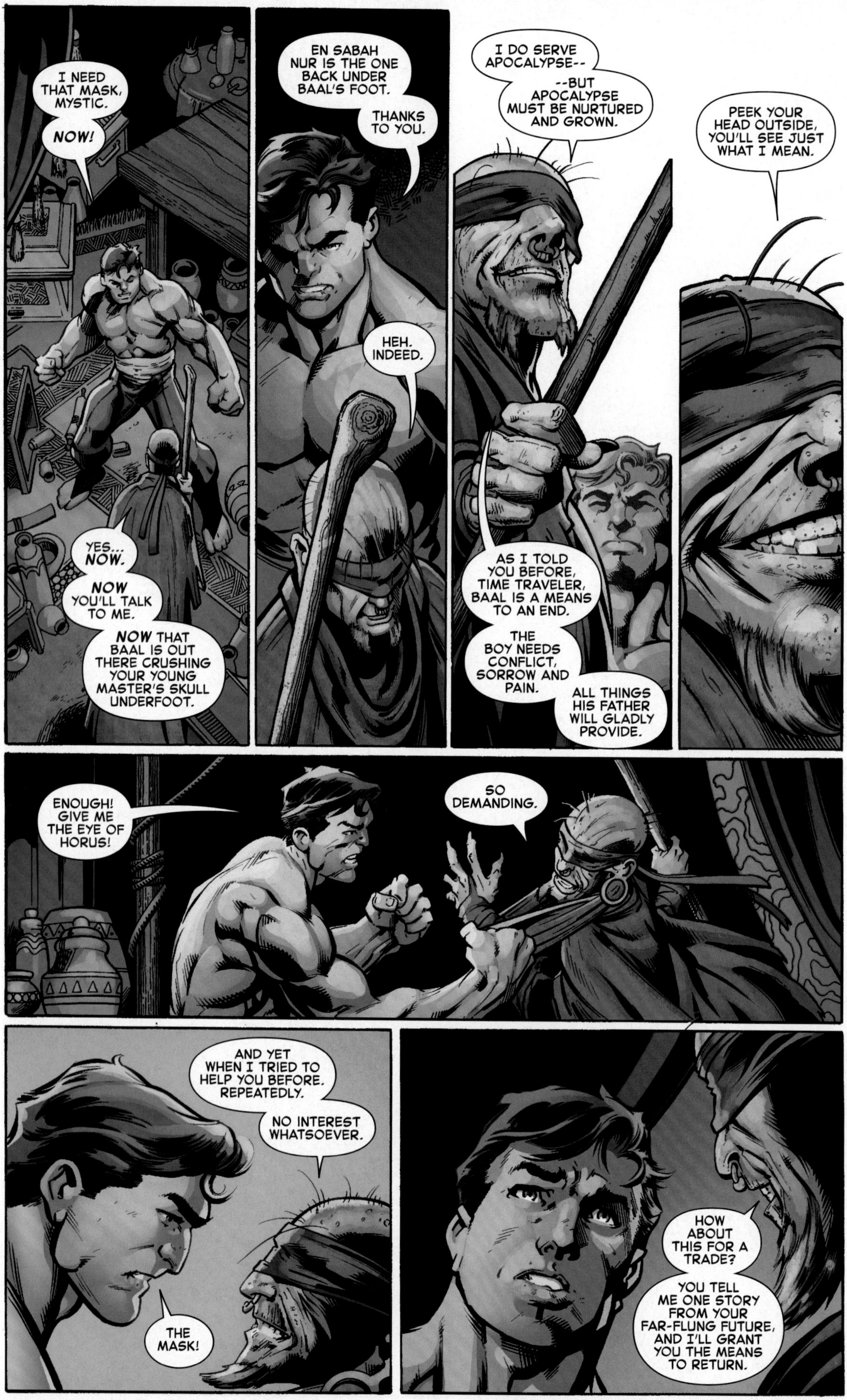

I NEED THAT MASK, MYSTIC.
NOW!
YES... NOW.
NOW YOU'LL TALK TO ME.
NOW THAT BAAL IS OUT THERE CRUSHING YOUR YOUNG MASTER'S SKULL UNDERFOOT.
EN SABAH NUR IS THE ONE BACK UNDER BAAL'S FOOT.
THANKS TO YOU.
HEH. INDEED.
I DO SERVE APOCALYPSE--
--BUT APOCALYPSE MUST BE NURTURED AND GROWN.
AS I TOLD YOU BEFORE, TIME TRAVELER, BAAL IS A MEANS TO AN END.
THE BOY NEEDS CONFLICT, SORROW AND PAIN.
ALL THINGS HIS FATHER WILL GLADLY PROVIDE.
PEEK YOUR HEAD OUTSIDE, YOU'LL SEE JUST WHAT I MEAN.
ENOUGH! GIVE ME THE EYE OF HORUS!
SO DEMANDING.
AND YET WHEN I TRIED TO HELP YOU BEFORE. REPEATEDLY.
NO INTEREST WHATSOEVER.
THE MASK!
HOW ABOUT THIS FOR A TRADE?
YOU TELL ME ONE STORY FROM YOUR FAR-FLUNG FUTURE, AND I'LL GRANT YOU THE MEANS TO RETURN.

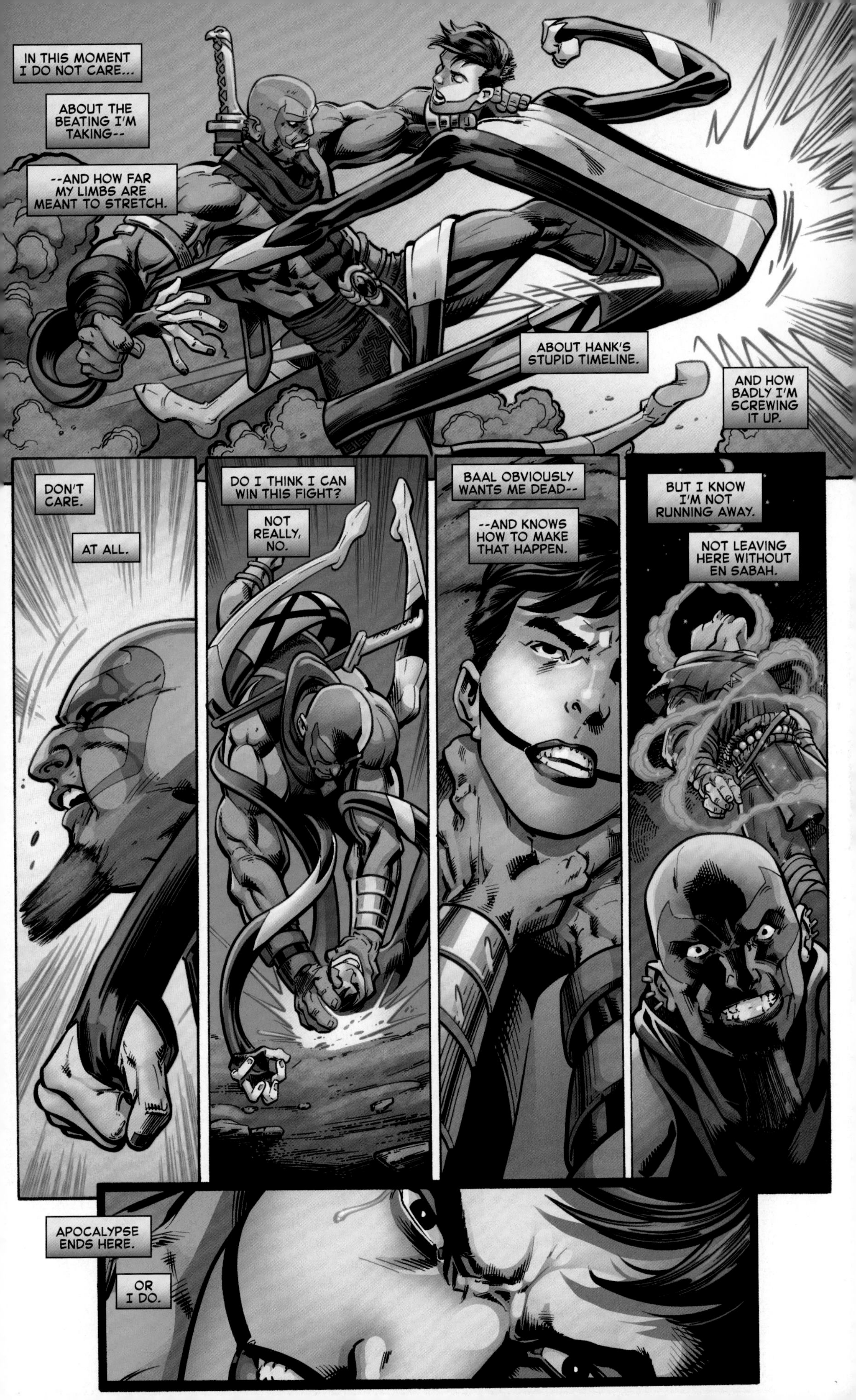
IN THIS MOMENT I DO NOT CARE...
ABOUT THE BEATING I'M TAKING--
--AND HOW FAR MY LIMBS ARE MEANT TO STRETCH.
ABOUT HANK'S STUPID TIMELINE.
AND HOW BADLY I'M SCREWING IT UP.
DON'T CARE.
AT ALL.
DO I THINK I CAN WIN THIS FIGHT?
NOT REALLY, NO.
BAAL OBVIOUSLY WANTS ME DEAD--
--AND KNOWS HOW TO MAKE THAT HAPPEN.
BUT I KNOW I'M NOT RUNNING AWAY.
NOT LEAVING HERE WITHOUT EN SABAH.
APOCALYPSE ENDS HERE.
OR I DO.

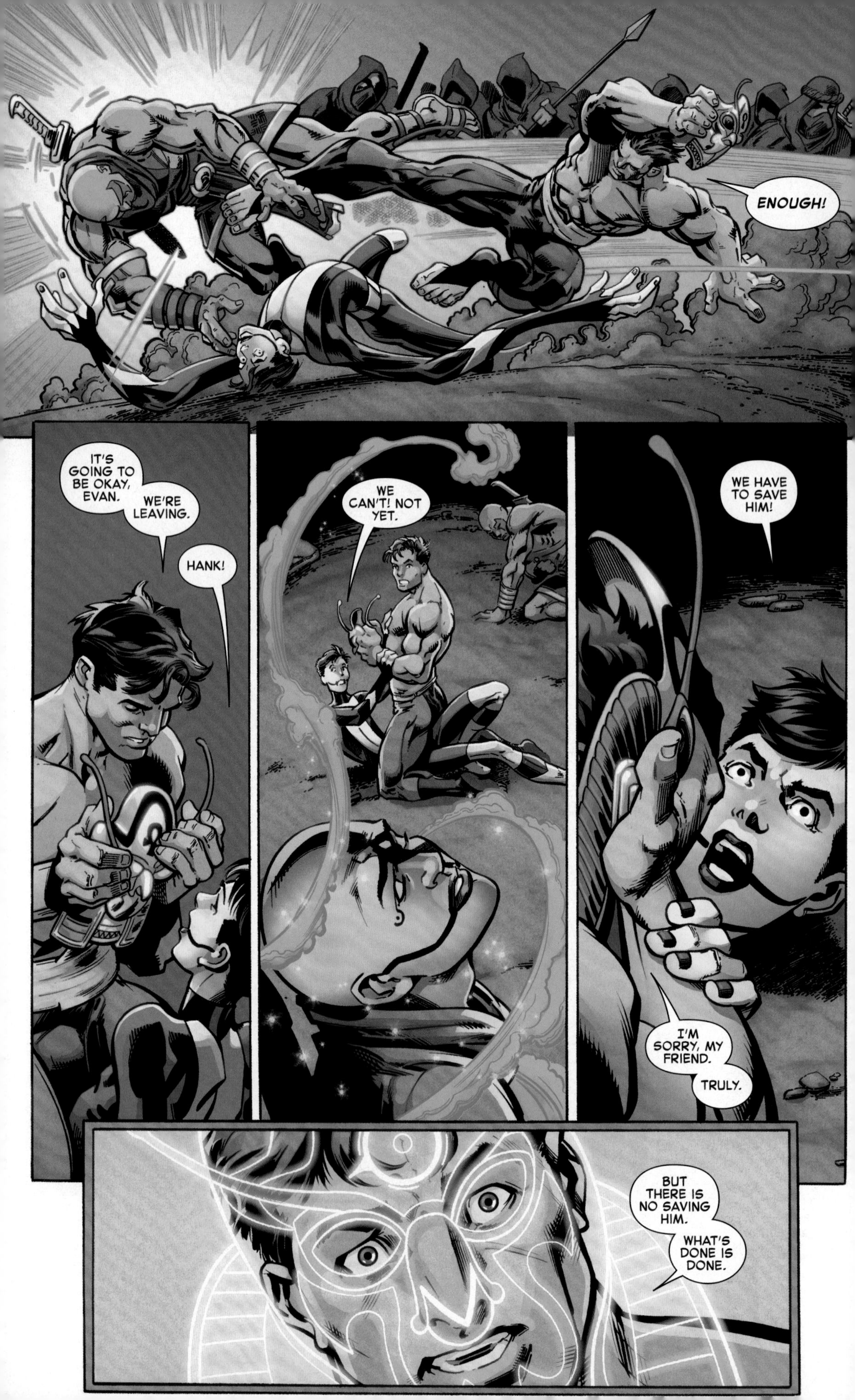
ENOUGH!
IT'S GOING TO BE OKAY, EVAN.
WE'RE LEAVING.
HANK!
WE CAN'T! NOT YET.
WE HAVE TO SAVE HIM!
I'M SORRY, MY FRIEND.
TRULY.
BUT THERE IS NO SAVING HIM.
WHAT'S DONE IS DONE.

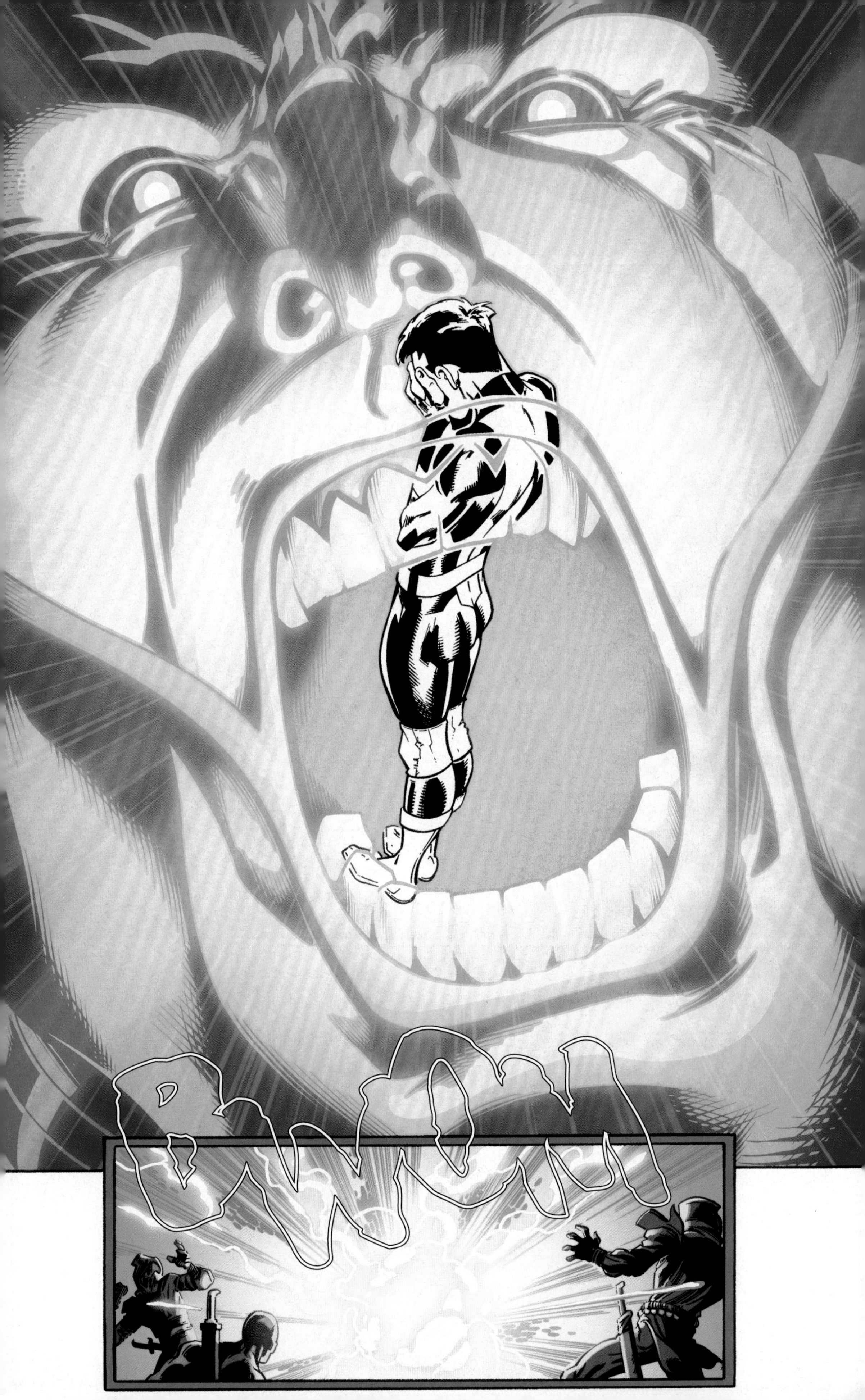
BWOM

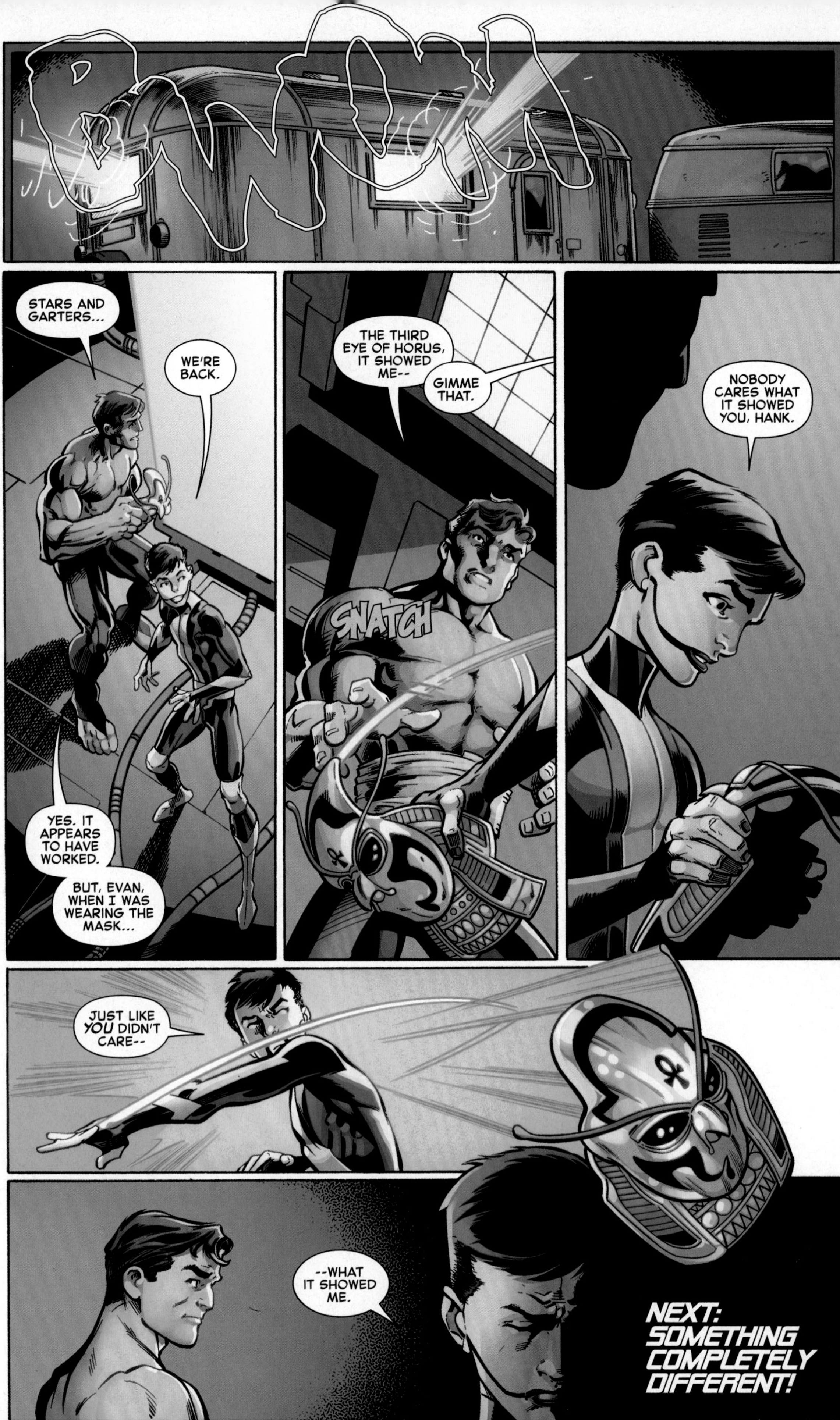
BWOOM
STARS AND GARTERS...
WE'RE BACK.
YES. IT APPEARS TO HAVE WORKED.
BUT, EVAN, WHEN I WAS WEARING THE MASK...
THE THIRD EYE OF HORUS, IT SHOWED ME--
GIMME THAT.
SNATCH
NOBODY CARES WHAT IT SHOWED YOU, HANK.
JUST LIKE YOU DIDN'T CARE--
--WHAT IT SHOWED ME.
NEXT: SOMETHING COMPLETELY DIFFERENT!

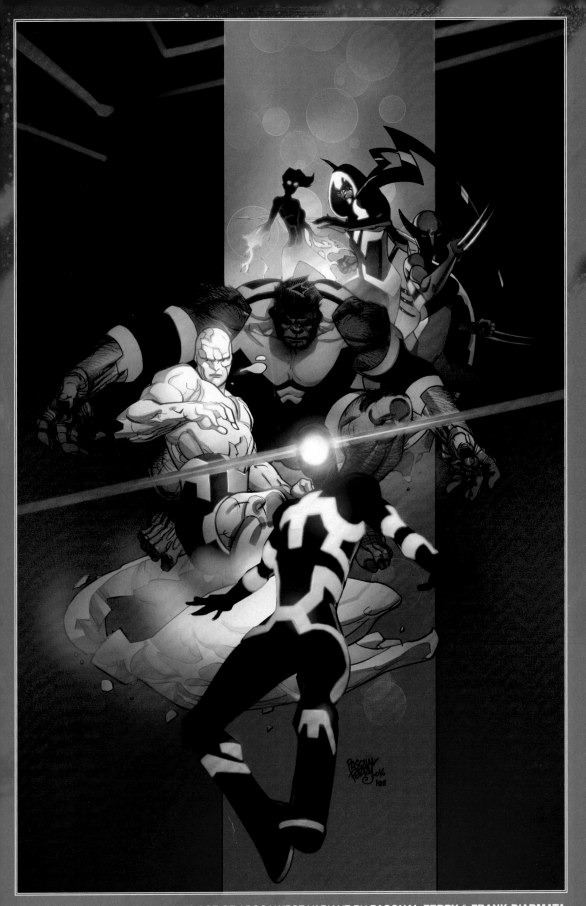

#9 AGE OF APOCALYPSE VARIANT BY **PASQUAL FERRY** & **FRANK D'ARMATA**

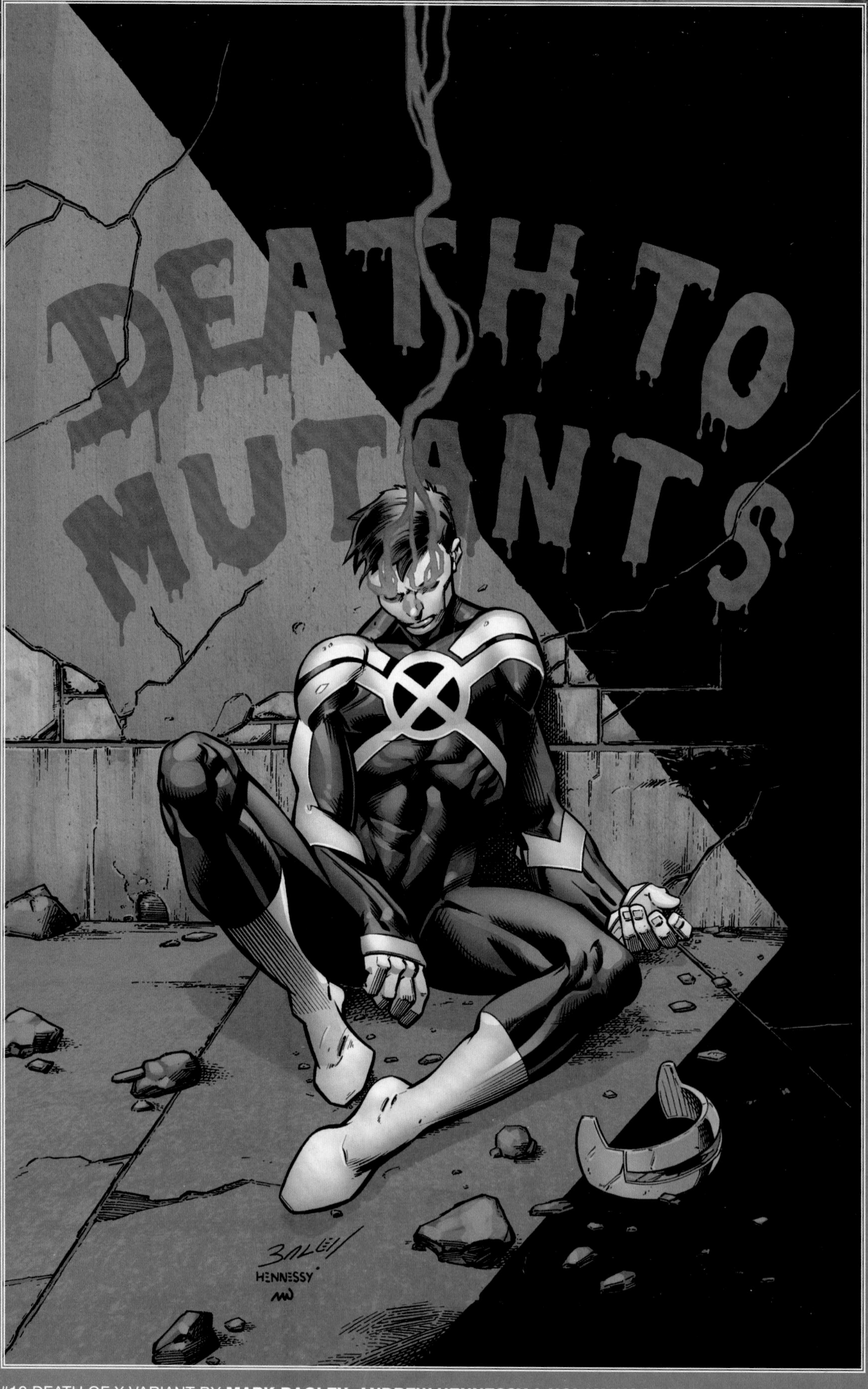
DEATH TO MUTANTS
BAGLEY
HENNESSY

#10 DEATH OF X VARIANT BY **MARK BAGLEY**, **ANDREW HENNESSY** & **NOLAN WOODARD**